THE Christian AND THE World of Unbelief

THE Christian AND THE World of Unbelief

Líbuse Lukas Míller

ABINGDON PRESS

New York *Nashville*

THE CHRISTIAN AND THE WORLD OF UNBELIEF

Library of Congress Catalog Card Number: 57-5078

Scripture quotations so designated are from the American Standard Version of the Revised Bible, copyright, 1929, by the International Council of Religious Education. Scripture quotations so designated are from the Revised Standard Version of the Bible, copyright 1946 and 1952 by the Division of Christian Education of the National Council of the Churches of Christ in the U.S.A.

SET UP, PRINTED, AND BOUND BY THE PARTHENON PRESS, AT NASHVILLE, TENNESSEE, UNITED STATES OF AMERICA

TO

F. M. Jr.

and

F. M. III

Preface

AFTER FINISHING A CONVINCING BOOK OF CHRISTIAN APOLOGETICS, ONE is sometimes tempted to give a sigh of relief and to assume that, at least in religious matters, surely the just-converted believer "lived happily ever after." This book is written in the conviction that perhaps it would be more to the point to say, in the same humorous and yet serious sense in which it is said about entering the married estate, that the man's real troubles were just beginning. The object of this book is to help the Christian believer realize that the life of faith must be lived in two worlds—the world as seen through the eyes of faith, and the world as variously deciphered or undeciphered by the unbelievers—and to help him find a modus vivendi in a situation so peculiar, so contemporary, and so perennial. In this book I use the terms "believer" and "unbeliever," not in an evaluative sense, but in the statistical sense in which all the inhabitants of the planet could be counted one way or the other, by their own admission. This usage not only gives the Christian a realistic idea of his minority status but also makes him aware that the unbelievers have a world of their own to live by—a world whose assorted basic assumptions, in spite of the many forms in which they are exhibited over the earth, are not so different from one another as they are collectively different from those implied in the Christian outlook.

The unbelievers' world is not all of a piece—but it is all of certain pieces that keep showing up again and again in the various areas of human endeavor, trying to make up a world that can successfully live by its independence of the Christian God. I have tried to present the problem of the believer's finding a modus vivendi in the two-world situation by taking up one after another, in the following chapters, several of the more important areas or realms of human experience—especially as they display the pieces of the unbelievers' world—and describing the believer's relationship to them. The introductory chapter, however, is somewhat different from those that follow, in that it tries to describe the believer's situation as such, as something that he takes with him into whatever area of experience he enters. The state of being "in" the world and yet "not of it" takes some getting used to. It is a gymnastic of the spirit so difficult that most of the time the believer finds himself zigzagging back and forth—that is, falling far short of the tension-in-balance ideally required for living simultaneously in both worlds during the aeon of expectation. This chapter, then, should be read as a prologue, a setting of the scene and an invoking of the atmosphere in which the issues of the subsequent chapters are undertaken.

I have not assumed for the Christian believer any special technical philosophy or school of thought, but I have assumed that he is one to whom the words and categories of biblical thinking, as well as the Christian witness to them in the ages since, have "come alive" to such an extent that he can no longer make basic sense out of his life and his historical situation in any other terms. The situation of the Christian believer who wishes to be a philosopher is a special case considered in Chapter III. I have also assumed in anyone likely to read this book some agreement with me as to the importance of the issues dealt with for the kind of biblically oriented life and thought just indicated.

In view of the fact that each of the subjects brought together here within the scope of one book easily invites volumes to be written on its own account—science, philosophy, social science, ethics, culture, and history—I must beg the indulgence of the specialized reader, for gross omissions, for many too-general statements, and for passing over the fine points of many a problem discussed. I can only hope that a certain breadth of outlook, a bird's-eye view of the situation, will compensate for such deficiencies.

Since this book is not concerned with apologetics directly, but rather takes up where apologetics leave off, I feel it necessary to state here in the preface, to avoid one possible misunderstanding, that this is not because I do not have the greatest respect for apologetics. I do not belong to that school which believes that the best defense of Christianity is no defense at all, for it is much too easy to confuse merely incorrect thinking with that which is by nature beyond the scope of logical expression. If Christianity is foolishness to the Greeks and a stumbling block to many, let it at least be made clear in exactly what sense this is so. Let us not add to the real difficulties of achieving faith the merely distorted and prejudicial thinking produced by a given historical situation, because of our unwillingness to unravel the latter and distinguish it from the former. In this sense the believer is never finished with apologetics, for the two-world situation is constituted by the mutual interpenetration of the one which announces and defends Christianity with the one which, by its very refusal to be convinced, creates situations that call for an ever new and relevant announcing and defending of the Word. "Go and teach all nations"—and what if they won't listen? Then we must make them listen, by going where they are and beginning there. And that is the basic task of apologetics, in every age to begin where the unbelievers are in that age. So, if any reader of this book feels offended because it takes the believer too much for granted, and is written too much from the side of faith, I refer him to the many good books of apologetics in which Christian literature abounds.

For helpful reading of all or parts of the manuscript in the various stages through which it passed, and for valuable technical suggestions, I am gratefully indebted to John Crowe Ransom, to Charles Joseph Stoneburner, and to Henry Cutler Torrey.

LIBUSE LUKAS MILLER

Contents

Chapter I

THE LIFE OF FAITH AND THE WORLD OF UNBELIEF

The two-world situation

FOR SOME TIME NOW THE POPULAR IMAGINATION HAS BEEN PRE-occupied with the details of space travel, the possibilities of reaching the moon, the establishment of space stations, and the prospects for starting all over again on another planet when the earth has been made uninhabitable as a result of atomic warfare. I should like to suggest that there might be an image in such space lore for the Christian believer, who has to live the life of faith in a world of unbelief. Perhaps he could think of this life after the pattern of an interplanetary expedition from another world, sent out to establish a colony of heaven on our planet, under somewhat forbidding and unpredictable conditions. The image would be up-to-date, and yet it would be descriptive of a situation that appears to be perennial for Christians. The believer in all ages has been something of a fish out of water, and has had to try to explain his discomfort by appealing to various pictures of his curious position in the world. The life of early Christians is described in *The Epistle to Diognetus* thus: "They reside in their respective countries, but only as aliens. They take part in everything as citizens and put up with everything as foreigners. Every foreign land is their home, and every home a foreign land. . . . They spend their days on earth, but hold citizenship in heaven." [1]

Augustine's City of God and City of Man arrangement was another such picture, and it tried to indicate the conflict between the two cities, as well as the nature of the ultimate victory. It embodied the Roman sense of orderly community of the entire human family by its use of the term *city*. Today, when actual attempts to impose orderly community on the whole world are being made by parties and peoples motivated by dogmas and desperations of various kinds, it is harder and harder to see in the City of Man that is likely to come, the foreshadowing of a City that might be of God. Similarly, the medieval picture of the Church as the mother, and of Christianity as the home which is always ready to receive the prodigal children whenever they have had enough of wandering, is based on a far too universal understanding of what Christianity is, to do for the believer's situation today. The same may be said of such a drama of redemption as the *Divine Comedy*, in which even the damned understand the rationale of their damnation. The city, the home, the drama: I do not wish to suggest that these pictures must be discarded, but only that they must be seen by the present-day believer in their historical perspective, as part of the inherited situation which has changed from what it was when they were proposed. It is as if the extraplanetary colonists, upon arrival, discovered that they must build their outpost upon the ruins and remains of previous attempts at colonization. Those attempts, to judge from the legends of the people and the temples still shown to the tourist trade, had been far more successful than anyone had expected, and then had almost succumbed to some indigenous disease.

Like the interplanetary traveler, the believer moving about in the world of unbelief must carry with him wherever he goes both his essential food and the atmosphere in which he can breathe. The essential food of the Christian believer is the Word of God made Flesh, and the atmosphere in which he can breathe is the actual God-relationship in which he stands. From these he must never wander far, if he expects to survive in the colonial situation. Unlike the subject of the standard space story, however, he need not exercise his imagination in trying to describe the odd characteristics of the race of creatures native to this planet: in all outward respects they resemble himself exactly, and it is rather to the task of understanding the invisible differences that he must apply his imaginative talents. Nothing is easier for him than to mingle indistinguishably with the natives, so that he is constantly tempted to leave his food and his air at home when he goes out into society, only to find himself suddenly gasping for breath and shaken with weakness in the midst of their most charming and solicitous hospitality. For they are friendly natives, mostly, urbane and skilled in all the civilized arts. They fan him with their words, offer him their food, open the windows, all to no avail—to everyone's embarrassment he must leave the party, and go back to his own sources of strength.

But it will not do to push this image very far, at least not without considerable amendment. In the classical space story the invasion of one planet by a species from another usually results in conflict for the enslavement or annihilation of either the visitors or the natives (a not too inappropriate image for the Christian invasion of the pagan world after Constantine). But the present-day believer does not feel that he arrives fully equipped from another world so much as that his becoming a believer makes him aware for the first time of the existence of the two worlds, and of the necessity for his learning to distinguish them. He is born or admitted into a curious symbiotic arrangement between the two worlds, brought about over the years by mutual infiltration of influence between the colonists and the natives. To make the image work better, then, we should have to postulate the invasion as having taken place at a remote time in history, long before interplanetary travel was dreamed of, and, as so often happened in the case of earthly tribal clashes, the victorious invaders becoming in the course of centuries thoroughly assimilated and "conquered from within" by the natives. This amendment does greater justice to the present confusion, overlapping and interpenetration of the two worlds, but it loses the advantage of impressing upon the believer the strangeness and the essential lack of understanding between the two worlds, as well as his need for maintaining the life-giving connection with his world. Somehow both of these features must be maintained, for the life of faith in relation to the world of unbelief is characterized by just these two aspects of the "colonial situation": the sense of belonging to another world even while on a perilous mission that requires the intimate penetration of every aspect of the life of this world; and the constant struggle against assimilation and being conquered from within by the wily natives, who, so far from being a simple people, seem to possess inexhaustible talents for welcoming the invaders and putting them to work for their own purposes.

The pragmatic sanction

As the Christian faces up to his situation in order to try to visualize exactly what the colonization might consist of in the present time, he cannot help noticing that he is living in an age in which a great religious revival is supposed to be taking place. As a result of acknowledged cracks in the current civilization, now familiarly referred to as "the mess we are in," there has been a revival of interest in religion which might lead one to conclude that war and devastation had at last brought this hardheaded people to its senses, and that a *rapprochement* between man and God was actually under way. Faith, a word until recently not considered respectable in philosophical and scientific circles, has come back into circulation as a rallying cry. Atheists are expected to hide their beliefs out of common courtesy, like Protestants at a Catholic wake, and have been ruled out of order in foxholes. The churches are crowded enough, and every Sunday all over the land this multiple, expectant congregation listens patiently to the regular explanation of how all our troubles, individual and collective, domestic and international, can be traced to the lack of religion in the lives of our people.

This argument, unfortunately, becomes more and more self-contradictory as it successfully draws more and more people into the churches, and one wants to inquire into just what is meant by religion, and what the people expect of religion, in the present "religious revival." That it would seem to be more correctly described as an *ethical* revival is indicated by the pragmatic nature of the sanction with which religion is being reinvested. Stripped of all sentimental trimmings, the pragmatic sanction runs somewhat as follows: Several generations of ardent skeptics and skeptical science worshipers have reared their young to believe that moral standards are a matter of geography, and have placed at their disposal the power released by applied science. Professing astonishment when the moralists of different geographical origins challenge one another to a fight to the finish that threatens to undo the earth at the seams, these wonder-working skeptics hasten to add that, of course, there must also be a science of human nature, a technology of conduct, analogous to the technology born of the natural sciences, to prevent such outbursts in the future, or at least to control them. Unfortunately, there has been something of a cultural lag: the sciences of man have permitted the natural sciences to outstrip them. This condition must be remedied as fast as the progress of the social sciences will permit, but meanwhile, *meanwhile,* life must go on, men must live and act and adopt some principle to guide them. Meanwhile we must have faith. In the

Western world at least, where it is "indigenous," Christianity will do as an *interim ethic*, valid only until a more developed science of man will yield more incontrovertible evidence as to man's proper obligation and destiny. Christianity is to be not only tolerated but encouraged because it produces certain immediately desirable results in conduct. It may be that some of the more obnoxious aspects of the Christian religion, such as its claims to "truth" and its peculiar god, will have to be neutralized by means of adroit redefinitions that every sane person can accept, but it would be most unpragmatic not to admit that believing in something, in this interim period, makes the task of preserving "ethical values" easier.

The pragmatic sanction has the support not only of scientists but of generals, statesmen, philosophers, and educators. These are the doctors of the ailing civilization, and they are faced with the demand that they do something for the patient right away. They recommend faith because it is a medicine that is purported to have worked some remarkable recoveries in the past, but also because they are desperate and must be willing to try anything. It is as if, while arguing and wringing their hands in the consultation room, the doctors happened to look in a cabinet where in a dust-covered bottle they found an old-fashioned remedy that used to work pretty well. There being nothing to lose, and this being hardly a time for professional pride, they rush the medicine to the patient. But either it has turned sour over the years from sitting in the cabinet or it has become too strong from evaporation: the patient makes a horrible grimace and backs away. He is quite anxious to be cured, he says, but surely in this age of pills and shots he cannot be expected to swallow *that*. So finally the doctors appeal to the Public Health Service, Morale Division, to spray the ambient atmosphere, not only with DDT, but also with cloudy signs and semblances of faith, so that men may become infected unconsciously with its essential attitudes, at least for the time being.

If only the name of God can be mentioned often enough in the speeches of statesmen and educators, in the titles of best-selling books, and in the confessions of war correspondents and bomber pilots. If only the lives of some true believers can be held before the public as exemplars of bravery or endurance. If only the name of religion can be reinvested with its halo of sanctity, and unbelief made to feel ashamed. "Let there be faith!" the generals command, the scientists concede, and the educators implore, in their various intonations; and this chorus, swelled on the other side by the loud antiphon of "I told you so!" issuing from the churches, makes up the standard hymn singing of the present religious revival.

A hundred years ago that Danish *infant terrible* Kierkegaard complained that there was no point in trying to become a Christian when everyone assumed that you already were one; or, rather, that this was the most difficult of all tasks, almost an impossibility. It was as if a naughty boy tried to arouse the neighborhood by dressing up as a lion, only to find that everyone had adopted lion skins as the standard Sunday dress. Since Kierkegaard's day the question of what it means to become a Christian, or to live the life of faith in the modern world, has received several more ironic twists. Official Christianity lost its intellectual respectability under the impact of the scientific attitude, and this might have been a wonderful thing if it had made people aware simply of the inadequacy of the exclusive intellect. But at the same time that large-scale disintegrations in public and private life manifested the neglect and perversion of the nonintellectual aspects of man, intellectual respectability itself took a shift from the theoretical to the practical. Now, under the pragmatic clamor for results, and especially for therapeutic results, Christianity, dismissed from respectability as a dogma, threatens to become reinstated into respectability as a technique.

One might ask, why shouldn't the believer rejoice in this new honor conferred upon his faith? And perhaps he should—up to a point. But it is a little like asking, why shouldn't God rejoice that man, when driven to the point of desperation, will in some cases finally turn to him? This is the realistic question that must be put to all who would like to be optimistic about the present religious revival. Wars are always accompanied by a resurgence of religious interest, entirely aside from the question of the causes of war. The dead bear witness to the transience of life in a way that seems almost to belabor the point, and the survivors discover that it is possible to lose everything that is ordinarily deemed essential to bearable living, to lose not only possessions but family and friends and health, to be the witness of unforgettable crimes; and still to live and find this transient life precious, or at least hopeful. The religious faith born out of such extreme need may be sincere enough at the time, no matter how primitively expressed and felt, but one has to ask what happens to this faith when "normal" conditions are restored. If religion is man's natural reaction to bad times and skepticism his natural reaction to good times, the religious optimist must either decide in favor of perpetual war and disaster or he had better consider the possibility that war and disaster do not so much make man religious as they reveal that he is fear-ridden and inclined to be superstitious.

For the believer the pragmatic sanction merely complicates his situation. It means that he will be discovering essential unbelief in the most unlikely places. It means that, having put in its place every lesser allegiance in the hope that none but God might use him, he will become aware that someone else is using him, but not for the glory of God. It means that he will sometimes have to bear witness against what seems like the most persuasive argument in support of Christianity brought forth so far: that it will save our civilization. For, of course, there is a great deal of truth in the pragmatic sanction. The fallacy of the pragmatists does not lie in their making the none-too-clever observation that if everybody were a Christian the world would be a more Christian place to live in, or even the more sophisticated deduction that if civilization needs faith to make it run faith must by all means be encouraged. It is their all too logical, ends-and-means-engineering manner of going about it that betrays the fact that the prophetic denunciation of *this* civilization which is concealed in the pragmatic sanction of Christianity has not touched them at all. They do not seek the kingdom of God, nor his righteousness; they simply would like to have "all these other things" added on to their own kingdom. They do not wish to serve God; they wish him to serve them. They do not repent; they calculate. But, for all of that, the possibility of repentance is always there, and so the believer must not allow the peculiar atmosphere of the pragmatic sanction, the sense that he is being used, to dismay him. He must face it with hope, as he must face all unbelief with hope if there is to be any hope.

Hints, clues, and outward signs

The pragmatic sanction betrays the degree to which all is not well with the unbelievers' world even by their own standards, and that at least at the present time they are sufficiently exasperated or desperate to try anything, even Christianity, to cure their ills. This situation is therefore full of possibilities as well as full of the most baffling ambiguities. To pick his way with any assurance through the maze of crisscrossed motivations and ideologies which any "piece" of their world presents, whether the context is personal or social, philosophical or political, would require the believer to be a wizard of omniscience, possessed of X-ray vision into the human heart and some kind of miraculous knife for dissecting and laying bare the causal connections of human history. But, of course, he is equipped with nothing of the sort. At least if he thinks he is, his own mistakes and the experience of complexity in actuality will soon disabuse him of this notion. What he is equipped with is more like a pair of glasses, neither rose-colored nor dark, which provide him with a different way of seeing things whenever he chooses to use them.

The world looks different seen through the eyes of faith, and yet it is the same world that he and the unbelievers both look out upon. The "objective" evidence is the same for all. All look out upon the same woods and fields and hills, upon the same cycle of cosmic and terrestrial functions, the same rhythm of weather and vegetation, the same daily endeavor, waste, and hope of human life. All inherit the same historical antecedents; the same cultures and civilizations of the past and present are spread out for everyone to see who wishes to examine the efforts of man to decipher the universe from the earliest time to the present. All submit to the same providence or fate: fortune and misfortune, war and peace, the seasons of the individual and the seasons of society, the sun and rain of personal destiny, fall no less upon the believer than upon the unbeliever. It is the interpretation, even in the most elementary terms, that is different.

To the believer this multiverse of objective form and function, the ceaseless straining of vitality, the endless birth, maturity, decay, and death, the indefatigable effort, failure, and renewal of effort, while not understood, is believed to be the outward manifestation of a single event—for that is in part what it means to believe in one God who is creator and redeemer and lord of history. To the unbeliever the same collection of facts and events spells, according to various temperaments, a bag of tricks he must learn to outwit; a hectic, sometimes pleasant but generally pointless interlude between two peaceful eternities of nothingness; a treacherous bog that threatens to swallow him up; or a cruel game in which he is lured on by thoughts of victory to make his play, but in which he is always at last the loser—for these are some of the things it means *not* to believe in one God who is creator and redeemer and lord of history.

The fact that the objective evidence is the same for all interpretations is something the believer should put down for a good thing and never forget. It is a clue as to where a common ground can always be found, the limit of the two-world situation where the two worlds overlap so neatly as to coalesce, an ever-present point of departure for new beginnings, especially new attempts at communication when old words fail. This fact also means that the objective evidence cannot be used argumentatively in support of any interpretation, since it lends itself selectively to many different interpretations and thus becomes for all of them in its totality ambiguous. This is also a good thing; it puts all clever heads on the defensive, and turns attention to the so-called subjective or inner attitudes and dispositions of men as the source of the different interpretations. But if the believer will examine himself and his unbelieving contemporaries in the matter of subjective equipment, he will discover that here too he differs from them in no perceptible way. There is nothing in the way of attitudes and dispositions they are capable of that he is not capable of; he is as much a human being as they, with human hopes, human desires, human needs, and human failings. Just as there is no biological difference between him and the natives, so there is no psychological difference; at least no test can be devised to prove it. Even such a popular item as "integration of personality" will not do, for thousands of years of Oriental religion, as well as primitive religions and modern political religions, have shown the possibility of integration of personality about a great variety of ideas and values. Nor can he find in his own constitution any special "talent" for faith, any predisposing factor, such as moral sensitivity, or yearning for the eternal, which cannot also be found among unbelievers.

Finally, if he is persistent, he will discover, perhaps to his own surprise, that he does not differ from them even in the most obvious distinguishing factor resulting from his special position as interplanetary visitor from another world: his strangeness to this world. The natives make a great show of being very much at home in their world, but closer inspection reveals that each one harbors somewhere in his secret places the feeling of strangeness in this world that he constantly tries to forget about or escape from. There are moments in the life of man on this planet when he finds himself suddenly looking at his world as on the dead body of a friend. It is the same body he knew in other times, but silent and indifferent, stripped of all familiarity, a stranger to him and he a stranger to it. "What have I to do with you?" he asks, an icy loneliness enveloping him, and in that moment both the spiritual consolations of religion and the reasonable explications of science or of common sense seem equally distant, inconsequential fairy tales, invented specifically to divert the human consciousness from the terror of naked being. Men do not live long in this agonizing moment. Death, insanity, or animality seem preferable to a prolonged contemplation of uninterpreted reality, and, therefore, a great part of human activity, all that is not concerned with the bare sustenance of life, can be construed as a half-conscious struggle against this moment, an endless distraction, or a rushing to the rescue with ready-made meanings and purposes.

That men are capable of feeling this strangeness in the midst of the only world they say they know is another hint or clue for the believer as to the nature of the two-world situation. Apparently the natives are not as native as they have to pretend to be. The picture must be revised again to include the possibility that this race of beings also belonged to another world, but that they have lost the life-giving connection with that world, and have become over the years "adjusted" to the living conditions of this world, some of them so well-adjusted that they hotly disclaim even the possibility of any other world.

The children of this world are great believers in outward signs. They are always looking for something, like Athenians, preferably some new thing, and, whenever they think they have discovered it, their first reaction is to organize a group or build a building on its behalf, or both. They judge the strength of the Christian invasion in any country by the numbers of church attenders, the numbers of Bibles sold annually, the size and number of cathedrals that are landmarks.

That this propensity is not a manifestation of the present times, not even of the pragmatic rage for results, but something characteristic of the species, is shown by history. Emperors have been converted to the alien cult by being impressed with the magnificence of its forms of worship. The Middle Ages covered the countryside of Europe with the outward signs of the cult's most ascetic manifestation. Popes and kings fought with equal determination for outward signs of power.

These people demand signs and wonders, and yet the strange thing is that when the signs and wonders are given to them they are somehow not convinced, and demand more signs and wonders. For example, in asking for the credentials of Christianity, they demand of the believer that he show them some outward signs by means of which one may detect and acknowledge his superiority to the unbelievers. But should he naïvely show them a few, they dub him a pious fraud, and rightly so. For they are themselves a pious people, who have mistaken the outward signs for the reality signified, but it is easier for them to detect the fraudulence of piousness in the case of a reality they do not believe in.

The businessman who is supported in his life by the monuments and ceremonies of commercial success, the educator who is impressed by the institutional grandeur of universities, the civic leader who is thrilled by the intricacy of a city's traffic or sewage-disposal system, the statesman who is uplifted by public demonstrations—all these are pious people. And when their piousness is challenged, they cannot understand that it is not the outward signs that are to blame, nor that it is not a question of getting a different set, or of having none, which is impossible, but always and only the mistaking of the sign for the reality. In the words of a phrase of Kierkegaard's, they do not wear the clothing of this world loosely enough; in the words of the Bible, they are an idolatrous species.

The simultaneous demanding and distrusting of the outward signs of the reality of Christianity represent a kind of loss of innocence that makes the situation of colonization quite different from what it was in the early missionary efforts of this religion. When everything that might serve as an outward sign (and something must so serve, else there cannot be even communication, much less incarnation) has become tainted with the distrust of skepticism, and the reproach of historical guilt, what is needed by the believer is a new kind of innocence. The new kind of innocence must be undismayed and tough, accepting the situation, and yet affirming outward signs both old and new without denying whatever truth is contained in both the distrust of skepticism and the reproach of historical guilt. And this innocence must be forthright enough to point out to the people that they can hardly afford to be overly fastidious about their clothing, or that of the Church, when they have soiled all the available cloth.

Temptations

It having pleased God to begin on this earth a new dispensation which shall also be its true restoration, and the believer finding himself by a curious second birth born into this dispensation as into the outpost of another world, the question that arises for him is: What is demanded of him that is not demanded of all in this refractive atmosphere of double images, where everything is the same for the two worlds and yet different? What is the real meaning of the believer-unbeliever dichotomy for him, and to what special temptations does it make him subject?

The first temptation that he must learn to resist is to take his cue for the meaning of this distinction from the unbelievers. As the pragmatic sanction indicates, the unbelievers have all kinds of definite ideas as to what the distinction is, and even when approving cannot avoid putting it in invidious terms. Believers are people who think they are, and in some cases actually seem to be, holier or happier or better behaved than unbelievers. The pragmatic sanction is based on the practical admission that we could all use a little more of these qualities, or related ones, in the interim while it is being decided by the research foundations what we really ought to be. That all these qualities turn out to be ambiguous, and, upon further definition in Christian terms, paradoxical, should be a warning that any distinction in terms of invidious comparisons had better be avoided.

What is really demanded of the believer is that he bear witness to a certain truth, and the bearing of this witness may take such different forms that if he should also happen to be what the unbelievers call holy or happy or well-behaved, it may be an optical illusion or a coincidence. In any case, his own understanding, as a redeemed sinner who is to bear witness to Christ, of what holiness or happiness or good behavior might mean under these circumstances, is so different from theirs that the resulting mutual misunderstanding is likely to be almost comical.

An age of unbelief, in contrast to an age like the Middle Ages, is like a rare opportunity especially designed to show up this neutral, factual, or what the natives would call "nonvaluative," aspect of faith. So you are a believer! Shall you congratulate yourself on this fact? Or allow others to congratulate you? In an age like the Middle Ages, when everything in the atmosphere was conducive to the encouragement of faith, when belief was nurtured from the cradle to the grave and every human institution consciously or unconsciously reflected the commonly inherited Christian tradition, men might have been tempted to congratulate themselves on their faith. The evidence of the Reformation would seem to show that they did just that, and became pretty complacent about the part they were able to play in bringing new believing souls to God. In an age of unbelief the atmosphere is sufficiently unpropitious and even hostile that at least this temptation does not arise, and faith seems less like an achievement than like a destiny, even like a miracle, and a rather embarrassing miracle at that.

Especially when engaged in direct evangelism does the believer become inclined to regard faith as a miracle: when he tries to bridge the gulf between the two worlds from his side, or, even more, when he observes some who are trying to bridge it from their side, who would like to believe. He is filled with the desire to give his faith to others, to share it, not to hoard it as a secret possession, but to spread it abroad as the blessing which in spite of all embarrassment he has found it to be. The more he loves the men of this earth in a more than superficial way, the more he is concerned to bring to them the salvation of faith. Whether it be by the rational persuasiveness of philosophy or theology, or by personal witness on behalf of the biblical truths, or by pointing out the "signs" in history, or by works of love and mercy, the believer, by whatever he does, hopes that he may make it a little easier for someone else to believe.

This is his function as colonist. But the more he tries, the more he is made to realize that all his efforts can only bring another man to the edge of the gulf. The final "leap of faith" the most ardent believer can neither force on the unwilling nor guarantee to the seeking. In the absence of the psychological and cultural power of the Church in society, it suddenly becomes apparent that here neither bribes nor threats nor promises nor assurances of any kind are of any avail. He knows that *he* did not become a believer because of this man's unimpeachable life or that man's unimpeachable argument. What is ordinarily obscured by the very presence of a strong church becomes laid bare in the bareness of an age of unbelief: that faith is not a matter between one man and another, but always finally only between God and man, an act of love between God and man which is for man always the embarrassing miracle.

The knowledge that the situation of evangelism brings him that he is not in ultimate control of the situation, even though it makes his relationship to the unbelievers more difficult, is a salutary realization for the believer, the token of his relationship to Him who is, and the badge of a real servanthood. It saves him from the horrible suspicion that faith is just another human idea, another philosophy, an extra-extra-clever solution to the human predicament. If faith were a matter for human disposal, then it would be the grandest of illusions about this world, and the most Machiavellian of deceptions about the self. The knowledge, available only after faith, that by himself he could never have believed, as well as the knowledge that by themselves the unbelievers will never be able to believe—this is the earth-transcending fact which strengthens and upholds the believer in his forever-ridiculous position of one who lives and hopes and labors for something which it is not in his power to give.

But if in an age of unbelief he is not tempted to make of faith an easy thing, nor even to congratulate himself on it, other temptations lie in wait for him. The most proprietary of these (not the general run of human temptations, but such as appear to be tailor-made for the believer) arise from two opposing desires within him, or, looked at externally, from two opposite reactions to the characteristic discomforts of his position. There is, on the one hand, his unwillingness to bear the isolation into which both the intellectual and the practical aspects of his faith repeatedly push him. He wants to be "at one" with mankind, not to be always "against the world." It is perhaps an irritating surprise to him that his faith, which is concerned with the most basic unity of all men, should cause him to feel isolated in an alien world, cut off from his fellow men as much by tolerant as by hostile misunderstanding. On the other hand, there is his need and desire to renew and purify his faith; to return to its source for strengthening; to protect it from subtle invasions of unbelief due to imitation and conformity, and from betrayals due to compromise and cowardice.

The first set of desires will lead him to attempt all kinds of *rapprochements* with the unbelievers. Of course, he is always in the act of "approaching" the unbelievers, as one who bears witness to that which they do not believe. But as soon as this becomes an attempt to overcome at all costs his unwanted isolation from them, there occurs an ever-so-slight shift of emphasis in the approach. He is tempted to minimize the differences in outlook and motivation and to concentrate on all possible forms of co-operation. This usually means some outward activity, and here, after all, there is so much to be gained by concerted effort! The unbelievers are neither lazy nor stupid and are, on the contrary, full of all sorts of ingenious schemes for human salvation, some on a world-shaking scale.

With many of these plans for human happiness the believer will find himself in partial agreement, or at least he will find himself able to give them his support as partial plans. But the unbelievers, lacking any transcendent frame of reference, will be disposed to regard each his own particular plan as the all-sufficient purpose for man, and to demand for it an undivided allegiance that the believer can hardly give. There thus arises the familiar situation where the believer and unbeliever find themselves working in close co-operation on some program of "works," but it is as if a wall separated them. From the viewpoint of the believer the unbeliever wants the right things for the wrong reasons, while from the viewpoint of the unbeliever the believer's center of allegiance is elsewhere; he has not staked all on the program and cannot be trusted.

At this point the temptation for the believer will be to say that only the results count, the motivation doesn't matter; and when the results themselves reveal the difference of motivation, he will be further tempted to put off as long as possible the need for drawing a line somewhere, or to obscure it with rationalization. He will become painfully aware of all that he owes to his fellow men, especially the unbelievers among them, and may attempt to discharge this debt of gratitude by pointing out to them that he is also a useful member of society, he has their best interests at heart. He may even catch himself repeating the arguments of the pragmatists about his function as a moral leaven. In the realm of thought he will be tempted to search for some philosophy that is able to embrace everything and thus supply himself and them with a common ground, and, finally, he may even be tempted to make of his faith a secret, that the unbelievers might not be offended by the implied deficiency at the foundation of their existence.

The betrayal into which this set of temptations finally leads him will then throw him into the opposite set of temptations. Here he will be tempted to deplore that he was born into this age, and to think with nostalgia of some golden age of the past, such as the idealized Middle Ages, when faith was at least a virtue. He will be tempted to pursue a plan of personal perfection, to withdraw into himself, become absorbed in his private salvation and let the rest of the world go its way, as it seems determined to do anyway. After all, the attainment of religious maturity and spiritual versatility is a lifetime job in itself, and must he not transform himself before he can hope to transform others? He will at any rate be tempted to confine his associations to the company of his fellow believers, for here there is such warm peace, such a friendly rivalry in the doing of good, such a sense of reassurance and solidarity. When he finally realizes that this is also a betrayal of him who came to minister not to the healthy but to the sick, when he sees that God himself has not so forsaken the world as a satisfied churchgoer, then,—well, then he will again be ready for the first set of temptations.

If we were speaking here of mechanical forces, there would, of course, be some point at which these opposing tendencies just balance. Ideally the believer should be able to walk along a knife-edge path that lies just between these two opposing sets of temptations. But the disposition of the spirit is not to be thought of as the resultant of the summation of opposing forces, for the spirit is not a dead force but a live response, and there exist no ideal believers, only particular human beings struggling with one thing at a time who hope and pray that they may be accounted believers. So the believer is shuttled back and forth between these two opposite sets of temptations and in this process he learns something of the perennial instability of this kind of life, its inability to settle down into any fixed attitudes, or to rest on any established achievements.

Further reflection on this situation may teach him that what he is involved in is not a local or historical problem but the eternal problem of eternity re-entering time, time and again. It is not even the special problem of an "age of unbelief," for what age is not also an age of unbelief? And what believer is not also an unbeliever, a merely hope-to-be believer? He who knows that faith and love in relation to God are ultimately indistinguishable, also knows himself for an unbeliever. For he knows that as he did not love enough he did not believe enough, and as he did not believe enough he did not love enough. But if at any time he did believe and therefore love, and if at any time he did love and therefore believe—if only for a moment, and in the hope of another such moment—then in that moment all the contradictions and peculiarities of his position as a believer sprang into existence. And in that moment, as believer, he observed them and accepted them gladly and made them his own. While in between such moments, when he knew himself for an unbeliever, he perhaps resented these contradictions and peculiarities, considered them a "burden" of faith, and was tempted to drop them and make peace with this world. But at the same time he clung to them in hope, in the hope that he might after all become a believer again, that his "burden" might again become "light." And then he knew himself again for a believer, in that he did not, he could not, give up the hope of again becoming a believer.

This world's possibilities

In such precarious struggle of the spirit is the faith that is to transform this world delivered into the world, defeated, and withdrawn to its source for strengthening in order to emerge again. But this does not happen in a vacuum, nor in an imaginary realm above the world. It happens in the context of this world's possibilities seen in a perspective that implies the other world, and from that perspective this world's possibilities become faith's opportunities. This world's possibilities are the various areas or realms of life such as the several to be considered in this book in relation to the believer.

In an age of unbelief it becomes obvious that this world's possibilities are already being used, not as opportunities for redemption, but as idolatrous and destructive substitutes for faith. In relation to the world's possibilities the believer must not place himself in competition with the unbelievers. He is to leave all blueprint-making and utopia-constructing to them, on the ground that the world already has a structure. The world's possibilities are discovered, not created, by men, but the human actualities are formed by men out of the discovered possibilities. The several aspects of life artificially distinguished by thought for convenience in handling represent in their totality a certain quality of human life—call it knowledge, relatedness, awareness, consciousness, sensibility, or simply being—that is the object of redemption, the "thing" that is in need of being redeemed.

This totality is far from simple; at least for the human mind to reflect on it means to look at it from different angles one at a time, producing a fragmentation constantly in danger of being mistaken for chaos. The demand for simplicity, however, is here the very temptation to be resisted. It arises naturally from the fact that the consciousness of the totality of being happens only to a single one, a person, who mistakenly concludes that his life would be easier and his personality more integrated if the possibilities he sees in the world could be simplified. This is because he seeks the unity of his personality in some simple relation to the world. But the believer's unity of personality is centered in his relation to God, not in any simple, know-it-all relation to the world, so he can afford to face a complicated world with equanimity, and to resist all attempts at simplification that violate life for the sake of an easy integration of persons around the wrong thing.

He will find in his approach to the several realms of life that the unbelievers demand a simplification of a given aspect just to the degree that they would like to use it as a substitute for faith (for example, their use of history as a world philosophy). However, in his searching out of the redemptive possibilities he must sooner or later say something in word or deed, in the saying of which he himself will risk oversimplification and misunderstanding, a risk which he must take. Unavoidable simplification may be harmless as long as it is understood to be representative of life, not constitutive of it.

After the warning against the temptation to simplify, the believer needs a guiding principle which will be the same for the several realms or areas of life no matter how diverse their interests, and that means that the principle must be grounded in the Christian's own situation rather than in the variety of perspectives reflected in the world's possibilities. But the believer's situation is that of one who has to live in two worlds at the same time. These two worlds are constituted by his faith in the God who is both creator and redeemer. The world as created good by God he never sees. But in the unredeemed world, the fallen world, he must learn to find the traces and evidences of its original goodness, and the structure of its good possibilities and good limitations. This simply means that he must learn to the extent that his abilities allow, what life is actually like, not letting himself be distracted by any of the romantic illusions or clever escape devices which at least some of the unbelievers have invented to shield themselves from its reality.

In this search for the way things really are, the believer will find many opportunities for collaboration with the unbelievers, at least up to a point, and up to that point he should rival them in openness for knowledge, especially where that knowledge is pertinent to the redemption to be effected. He should, in any case, at all times be willing to learn from the unbelievers, that he may know what they know and something more. The point at which the learning from the unbelievers must change into a passing of judgment upon them will be very different for the different areas of interest. It will be the point at which the distortion of the original goodness of creation becomes evident in the revealing light of the Christ norm. Christ is the searchlight that reveals both the outlines of sin in the fallen world and the outlines for its divine restoration. It may be only by a very roundabout way that the point at which the criterion of Christ can be applied is reached, so beguilingly kaleidoscopic and apparently disinterested are the varied activities of men, but wherever the categorically human, the concern of man as man, can be uncovered and studied behind all the swarming of busyness and enthusiasm, there is the vulnerable spot.

Increasingly to learn to see the world as created good by God, to reveal and judge its human distortion by applying the criterion of Christ, and to bear witness in word-deed to its redemption in the power of the Holy Spirit: these three are the forms of the believer's opportunities in relation to the different aspects of life which are the world's possibilities.

Chapter II

FAITH AND KNOWLEDGE

The claim of faith to be a kind of knowledge

WHEN FAITH EXPRESSES ITSELF IN WORDS, IT TENDS TO TAKE THE FORM either of doctrine or of poetry, both of which try to witness to some kind of truth about man's knowledge of the world, of himself, and of God. Throughout the history of Hebrew-Christian religiousness both types of expressions of faith have occurred, and we may take Thomas Aquinas' *Summa* or John Calvin's *Institutes* as examples of the doctrinal, and the Psalms or Dante's *Divine Comedy* as examples of the poetical, expression of faith. However, poetry and doctrine are the fragmentary, cultural by-products of a condition of the spirit which even in a personality not gifted for such expression may be something more complex, many-sided and all-embracing than even poetry and doctrine between them can encompass.[1] It is perhaps the distinguishing mark of Christian faith, as against the kind of belief exacted by other religions, that it makes this totalitarian claim upon the personality, so that neither will, nor feeling, nor intellect, nor imagination, nor activity, nor passivity, nor any other human capability, can be made impervious to its penetrating power.

A man does not become a Christian believer by cutting off or inflating his intellect, suppressing his will or exaggerating it, suppressing his feelings or exaggerating them, becoming strictly active or strictly passive, as, for example, a man might be said to become a disciple of the Buddha by cultivating the psychological attitudes appropriate to what his intellect understands by the meaning of nirvana. Neither does a man become a believer by deciding in his mind to call Jesus the Son of God, in the way that a man may be said to become a Mohammedan by subscribing to the doctrine that Allah is the Great One and Mohammed is his prophet. This is what happened in the history of the Church when whole nations were "baptized" in the name of the Lord by the decree of the ruler, or what happens today when they are so "baptized" by the decree of custom. A Christian believer is one who has permitted the invasion of his life, perhaps only gradually, and by imperceptible degrees, and certainly not without some resistance on his part, by what may have been originally a one-sided commitment, but which, precisely because it was an honest commitment, eventually became a many-sided commitment, just as many-sided as the natural limitations of his personality allowed.

The implications of this totalitarian claim of Christian faith on the human personality have seldom been understood in the history of Christianity, and are still less understood today. The periods of Church history with their special characteristics, such as periods of great theological controversy, or of ascetic retreat, or of social transformation, or of missionary zeal, are as much a witness of this total claim of faith on all that is humanly possible as they are also the response of the spirit and flesh to the possibilities and limitations of special historical circumstances. Nowadays this ability of Christian faith to mean, and to have meant, so many different things to different men and different times is considered detrimental to the claim of Christianity to be the "truth," for the latter, if expected at all, is expected to show itself in the form of some uniform law of nature or of history. In this chapter we are concerned with only one implication of this claim on the total personality: namely, the fact that faith, whatever else it may be, must also be regarded as a kind of knowledge, and how this fact brings it into conflict or co-operation with other kinds of knowledge.

The problem generally considered under the time-honored rubric of "science versus religion" needs a restatement. As long as it is thought of as a conflict between specific scientific discoveries and various misunderstandings of nature found in the Scriptures or Church tradition and history, it can be resolved all too simply by granting the validity of the former in their proper field of reference. The fact that the granting of this validity does not cause people to become Christian (as if that had really been the chief obstacle) or that it causes them to become religious for the wrong reasons (as pointed out in the previous chapter) shows how much more is involved in the question than simple factual contradiction. What is here involved is the question of whether modern man has really invented knowledge or whether knowledge, in the broader sense of a meaningful patternmaking out of all kinds of experience in whatever categories are capable of producing a pattern, is not tied up with the very concept of man and as old as man on the earth. Looking at the situation in the Bible, a Christian believer can hardly maintain that the creatures whom God there addresses as men were not really yet men because they were so sadly remiss in that particular kind of patternmaking out of a particular aspect of experience that now goes under the name of science. On the contrary, the very fact that God addresses them as men would seem to indicate that their patternmaking in the realm of religious experience was already sufficiently adequate to make them feel responsible before him, or at least not exonerable on the grounds of ignorance. Nor were they devoid of other kinds of knowledge, such as that of practical affairs, war-making, power politics, aesthetic expression, moral argumentation, and even cosmic speculation—all in various degrees of conflict or co-operation with their religious knowledge.

When the question is put, "science—and x—and y—and z and also religion," the either/or connotation is removed from the disjunction with religion, but by the same token a measure of responsibility is injected into the relationships between all the different kinds of knowledge, precisely in so far as they are knowledge and not illusion. The claim of faith to be a kind of knowledge must mean at the same time the acceptance of this responsibility. It must be admitted that when man's knowledge is defined in this broader sense, it takes on more the look of a patchwork quilt than a single golden measuring rod or principle that can be applied to all kinds of experience universally, but to admit this is to deny neither the validity of the patches nor even the possibility of their fitting into some over-all pattern. In its aspect as knowledge the Christian faith is a meaningful patternmaking out of that aspect of experience concerned with the wholeness and ultimacy of life, in terms of categories of interpretation (mythical and historical) derived from the Old and New Testaments.

The difficulty that arises from this claim at the present times lies in the fact that to the modern mind the statement: faith is a kind of knowledge, is a contradiction in terms. In the face of a contradiction in terms everyone is instantly thrown back upon his "intellectual honor." He fairly bristles with philosophical integrity, and he feels he must break off intellectual relations with all who wish to entertain such a notion. However, that this is actually the way many an honest intellectual feels about it is betrayed by the fact that the more broad-minded among them have no objection to faith as such. Let there be plenty of faith, they say; let all who feel temperamentally so inclined believe all they wish, especially if this makes them happy; let the whole world become religious. Only let not a single soul claim that a single one of the assorted religious beliefs men hold represents a kind of knowledge. For if we have to have faith about something, it is because knowledge of it is not yet available; and if we have knowledge, we no longer need faith.

The movement in philosophy with which this attitude is most closely identified is positivism. It must be discussed before the rest of philosophy can be discussed, because if its attitude on knowledge is allowed to stand unchallenged, there would be no more room for the claim of philosophy to be a kind of knowledge than for the claim of faith, or any other partly cognitive activity of the human person. The development of positivism is a curious and instructive phenomenon from the standpoint of the believer's effort to understand the unbelievers' world, for it reveals both the desire for some kind of absolute certainty and the optimistic willingness to assume the control of nature as driving motives behind at least part of the scientific enterprise. The very connotations of the word "positive" include the meanings of "certain" and "good." As originally used by Auguste Comte, it meant the kind of knowledge that presumably results from the application of scientific method to all areas of experience, historically destined to replace as outgrown two previous kinds of knowledge attempted in the past, the mythical and the metaphysical. Positivism developed historically as the logical extreme position of the more vague and venerable philosophy of naturalism, much older than the scientific method. In tending toward the logical extreme, positivism represented a kind of critical self-examination on the part of the natural sciences as to the implications of their method for the results, especially when it came to the question of philosophizing over these results.

During the age of the Enlightenment the rather vague philosophy of naturalism combined with the scientific method to produce not so much clear thinking as a wave of enthusiasm. Just as classical antiquity in its humanism had assumed that "man" was a definite something, and medievalism in its theocentricity had assumed that God was a definite something, so the naturalism of the Enlightenment assumed that "nature" was a definite something. "Nature" included the totality of bodies and motions, of structures and functions and processes that man could become aware of, and the scientific method was the tool by which he found out their interrelations. The earlier naturalists, who were still mostly rationalists, and whose attitude toward nature was still romantic and wishful rather than empirical and objective as the scientific method demanded, included man's body in the concept of nature, but had some reservations about his mind. Whether through instinct, or through theological prejudice, or just through a conservative desire to maintain possible contact with the time-honored notions of the soul and of God, it occurred to these early naturalists that that which is the observer of nature, its chronicler and cataloguer, cannot be exactly identical and continuous with that nature itself, and that even in logical terms the totality cannot be comprehended by a part of the totality, except if that part exist somehow outside that totality, or have some special vantage point over against it. This "part outside" might be the "soul," and the totality might be thought of as God, so that the scientific naturalism would be nothing but a new method of seeking knowledge of God—an attractive idea which silenced much theological opposition and aroused religious enthusiasm for the new science.

But the more the naturalists settled down to the sober and laborious task of actually studying nature by the scientific method, instead of merely rhapsodizing over the possibilities of it, the more it became evident that there was no excuse for maintaining the distinction between "nature" and the human "soul," at least not on scientific grounds alone. And by that time the enthusiasm for the new kind of knowledge had carried away the naturalists to the point where they were convinced that scientific grounds were the only grounds worth considering. On scientific grounds, then, there was no way to draw a line between the mind that studies nature and that nature itself, and in witness to this there sprang up the new science of psychology, which applied the new method to the mental and emotional reactions of men as best it could. The fact that an enormous quantity of observations and correlations in this field was soon forthcoming seemed abundant verification of their assumption, and so the human soul was on scientific grounds unceremoniously incorporated into nature, a rather peculiar bit of nature, and God soon followed as one of the rather peculiar ideas entertained by that peculiar bit of nature from time to time.

It is quite true that there is no way of drawing a line between nature and the human soul, or the special quality of manhood, consciousness, spirit, transcendence, call it what you will, *on scientific grounds alone.* All this statement means is that there is no way of limiting the kind of subject matter to which the scientific method may be applied, if anyone is willing or determined to apply it to anything under the sun. The real question to ask is—what kind of knowledge will it produce when so applied? There is nothing to stop anyone from applying the scientific method, let us say, to a poem, including in the study all the historical, biological, psychological, physical, chemical, geographical, meteorological, and other data that can be assembled and verified about the writing of it and the reading of it. The question then is, is this kind of knowledge really adequate to the subject, does it tell us all there is to know about the poem, and, if it does not, if there is a residuum, however small, that the scientific study of it does not touch, must we, if we are to be accounted orthodox in the scientific faith, exclude all such further meanings or intimations from the realm of knowledge and let only the scientific description of it claim this intellectual standing? The same can be asked about the now so-called soul of man. Certainly a scientific description of it can be attempted—behaviorism is such an attempt—but what sort of knowledge of souls does it give us? Does it give us anywhere near as accurate, complex, and immediate understanding of our fellow men, for example, as even the most casual introspection into our own "souls" can give us, or as a deeper and more imaginative probing by means of literature might give, into regions where no scientific method with its measurements can reach?

By now, however, such a question could no longer be asked within science itself, for science had become, in the minds of most intellectuals, synonymous with the only real knowledge. It would have to be asked, if at all, from some point outside science, such as philosophy, which presumably dealt with more aspects of knowledge than only the scientific. But, alas, the scientific mania had already begun to eat into the foundations of philosophy, putting philosophy on the defensive with its sure and demonstrable laws, and raising the question of whether philosophy were any longer necessary or useful to men, since science now pointed the way to real knowledge. Before this new avalanche of facts and correlations, laws and hypotheses, experiments and their generalization, the philosophers themselves were the first to retreat overawed. They made haste to accommodate this boisterous, lusty, and aggressive child of the human brain which by its amazing growth and success threatened to drive all its parents and relatives out of the house, so that soon there would be only three valid disciplines for the human mind: science, applied science, and philosophy of science. The latter was rapidly becoming the last-ditch stand of philosophy, the only place where philosophy could still find a *raison d'être*, and that only in so far as it vouched for the validity of science against theological prejudice and traditional philosophical schools.

The logic of logical positivism

It was as applied to the problems raised by the "new physics" at the turn of the century that positivism first became a rigorously thought-out epistemology, after having been at first only a vague, science-glorifying outlook in the hands of Auguste Comte and the philosophical naturalists. The breakdown of the classical Newtonian mechanics and its reconstruction under relativity and quantum mechanics provoked a re-examination and reinterpretation of physical concepts and the nature of physical theories that could not stop short of the theory of knowledge itself. This is because in physics such general or abstract ideas as space, time, matter, energy, causation, determinism, had to be dealt with concretely, in terms of physical acts, and the concrete results turned out to make not much sense in terms of the same ideas as they appeared in everyday life or common-sense usage, or even in philosophical discourse. But even before the advent of the "new physics" positivism received a ready hearing among physicists, for physics was probably the first science to feel the need of being rescued from the enthusiastic claims and unscientific pronouncements of its stanchest supporters. Physicists became interested in positivism because they saw in it an attempt to make science more empirical, less humanistic, more accurate in its terminology, less given to speculation and more to observation, more rigorous in the formulation of conclusions, and more noncommittal where conclusions were not justified.

The pressing need, these physicists thought, was to remove from the words that were used in physics any animistic, or humanistic, or teleological implications which adhered to these words as a residue from Aristotelian physics and from everyday, common-sense philosophical notions. The purpose of science was declared by the positivists to be the establishment of connections and relations between elements of perception, and nothing more. Such words as "force," "energy," and "matter" were declared to be nothing but symbols for certain observable relationships among the elements of our experience, and any inclination to regard them as something "real," that "existed" somehow of its own accord, was considered an illegitimate instrusion of metaphysics into science. Perceptual experience was the raw material out of which science was built, and the finished product was a relationship, as exact as possible and preferably expressible in mathematical terms. If in the course of trying to understand or to visualize a relationship it was necessary to construct models or pictures, this was all very well as long as these pictures and models were remembered to be just that, and were not taken to have a reality of their own. The pictures and models were, of course, also taken from experience, otherwise their elucidatory value would be nil, and they were then doctored up to fit any new facts that came to light.

In this way scientific knowledge became the representation of certain relationships in experience by analogy with models or pictures from other kinds of experience, preferably with the kind that is subject to mathematical treatment. The planetary model of the atom, for example, was not to be taken as a theory of atomic *structure*, which presents to our eyes the form and shape of something that really exists on an invisible scale, but rather this theory was to be taken merely as a model or "construct" made by and for the imagination, which constituted a convenient summary for many experiments, a practical shorthand for the diversity of facts observed about the atom. The whole atomic-molecular theory was itself this kind of model, or picture analogy, for summarizing the phenomena of gases, liquids, and solids. The most that could be said in a philosophical way was that the elements of *this* area of experience behaved *as if* they could be adequately represented by a model or concept from some other area of experience, preferably some fairly common concept on which there is general agreement. Thus it is fairly easy to get general agreement on what is meant by a picture of small particles having mass and moving with uniform velocity and suffering collisions. The experience of billiard balls is immediately called to mind. But from the statement that the behavior of gases can be represented by such a model, to the statement that "reality itself" consists of material particles on a suitably small scale, is an unwarranted leap from the realm of experience to the realm of metaphysical speculation. It is an attempt to create an independent, self-existent universe out of what are merely helping ideas or pictures or analogies employed in the endeavor to bring orderliness out of the chaos of our perceptions.

The hostility of positivism to metaphysics was due to the fact that of all the various nonscientific meanings that still clung to the words used in physics, it was the metaphysical ones that pretended to be able to interpret the "broader significance" of the physical results, and of scientific results generally. Positivists therefore saw two good reasons for getting rid of metaphysics entirely, besides the need for stricter terminology: (1) they thought they could rid the whole program of science of the preoccupation with unanswerable questions; and (2) they thought they could establish a mode of expression for the scientific concepts that would not have to be changed as one passed from one science to another, but would form the basis of the unification of the several sciences.

(1) According to the positivists a proposition in science had to contain a statement about observables, or the directions for reaching some observables, through logical implication, however involved and remote the process might be. Statements which did not contain any ultimate reference to observables were without means of verification, and were to be thrown out of court. They were declared to be meaningless, or illegitimate statements. This amounted to the setting up of a three-valued logic, in which propositions could be declared true, false, or meaningless. Into the last category came the innumerable questions that arose, according to the positivists, when certain words in physics were used with the metaphysical meanings that had accrued to them during their long service in the classical schools of philosophy. Such questions as, "Does nature obey immutable laws?" or, "Are physical events determined in advance?" or, "Is matter or energy

more fundamental in the structure of the universe?" could never be decided in terms of observables, and, if we confined ourselves to observables, we would not even think of asking them.

(2) Somewhat the same situation obtained when one passed from the concepts of one science to those of another. Here the monistic metaphysical notion that all concepts must be somehow reducible to an irreducible lowest common denominator, which was then declared to be the "real" or the "thing in itself," raised insurmountable barriers and endless philosophical controversies between the several sciences. Thus when the concepts of biology did not readily "reduce themselves" to the concepts of physics and chemistry, there arose the acrid controversy between the "mechanists" and the "vitalists," the former insisting that only concepts which were thus reducible should be used in biology, the latter proclaiming that the facts of biology could never be comprehended in merely physicochemical terms. To the positivist this was another one of those "meaningless" questions which would never arise if scientists confined themselves to observables, and the relations between observables. The very idea of "reducing" one concept to another, so-called more basic one, was clearly a metaphysical notion. All that this could mean in positivistic terms would be that a relationship had been established between the observables involved in two concepts, or that one concept was more "economical" than another in that it could be used to replace several more involved ones. It certainly did not mean that one concept could "explain" another concept, and thus precede it in the scale of "fundamentalness." Positivistically speaking, all relationships between observables were upon an equal footing, and while some relationships were more close to the immediate observables and others more remote, there could be no question of this or that one being more fundamental. On this understanding of the concepts used in science the positivists hoped to bring about a unification of the several sciences.

It was inevitable that such a critical scrutiny of the individual words and phrases used in science would eventually lead to the analysis of the logical structure and function of language itself. The logical positivists maintained that language was nothing but a set of words or symbols, plus a set of rules for the combination, substitution, and transposition of the words or symbols such that, for any given set of rules, a set of words or a proposition could be declared logically correct, logically incorrect, or logically meaningless. Therefore, the language of science must be made to consist of a set of words or symbols plus a set of rules for their combination, substitution, and transposition such that the resulting propositions could be declared scientifically true, scientifically false, or scientifically meaningless. But since, to be scientific, a statement had to contain an ultimate reference to observables, these ultimate statements of observation, in the form of "A says he observes thus and so, at such a time and place," became the primary elements out of which the whole language of science was to be constructed, even to the most general hypotheses and the so-called laws of nature. In other words, the positivistic language did not deal with objects or events but only with statements of observation, and logical statements about statements of observation.

The ordinary language of objects and events—which they called the "material language"—could be used for convenience, but only in so far as it was at any point translatable into the language of statements of observation, and statements about such statements—which they called the "formal language." This was to insure that at no point in the language of any science would there be permitted the introduction of objects or entities or events for which no statement of observation could be reached—in other words, objects or entities which made no observable difference in the observable world.

For the positivists all the traditional problems of philosophy about which the various schools of philosophy took issue—such as realism and idealism, fate and freedom, being and becoming—were pseudo problems resulting from the illogical use of language. They consisted of the indiscriminate mixing up of objects or entities for which there were statements of observation with objects or events for which there were none, a fact which could easily be demonstrated by the logical analysis of the language they used. The logical analysis of language therefore remained as the last shred of philosophy, but it was not called philosophy, because it rejected all metaphysical presuppositions and implications. It was rather called the first step in science. Science was nothing but applied logic of language—that is, "the logical analysis of terms, statements and theories proper to the various departments of science" according to the rules prescribed.[2] All problems other than this were declared to be nonsense problems, because they were concerned with the relationships of nonsense propositions.

The logical positivists simply ignored, or did not allow to be raised, the question of the metaphysical presuppositions of the logical analysis of language. In other words, they did not allow the question of existence to be raised, only the question of observation. They did not seem to see that the founding of science on the logical analysis of language presupposes that the world which science investigates, even if you call it *a set of observables*, is such a world that a set of logically correct propositions about it yields sense rather than nonsense. The truth value of logic itself was simply assumed by them, not proved, which is a denial of the claim that logical positivism is a philosophy without metaphysical presuppositions. Those logical positivists who saw this difficulty answered that they were not interested in truth value, with all its implied overtones of "existence" and "reality," and they were quite willing to admit that thereby the whole enterprise of science became a "game"—a game whose object was to demonstrate the possibilities of logical relationship in any given collection of empirical data. What they were much more interested in was to show that the game of science was the same sort of game, no matter what the observables, and, therefore, that strict adherence to the rules of the game would bring about a true logical and empirical unity among all the sciences.

In spite of this sophisticated reasoning there was little acceptance for the positivistic outlook in science until the advent of the relativity and quantum theories in physics, when it suddenly achieved a leap in popularity as being the only point of view that could reconcile the relativistic concepts with their classical antecedents, and remove the apparent contradictions which the new physics entailed. At the same time there appeared a further refinement of the positivistic methodology which demanded that not only must a statement in physics contain a reference to observables, but it must also indicate the operations by which the observables are observed. It was claimed that observables could be unambiguously characterized only in terms of the operations by which they were determined, or measured, and that observables which were determined by different sets of operations were really separate and distinct observables and should not be comprised under the same concept. For example, the concept of space acquired different meanings depending on how the space was measured—whether by means of rigid bars, as in the space of everyday life, or by means of the speed of light, as in astronomical space, or by means of the wave length of light, as in subatomic space. Much of the confusion which the new physics seemed to entail resulted, the positivists claimed, from our very human transference of the concept of space, as experienced and measured in everyday life, both to the subatomic and to the astronomical levels. Such a question as to whether space is Euclidean or not could only have meaning when referred to the operations by which the space was measured: thus, the space which we measure with meter sticks is Euclidean; whereas, the space we measure by timing a beam of light is apparently not Euclidean. The question, "Is empty space, unmeasured space, or space-in-the-abstract Euclidean?" is a meaningless question.

In a like manner not only the concepts of space and time and energy and matter were "disontologized," or deprived of their in-the-abstract meaning, and closely tied up with the human means of apprehending and measuring them, but also such concepts as causality and determinism. The idea that the concept of causality implied a *necessary* connection between successive elements in an isolated, repeatable train of events was replaced by the idea that causality is merely a concept used to describe the *routine* aspect of experience, for such terms as "repeatable," "isolated," and even "successive," apply in a strict sense only to idealized systems, which cannot be realized experimentally. Similarly, the idea of determinism, just to be expressed, always had to refer to the idealized Laplacian mind, which could know all events in the universe at the instant A, and thus be able to predict them at the instant B, an interesting flight of fancy, but hardly a concept that could have empirical meaning for the limited human mind. The concepts of causality and determinism were, of course, used by every scientist to order the elements of experience—a kind of cosmic card-catalogue system whose purpose was to file away every event at its proper time and place of occurrence. To this the positivist had no objections. He merely warned against raising these ideas to the status of "entities," having some transcendent, nonobservable, metaphysical meaning aside from the event they were supposed to order.

Now there were many physicists of the metaphysical school who were willing to go a good deal of the way with some of the positivistic interpretations of physical concepts. They saw, at least, that a certain clarity of thinking would result if, for example, such words as "force" and "energy" were carefully defined in terms of the strict and specialized meaning they were intended to convey in the specific experimental or mathematical situation in which they were being used, over against the innumerable vague and fuzzy meanings that such words could imply in general usage, or even in the context of some other scientific situation. Thus if positivism were merely a philosophically noncommittal effort to give the scientific language a drastic cleaning up, there could hardly be any objection to this from any scientist, no matter what his private philosophy.

But on closer inspection it turned out that positivism was not only *not* noncommittal about philosophy, but that, in spite of its own disavowal of metaphysics and its claim that it was not a metaphysics itself, but only a logic of science, it was actually almost indistinguishable from certain already well-known philosophical positions, such as subjective idealism and solipsism. This was pleasing to some of the metaphysical physicists, who were already philosophically inclined to subjective idealism or to solipsism, and not pleasing to others. After all, the former said, the positivists were merely calling our attention to the human nature of all our knowledge, to the impossibility of knowing anything but the content of our own consciousness, to the impossibility of gaining knowledge of "essences" or "things-in-themselves" which transcend our own experience. The line between subjective idealism and solipsism is pretty thin, subjective idealism stressing the ideational and creative side of the subject's inability to get outside his own subjective experience, and solipsism stressing the sensory and passive aspect of this inability. But logical positivism leans toward both of them, depending on whether one stresses the logical or the empirical aspect of it.

On the other hand, even the "metaphysical" physicists who were realists, and therefore confident in man's ability to apprehend reality directly through terms-in-relation propositions, were pleased with some aspects of positivism, especially with the operational interpretation of concepts. To gain knowledge of reality, man had to act upon it, as well as be acted upon, as pragmatists and realists had always insisted; small wonder, then, that his knowledge had to be formulated eventually in terms of his acts. But always the idea of "reality" kept creeping in, because these metaphysical physicists all suffered from the peculiar inability to get rid of the idea of existence, which the positivistic language ruled out. It just seemed to these simple scientists that the whole scientific enterprise pointed to the existence of something, no matter what you called it, which allowed itself to be investigated in this particular way.

Consequently, most of these metaphysical fellow travelers of the positivists came to a halt when they arrived at the question of the convergence of theories. The most radical of the positivists insisted not only that our scientific knowledge was merely a system of constructs or models or analogies intended to summarize the multitudinous facts of perception in an orderly, logical, and economical way. They insisted also that, as between several theories which ordered the same facts with different emphases, there could be no way by which one could be called more "true" or closer to "reality" than another. In other words, they rejected the idea of successive approximation, the idea that science tries to make models and theories that approximate more and more closely to reality, that necessarily converge to a limit. Even the requirement of economy was not to be raised to a metaphysical dogma, so that the most *simple* theory that accounted for a given set of facts could be declared closest to reality. For example, as the constructs and models of physics came to be taken more and more from mathematics instead of from everyday life, and the mathematical "pictures" turned out to be aesthetic objects, theoretical physicists became divided along such lines as "elegant" versus "sloppy," so that the whole question ultimately reduced to a matter of individual taste. It would, the positivists claimed, never be possible to get people to agree on what was the simplest, the most elegent, the most logical, the most comprehensive, the most satisfying theory or set of constructs. If any individual scientist wished to call a certain theory the most satisfying to him, and therefore the closest to reality, that was his privilege, but it was a statement without scientific meaning, and without coercive value for other scientists who were not so inclined to regard it.

Here was the real parting place between the two ways of thinking, the positivistic and the common-sense-metaphysical. Either science was an approach to reality, in which case the theories of science, no matter how circumscribed and molded by the nature of the knowing subject and his relation with the world, must converge to something (that is, for a given set of data there must be a "best" model or analogy), or science had nothing to do with reality, but was merely a game in which we represent our experience in terms of models which may satisfy some and not others. Such were the alternatives bluntly put, and it is obvious that the radical positivists were entirely unconcerned if it were claimed against them that their conception of science had "nothing to do with reality." It was precisely against the introduction into science of the metaphysical notion of reality that the positivists took their stand. Science was a system of conventions, just like a game, and like any game it gave us back exactly what we put into it when we made the rules. We followed the rules only so that it would be an orderly game, and not because the rules might not have been different. To speak of science as an approach to "reality" is merely to be overcome by an emotional attachment to one particular set of rules and the particular set of models that conform to it.

The lesson of positivism

As far as actual scientific work was concerned, the two schools of physicists were indistinguishable. They used the same terminology, the same mathematical formulas, the same methods of experimentation. In their strictly scientific papers they understood each other very well. It was only when the question arose as to what broader meaning, if any, should be allowed to be attached to the scientific results that the disparity of outlook revealed itself. In practice, then, positivism itself appeared to be one of those ideas that made no observable difference in the scientific enterprise as long as one stuck to the observables. The real significance of positivism as a historical phenomenon was therefore not so much in deciding the fate of science as in revealing the human situation in regard to the possibility of accurate, dependable knowledge of any kind, and, from the standpoint of a Christian critique, in revealing something of the human motivation with respect to the desire for this kind of certainty.

The phenomenon of positivism showed: (1) that there is no such thing as a presuppositionless knowledge; (2) that any examination of the presuppositions of knowledge must end with the examination of language itself; and (3) that the certitude (in the form of exactness and dependability) of human knowledge is related to the degree of its quantitative-structural nature, not necessarily to the degree of its objective-subjective nature.

(1) Positivism believed that it is the purpose of knowledge to take the place of "faith" and therefore we must begin the quest for knowledge by consciously eliminating all the usual unconscious "faiths" and "beliefs," even those demanded by "common sense." But positivism did believe in the testimony of the five senses. This testimony was supposed to be the "positive" starting point. However, once one begins to question the presuppositions of knowledge, there is no reason why one should draw the line at sense experience. Why should I trust the testimony of the five senses? What do they give me except immediate, private awareness of the present instant, and what is so "positive" about that? Can it even be called knowledge, or is it not more like a dream or a hallucination? Even positivism had to admit that something needed to be added to sensory awareness to make it seem like knowledge, and so it appealed directly to logic, and indirectly to the consensus of judgments and the unproved assumption that man is a rational animal. But since the simple, common-sense-metaphysical belief in an objective world corresponding to the subjective sense awareness was ruled out as one of the unnecessary "faiths" or beliefs, the whole body of "positive" knowledge was left straddled over the objective-subjective hiatus: its raw material, sense awareness, resided in the subjective or private world, while its method of verification, essentially a counting of noses, or a census of all who claimed the same sensations and drew the same logical conclusions from them, resided in the objective or public world.

The more the questioning proceeded, the more it became evident that all kinds of unproved assumptions would have to be made if there was going to be anything that men could agree upon to call knowledge. One had to believe in the reasoning process itself, which seemed self-vindicating up to a point, but beyond that point was also not impervious to the mood of questioning. Why should I believe that what reason tells me constitutes a knowledge of the nature of things any more than what imagination or pure guessing tell me? How do I know that even the most elementary deductions from the most self-evident axioms of logic and mathematics do not constitute merely a way of "scratching an itch," or reacting to the peculiar human need for making order out of chaos in whatever way the structure of the nervous system will allow? But then one also had to believe in the whole apparatus of communication: in the ability of sounds to carry meanings other than sound; in the ability of words to render adequate descriptions of things; in the general uniformity of human minds; in the ability of memory to reconstruct the past, even the preceding instant; in the ability of imagination to construct adequate models or images for intangible ideas; in the validity of the process whereby the mind abstracts from the totality of its awareness such qualities as like and unlike, whole and part, genus and species, the one and the many—abstractions without which language could not handle the reasoning process, but which for that reason seem a little arbitrary. All this and more one had to believe to get even a little common-sense knowledge agreed upon, not to mention the more certain, quantitative knowledge that science was hoping to become, or other kinds of knowledge, where feelings and attitudes as well as sensations and deductions were involved.

(2) Positivism really admitted that there is no such thing as a presuppositionless knowledge when it shifted the basis of its argument from the content of the scientific proposition to the language of the scientific proposition. For whatever else knowledge may be, on the level of language knowledge is definition, and the dictionary is its standard of reference, not any theories of knowledge. But the dictionary is no presuppositionless collection of definitions: every part of it presupposes some other part of it, and the whole of it presupposes that there is some nonlinguistic starting point (bodily gestures, pointing) by means of which people can come to agreement on the simpler words and thereby work their way around to the more complex. When we enter a foreign country and have immediate need of knowledge, we do not ask concerning the native epistemology, but wave our arms, point, make faces, or ask for a dictionary. The more sophisticated the analysis of language becomes, the more it becames involved in its own circularity. Every semantic statement concerning how the meanings of words should be understood is involved in the circularity that the meaning of the words in *that* statement must be assumed to be already understood. This is why, when positivism tried to make rules about how the meaning of the words in scientific propositions should be understood, it found itself positing the rules of a game, in which the posited rules must simply be "granted." That this circularity of language, which is the reflection of its dependence on nonverbal factors, came out so clearly in the case of positivism (rather than in some other

branch of philosophy, or in literature) was due to the fact that positivism was so determined to start out the knowledge enterprise by taking nothing whatever for granted.

(3) Just as positivism's determination to take nothing for granted brought to light the variety and scope of the things that must be taken for granted, if there is to be anything called knowledge, so positivism's determination to increase the certainty or exactitude of scientific knowledge by meticulous definitions and rigorous adherence to the rules of the game revealed the extent and scope of man's actual uncertainties with regard to knowledge of any kind. For positivism showed, more or less incidentally, that even within the realm of the relatively certain scientific knowledge the certitude that could be achieved was directly related to the degree in which the subject matter could be comprehended in quantitatively descriptive, or mathematical, terms. In other words, the only aspect of the universe about which man could hope to obtain relatively *certain* knowledge was the physically structural, the regular, the abstractly uniform, the recurrent, mathematically describable aspect. The importance of this discovery was not appreciated and in most cases was misunderstood by the positivists themselves. The more dogmatic among them took the position that since this quantitatively descriptive aspect was the only one about which man could get relatively certain knowledge, that is the only aspect he should be concerned with, all else being a waste of time; or, even more pontifically, that that is the only "real" aspect, all else being illusion.

The unfortunate tendency on the part of the positivists to lapse into metaphysical pronouncements in the midst of their antimetaphysical campaign, because of their eagerness to have the whole truth on their side, obscured the importance of this discovery. For along with vicious dogmatism in science there usually appeared a vicious subjectivism in all other fields on the grounds that only the "objective" knowledge provided by science could be absolutized, while all other kinds of knowledge, religious, moral, political, historical, aesthetic, were condemned to the most hopeless relativism due to the arbitrariness of the subjective reactions of human beings.

This was really an excuse for refusing to be objective about the subjective life of man, an excuse which was removed by the placing of the locus of certitude in the degree of mathematical manageability of the subject matter, not in the degree of possible objectivity or subjectivity with regard to it. There are many fields that science can investigate about which it can be as objective as it pleases, but if the subject matter is too complex to allow of mathematical treatment, the uncertainty (in such forms as unrepeatability or too many variables) remains very large. For example, in the social sciences there is nothing to keep the social scientists from being as objective as they please, but even their most heroic objectivity does not secure the certainty of the results in the face of the bewildering, mountainous masses of data that must be co-ordinated if the subject matter is to be done justice. Once we grant the presuppositions of knowledge of any kind, which we have to do even for the sake of scientific knowledge, there is no excuse for confusing uncertainty with subjectivity, or certainty with objectivity. In this way vicious subjectivism with regard to all kinds of knowledge other than science can be condemned on the grounds that it confuses the complexity of the subject matter with arbitrariness, trying to escape responsibility for achieving as much objectivity as is possible, and for finding ways of describing the complexity piecemeal, or in whatever way the complex subject matter will allow.

If the foregoing analysis is substantially correct, the lesson to be learned from the phenomenon of positivism is that of humility. It appears that man as a being capable of attaining certain knowledge about anything at all is not in as favorable a position as he imagined himself to be in the first flush of his discovery of the scientific method. No one, least of all professional religionists, should object to that kind of positivism which concerns itself with making science more accurate in its thinking, since it is precisely accurate definitions and careful discrimination between what is known and what is not that encourage the mood of humility. Nor should anyone denounce positivism as being necessarily atheistic: the positivists could easily answer that charge by displaying God as one of their prize "constructs." The point at which the protest against positivism must be lodged is the point at which positivism becomes dogmatic and "metaphysical" and refuses to remain noncommittal concerning matters about which, on its own premises, it can have nothing to say. In this protest the believer can join with men of broad sympathies everywhere, such as artists, poets, humanists, historians, moralists, men of action, and sensitive men of imagination, who simply feel without analyzing too much that there is a great deal more to be known about man and his life than the quantitative aspect; and that if that is the only aspect we can have exact knowledge of, well, that's too bad, we shall just have to muddle through on the other aspects somehow, because they happen to be important for life.

But at the same time that the believer must protest the arrogance of positivism in trying to browbeat all other kinds of knowledge out of respectable existence in what amounts to the claim that "all questions that cannot be answered by science should not be asked," he should notice that, in so far as positivism is an honest self-searching on the part of science for its most irreducible certainties, a Christian understanding of man is able to give scientific knowledge a greater validity than it is able to give itself, or that positivism is able to give it. For there is always hidden in all the unbelievers' quest for certainty an absolutistic, all-or-none reaction: either human knowledge is absolute—that is, capable of perfection—or it is nothing, it is illusion. Either it is godlike knowledge or it is a deception, a mere "game."

They seem to be incapable of accepting the idea of a "creaturely knowledge," a knowledge which is admittedly partial, fragmentary, and always "in terms of the creature," but which is none the less valid knowledge for the kind of creature that man is, and, as real knowledge, is capable of making him, the knower, responsible. Paul, in complaining of how the heathen misuse their knowledge of God, says at the same time that they are "without excuse." This is because "the invisible things of him since the creation of the world are clearly seen, being perceived through things that are made, even his everlasting power and divinity." (Rom. 1:19-21 A.S.V.) By analogy other kinds of knowledge also make the creature responsible. The fact that there is mathematics, and the fact that many phenomena can be described in terms of mathematical relations, and that the predictability and control of nature depend on the degree to which this is so—all this must from a Christian perspective be affirmed as part of the created goodness of the world and as opportunity for use toward good ends. The redemption of this kind of knowledge certainly does not consist of denying its validity because of its partiality,[3] but rather in insisting on placing it in a larger perspective that includes other kinds of knowledge, especially the knowledge of man's destiny as a child of God created in his image and for his fellowship.

As for the aesthetic use of this kind of knowledge, the contemplation of the grandeur of the world's physical structure, this too can become the occasion of despair and defiance for man if it is not combined with knowledge of another kind of grandeur, the holiness and righteousness of the biblical Creator. If the unbelievers are alienated from the biblical perspective because it does not contain the latest theory on the expansion of the universe, they should be reminded that the biblical writers did not find out about the holiness and righteousness of God by studying the more limited Ptolemaic skies, but by studying the ways of men with one another, and the ways of nations, and through them the ways of God with men.

To end this chapter on a positivistic note, let me suggest a picture, model, or "construct" for the different kinds of knowledge. Imagine a large sea of ignorance. Appearing above the surface of this sea are scattered islands, each of which represents knowledge of a particular kind, covering a limited area and governed by its own characteristic features or rules. Some of the islands are in groups—for instance, the several sciences would form an archipelago, being close in subject matter and rules but still not so close that a one-to-one correspondence could be said to form a solid land-body out of them. Presumably a continent of underwater land unites all of these separate islands to form that totality of knowledge that systematic philosophers have as their goal, but which must be admitted to be accessible only to God. Intellectual integrity, in this picture, consists of not confusing the underwater connections, which are actually unknown to us as long as they do not emerge as part of one of the islands, with the particular rules and features that obtain in those islands that at the present time rise so high above the surface of the sea as to dominate the scene.

Chapter III

FAITH AND PHILOSOPHY

The believer's peculiar relationship to philosophy

IF THE CHRISTIAN FAITH IS IN SOME OF ITS ASPECTS A KIND OF KNOWLEDGE, a meaningful patternmaking out of life in the categories of biblical thinking, then philosophy is also a kind of knowledge, but its categories are different, and hence its goal is also different. Looking at the history of philosophy, and not too much at contemporary philosophy, which seems to be rather uncertain of its goal, we can say that the goal of philosophy appears to be the interpretation of the totality, of all there is, in terms of the consistency and comprehensiveness of clearly defined concepts. But theology is also concerned with the totality in a way, with the life of man in its wholeness and ultimacy, and this similarity of concern is what brings philosophy and theology together, though it by no means necessarily brings about friendliness and co-operation between them.

Philosophy rightly considers the Christian believer, in so far as he enters the realm of philosophical discourse with every intention of holding on to his basic Christian beliefs, as something of an imposter. Anyone who considers himself to be the "thou" who is addressed in the two great biblical commandments must be, to the free and uncommitted atmosphere of philosophy, as a foreigner in our midst. We cannot speak to him, even with the best of good will, without becoming aware that his deepest allegiance is elsewhere. He belongs to another country. Philosophy can hardly help regarding him with suspicion. The chief charge against him is that he does not need philosophy, because in a way (the implication is, in an intellectually inferior way) he already has the answers that philosophy is looking for. His God is his metaphysic, ethic, epistemology, all rolled into one, and his philosophical ideas, if he has any, are all in the nature of afterthoughts, of arguments after the fact; they are interpretations and insights, not reasons and evidences.

But philosophy is concerned with the development of reasoned beliefs. It is not interested in beliefs primarily as they are in their isolation true, or beautiful, or noble, or good, or practical, but only as they are consistent with what has been postulated. They may be all these other things too, but philosophy cannot handle them except as part of a reasoned chain of thought. This shows itself in the fact that even an irrationalistic philosophy, such as that of Nietzsche, seeks to explore the logical implications of its basic postulates. Any systematic philosophy, therefore, which does not wish to dissolve into poetic vision, or a single inspired insight, employs a coercive logic; it forbids beliefs which cannot invite the consent of reason (granted the basic postulate), and, conversely, it commands or enforces beliefs whose consistency it has not been able to disprove. It says: if you believe this, you must believe that. Such are the rules. Without these rules, philosophy rightly insists, the rational belief-building process cannot go on.

Philosophy therefore charges the believer with intending to evade the implications of a reasoned chain of thought before it is even started, with being merely "interested" in the operations of reason, not determined by them. For the sake of unprejudiced thinking the believer ought to be debarred from philosophy entirely. But since believers form an invisible company, and since philosophy cannot hand-pick her devotees, she asks at least that philosophical ideas stemming from faith be held in abeyance, be temporarily suspended, until reason has been given full and unhampered play over the issues in question. Systematic works in philosophy generally end, they do not begin, with a chapter on God.

But along with this suspicious and somewhat resentful attitude on the part of philosophy toward the believer, there is also a certain small element of envy and a considerable element of curiosity. In so far as philosophy attempts to bring about a unified picture of the world and of man's life and function in it, there is no denying that the believer has this already assured to him in faith, while the philosopher must struggle under the constant uncertainty that what he is after may be in point of fact unattainable, that the human mind may not be equal to the task, or that the world itself will not warrant the philosophical expectation. To be sure, the believer's willingness to jump to the conclusion without the preliminary intellectual groundwork can only be characterized as scandalous. Still, there is something to be said for having the goal thus constantly before one's eyes. As Kierkegaard observed, the philosopher may even look forward a little to his old age, when, having himself done all that is humanly possible, and the "system" still not finished, he might perhaps be allowed to indulge in a little faith.

It is, however, as an object of curiosity, as a fact to be explained, or explained away, that the believer is of importance to philosophy. Philosophy's excuse for existence is that it attempts a comprehensive, not a specialized, view of the world and of man. Any such comprehensive view must account not only for the existence of cabbages and kings and philosophers but also for the existence of believers.

This would be a simple matter if believers were all simple people, or poets, or artists, or visionaries, or reformers, or prophets—if, in short, they lacked only the philosophical faculty. Their believing could then be put down to their ignorance of the philosophical problems involved. But the fact that there are many believers who understand philosophy quite well, appreciate its aims and its niceties, yet who continue to set their religious beliefs ahead of their philosophical ideas, makes the believer into a problem for philosophy.

For suppose a philosopher wishes eventually and in some sense to admit the deity as a possibility into his philosophy—to crown his system with a final chapter on God. In so far as philosophy claims to explain things, and not merely describe them in more general terms than the several arts and sciences, he must validate his deity on philosophical grounds, not merely "permit faith." He must show the difference between himself and the believer, the one believing because of philosophy, the other in spite of it, at the same time being careful not to "explain away" the believer entirely, especially not the philosophically inclined believer, who, though he once believed in spite of philosophy, may yet be converted to believing because of it. Thus, the believer, who is merely tolerated in philosophy, may at any instant become the shining example of a philosophy that takes account of God. But suppose the philosopher wishes to do away with God as a philosophical possibility. He is then under the constant necessity of "explaining away" the believer, rationally, historically, anthropologically, psychologically. To him the believer is an ever-present reflection on the comprehensiveness of his philosophy, especially the believer who is quite aware of reason, history, anthropology, psychology. Thus when philosophy argues atheistically, the believer is a stubborn fact, while when she argues theistically, the believer may be a living proof, but, unfortunately, always a somewhat irrelevant proof.

Finally, and in spite of his many shortcomings, philosophy must regard the philosophically inclined believer as being to some extent a collaborator. To be sure, he has certainly put the cart before the horse, and is running the journey backward, but what does this matter if he should by chance hit upon a passage that is clear, if he should after all demonstrate that the journey can be made? Would not such a passage work both ways? If the believer is looking for a philosophical justification of his religious beliefs, and if he should be successful, and his philosophy sound, would not these beliefs then become a tenable advance for those who began at the philosophical end, who were looking for the religious implications, if any, of philosophical ideas? In any case, there is a common ground of endeavor here, and it is not up to philosophy to be too fastidious. So the uneasy truce between philosophy and theology continues, although the number of professional theologians whose works are eagerly read by professional philosophers is probably small.

All of these ideas, however, are the philosopher's understanding of the believer's relationship to philosophy. Now let us look at it from the believer's side. He acknowledges that there is surely some truth in philosophy's accusations against himself. He realizes that he has committed the gravest error of scientific methodology, that of prejudging the case. So that wherever philosophy tries to use the methodology of science, he is simply *persona non grata*. But even where philosophy permits itself the widest speculation, all his ideas are suspect. None of them can ever claim that intellectual trustworthiness that is supposedly guaranteed by an impartial and objective attitude on the part of the philosopher. His thinking must always have the appearance of being to some extent wishful thinking. In fact he himself must be suspicious of his own ideas on this account. Why, then, does he persist in a field where he is so obviously a misfit?

This question comes to him repeatedly in the course of his

philosophical studies, perhaps with greater frequency as time goes on and he begins to see his position more clearly, and feel its disparities more acutely. We have assumed all along that our believer has no intention of giving up his "cherished beliefs," as these are somewhat sentimentally and condescendingly called in philosophy. We have assumed that he really does cherish them, because they give real meaning to his life; that the only excuse for calling him a believer is precisely his unwillingness to give them up in the face of philosophy, or even to give them up temporarily, as a prerequisite for an impartial investigation in philosophy, conducted in the secret hope that he might get them all back again, with philosophical credentials attached. For if he has given them up temporarily, he has not really given them up. And if he has honestly and without hope given them up, if he has determined to accept the verdict of philosophy, whatever it may be, then we are not concerned with him here, for he can no longer be called a believer.

But the believer who wants to remain a believer does not need philosophy to help him do that. Not only does he not need philosophy, but he can hardly help noticing that philosophy is in a sense his greatest adversary and temptation, a powerful and ever-present potential threat to his beliefs, the very ones he does not intend to give up. And that, furthermore, he himself permits this to be so, just to the extent that he is willing to take philosophy seriously. In the name of all common sense he ought to try to discredit philosophy, or at least to point out its limitations on its own grounds, in order to secure his beliefs against its inroads. Many a believer has entered upon the study of philosophy with exactly this intention, to point out to philosophy its limitations on its own grounds, in order to "make room for faith." But this intention turns out to be quite futile, as soon as the believer realizes that any radical criticism he may offer to philosophy must be made on the grounds of the Christian faith and not on the grounds of philosophy, something naturally not acceptable to philosophy anyway. By means of this situation he then realizes the responsibility implicit in the unwelcome fact that this faith is also a kind of knowledge, a knowledge that came into the world to judge the world, philosophy included, not to be judged by the world.

But before turning to the examination of the present situation in philosophy, we must consider the easy solution to the believer's problem provided by the phenomenon of positivism as described in the preceding chapter. For it is surely in metaphysics that his clash with philosophy is most likely to occur, and according to the more popular version of positivism it would seem to be possible to get rid of metaphysics entirely, by calling it nonsense. This assertion was made on the basis of a linguistic analysis of the statements made in science to determine their necessary logical form. That form was then declared to be the only form which "made sense," so that all other kinds of statements became by definition non-sense statements, a reasonable enough claim within the limitations of the linguistic postulates set up.

However, the use of the term "nonsense" in this connection was surely a chauvinistic device, for it took advantage of all the derogatory and deliberately ridiculing meanings associated with the word in everyday usage. Not only metaphysics, but all verbal exchanges on any subject which did not conform to the logical form required of a scientific statement, became stigmatized by implication as the senseless mouthings of idiots. It would have been more correct to say that the metaphysical statements did not make scientific sense, or made "nonscientific sense" in the context of the specific definition of scientific sense laid down. But even this more modest and accurate statement of the case is somewhat misleading, for it seems to imply that the kind of thinking that goes on in science and produces the statements that make scientific sense is somehow *radically* different from every other kind of thinking, and even *discontinuous* with it, a magic key that unlocks a door in the basement of reality which otherwise presents man with nothing but closed doors.

But as a matter of fact and of historical record the kind of thinking that goes on in science is only a deliberately self-restricted form of everyday thinking, or thinking in less specialized fields, and it suffers or enjoys the same defeats and triumphs involved in any effort to force language to be the mediator of experience, literally, to be a go-between. For example, the analogies used in science as hypotheses are self-restricted to the kind which contain a variable that is identifiable with something measurable in the sense world, so that an experiment can be devised to see "how far the analogy will go." Positivism itself pointed out the "modeled" or "constructed" nature of scientific knowledge, even where the models or analogies have to be taken from mathematics in order to fit the verifiable variables. But the parts of the analogies or models for which no measurable variable can be defined or reached are just as much big, beautiful emptinesses as the supposedly empty-of-meaning statements made in metaphysics, ethics, politics, theology, literature, or anywhere where the analogies used cannot be so easily followed, or can be followed only in imagination, to see "how far they will go."

If language is to be the go-between, there is no escape from the necessity of describing one part of experience by analogy with, or in the terms of, another part. The statements: the parts of the atom behave like a certain set of equations; the growth of the embryo goes through stages like the evolution of the race; being is like matter; God is like a father; sin originates as in the story of Adam and Eve; the sea is like a sleeping beast; are not so *radically* different in kind from one another but that a charge of nonsense against one of them condemns them all. They may differ in degrees of verifiability or, better yet, in the kind of verification to be expected and the direction in which it is to be sought, but being all circumscribed by what acrobatics language is able to perform in public, they are hardly in a position to call each other bad names.[1] The current attempt to suppress the original exploratory analogies used in science and to publish only "coefficients of correlation" is a kind of intellectual dishonesty which backfires on the scientist by leaving him with no hypothetical indications as to what correlations to explore next.

The attempt of some neo-orthodox theologians to discredit philosophy in order to make theology invulnerable to its attacks by using the positivistic claim that philosophy is technical nonsense is also a backfiring procedure, for if philosophy is nonsense, theology is the same kind of nonsense. To complete this cycle of name calling, it is necessary only to recall that science is also nonsense, being only one type or species of the "game" of human knowledge. Admitting, then, that all human knowledge is in some degree nonsense (and this is only the secular version of the creatureliness of all human knowledge), we may cancel out the nonsense factor and observe that if theology must sit in judgment on philosophy, it will not be because philosophy is nonsense, or more nonsense than other kinds of knowledge, but because philosophy is in some way harmful or dangerous to man from the standpoint of his destiny as a child of God. Philosophy could scarcely be harmful if it were pure nonsense, and it would scarcely be necessary to "protect" theology from its attacks if it were nonsense in some way that theology is not. As a matter of historical fact the attacks of philosophy on theology ever since the Enlightenment turned out to be the best thing that could have happened to theology, for they made theology re-examine itself to see what its real tasks and terms were. The easy solution to the problem of his relationship to philosophy offered by positivism must therefore be declined with regrets by the believer, for it is illusory.

The present situation in philosophy

At the beginning of this chapter I suggested that to get a definition of the goal of philosophy one must look at its history rather than its contemporary state, for at the present time there exists a great deal of uncertainty among philosophers themselves as to what the goal of philosophy should be. Although there is quite a temptation today to attach the word "crisis" to practically every human activity, it might not be too far wrong to say that, alongside the critical times through which we are passing historically, philosophy is undergoing an internal crisis, and has been in the throes of such a crisis, for about the last two hundred years.

The crisis centers around the various answers that can be given to the following questions, all somewhat embarrassing to philosophy, whether they are put in a hostile or in a sympathetic mood: Hasn't philosophy finally worked itself out of a job? Having handed over to the sciences, with its blessing, as well as with numerous logical refinements, the formula for the scientific method at its surest, what else is there left for philosophy to do? Surely philosophy cannot do the work of the sciences themselves. Has not the time perhaps arrived when philosophy, like the central state in the promised utopia of communism, should quietly wither away? And isn't that possibly just what we are witnessing in the contemporary uncertainty about philosophy's goal—the actual withering away?

I hasten to add that even giving the expected affirmative answer to these questions would not mean that philosophy would disappear as a study. There would always be the history of philosophy, the long, long train of thought that led to the present conclusion, and logic, the defense of that conclusion, and semantic analysis, the philosophical attempt to find out just what the various nonscientific pursuits of men are trying to accomplish when they use language. Such a study of philosophy would, however, be more like one of the "finished" studies—for example, like the study of classical Greek—than like the growing, developing, and cumulative concern, full of lively and portentious issues, that philosophy has thought itself to be in the past.

At first glance these questions that define the crisis in philosophy seem all of them to be loaded with a positivistic slant. Only a dogmatic positivist would want to declare the obsolescence of philosophy as the direct result of the advent of science, and surely it was positivism that so brashly announced the end of metaphysics as a form of knowledge. But a closer inspection of both the questions and the present activity in philosophy will reveal that uncertainty about the goal of philosophy reflects not so much positivistic brashness as realistic cautiousness and historical circumspection. It's not that science is the only knowledge, but that it's the only "safe" knowledge, as far as it goes. The day of the system builders is over. Nobody wants to go out on a limb like Hegel did, only to become ridiculous when the sharp saw of some technical logician prunes the limb from the tree.

Furthermore, if you take the sciences seriously, which all modern philosophers do even if they do not grant them an exclusive claim on knowledge, you must pay attention to what the sciences are discovering, and this always has the quality of tentativeness, approximation, and incompleteness of any empirical enterprise. Nobody wants to write a grandiose epistemology, a la Kant, for example, when several different schools of psychology are investigating several different theories of learning with varying results as to their probable soundness. Thus a cautious philosopher, who does not want to get caught saying something that some special science will eventually disprove, or else will demonstrate in a much more satisfactory way than any philosopher could, must keep an attitude of suspended judgment on many of the interesting problems which used to form the meat and sauce of many a striking philosophical viewpoint. On the other hand, if you take language analysis seriously, you become so impressed by the sloppiness and inadequacy of all verbal forms when compared to any definite realities they are supposed to describe or convey, you are tempted to come to rest in the now famous dictum of Wittgenstein: whereof one cannot speak, thereof one must be silent. (In spite of which he managed to write a fat book thereof.)

Thus we arrive at a picture of the cautious and circumspect present-day philosopher as a man whose judgment is suspended by the incompleteness of the scientific findings, and whose tongue is paralyzed by the demonstrated inadequacy of language.

Of course, this is a picture in extremes, perhaps of philosophy *in extremis*. I put the picture in extremes to make it quite understandable that there had to be, and has been, a reaction to this situation, this impasse in philosophy. The reaction has come from common sense and from human need—that is, the need for guidance. Common sense, that unrefined source of all refined forms of knowledge, phrases its protest thus: Very well, then, let's admit all this. Let us admit the incompleteness of all knowledge, and the inadequacy of language. What of it? We have to do the best we can with what we have. Where would science be today, not to mention the various humanities, if our philosophical ancestors had been so cautious as to allow themselves to be immobilized and rendered mute by these two obviously perennial conditions of man's position as knower? You are to be commended, gentlemen of philosophy, on your new humility, but there's such a thing as overdoing it.

The human need for guidance, on the other hand, phrases its protest somewhat like this: There never was a time, in the whole history of the world, when there were more bits and odds and ends of knowledge lying around in heaps. Who, if not a philosopher, is qualified to try to make some kind of sense out of this conglomeration, to arrange the bits in some kind of order and provide the whole with some unifying ideas? If the philosopher refuses to do this job, on the grounds that it is not "safe" to say much of anything, someone else will surely attempt it, and that without either the controls or the motives that philosophy has traditionally supplied: reason, and the desire for truth. Human need sees in the cautiousness of contemporary philosophy not so much humility as a concealed perfectionism (for instance, in the implication that it is better to be silent than to speak imperfectly), and human need regards perfectionism as a luxury that the race of men cannot at present afford.

In response to both the appeal of common sense and the appeal of human need, there have appeared and are still appearing a significant number of "neo" viewpoints in philosophy, such as neonaturalism, neorealism, neohumanism, Neo-Scholasticism, Neo-Socratism, Neo-Kantianism, and even Neo-Hegelianism. Each of these schools is reaching back into the history of philosophy for a major idea that once served a unifying function, and is trying to see if that idea, properly corrected for advances in knowledge, and properly repentant of its errors in the past, might not be made to serve that function again. In addition to these, and sometimes under one of their auspices, there are those philosophies which take as their unifying idea, or guiding "metaphor for the whole," a particular feature or structure or process from one of the several sciences. Examples here would be Whitehead's organicism, Bergson's vitalism, Karl Heim's dimensionalism (patterned after relativity theory), the various kinds of evolutionism, and, finally, the various kinds of ontology and philosophical anthropology patterned after depth psychology, now usually called existentialism.

There is thus no lack of candidates for the office of unifying idea, or group of ideas, and I am sure I left out of this summary list may equally worthy of mention. Such a list merely shows that at least some philosophers today, in response to the appeals of common sense and human need, and in despite of the warnings of the cautious analytical philosophers, are willing to take up once more what has traditionally been thought to be philosophy's job, "the interpretation of the totality, of all there is, in terms of the consistency and comprehensiveness of clearly defined concepts," the definition used at the start of this chapter. A real tension is perceptible between these two kinds of philosophers, for the "unifiers" are on trial, as it were. They are trying to answer the internal-crisis questions about whether philosophy has a job to do, other than logical analysis, by doing the job, under the jaded and critical eyes of the analysts, who claim that all of the history of philosophy witnesses to the fact that it can't be done.

At this point I should perhaps indicate something of the nature of the discussion to follow. It is not within either the scope or the function of this book for me to present a systematic exposition of "my philosophy," in so far as I have one, even though, inevitably, some of my philosophical predilections appear throughout the book. Such an exposition would have to be the province of a far more technical and extended discussion—in other words, the subject of another book. The function of this book, in this chapter, is to show the peculiar position of any believer, but, of course, especially the philosophically inclined believer, that arises out of the fact that he enters the field as one who already believes the essentially Christian teachings. It is no more true of philosophy than of any other realm of effort that one has to understand and solve its problems *before* one can believe (as a Christian). But neither is it quite true that one believes *in order to understand* (philosophically). One believes, as a Christian, in order to save one's soul unto God's service, in order to accept God's grace and truth in Christ, in order to be reconciled to God in Christ. These evangelistic phrases describe the situation much better than either philosophy or common sense, because they establish the right order of precedence.

If, after the establishment of this "first" relationship, the saving faith, it turns out that a believer achieves some new insights into particular areas of experience and thought, some Christian insights, this fact must from a philosophical standpoint be regarded as "pure gravy," and from a theological standpoint as the leading and suggestion of the Holy Spirit. But we must never allow a situation to arise in which it is implied that *only* the philosophical believer can really believe, because he has understood and solved all the problems that philosophy raises. And even the notion that Christianity can be shown to be the "best philosophy" must be handled with the greatest care, lest it lead people to desire it out of a motive like intellectual pride. Nowhere in the Bible is it suggested that the faith there demanded for the truth there disclosed will give the believer a God's-eye view of everything. The latter view would rather seem to be promised by idealistic philosophies, as we shall see in a moment.

So the thing to remember, in the discussion that follows, is that the believer is not looking for philosophical justification for his beliefs in the sense that he is asking philosophy's permission to believe. Justification in this case means that he is looking for philosophical ideas that are able to *do justice* to that which he believes on other grounds. They must do justice to that rich configuration of relationships and beings and events that constitute the biblical picture of God's historical self-revelation, and at the same time do justice to the many experiences that man is able to have and observe outside of or in addition to the faith experience. That much at least would surely be what is meant by a "unifying" idea, or group of ideas, the supplying of which has traditionally been considered to be philosophy's job.

In passing in review the many candidates for the office of unifying idea, supplied both by the history of philosophy and by contemporary schools, the believer will soon notice that a great deal of the struggle and disagreement among the various viewpoints arises from the effort to define what the nature of such a unifying idea must be beforehand—that is to say, before it is applied or demonstrated in detail. This is an effort to circumscribe the kind of ideas that are to be allowed in philosophy, if philosophy is not to change itself into something else—such as poetry, or mysticism, or propaganda. For instance, we have already noted that philosophy is committed to the use of a coercive logic, "if-then" propositions, for otherwise it cannot have consistency as its goal. Likewise it cannot handle isolated insights or visions that seem to have no necessary implications for anything else (although it might wish to be able to account for them by reasoned beliefs). Right from the beginning there is this large division in philosophy over the question of what the real "given" of philosophy is: is it the "raw" experience that reason tries to make order out of, or is it the reasoning process itself?

This turning of reason on itself—distinguishing the inductive and the deductive aspect and trying to decide which should come first in philosophy—is the cause of that division according to which all philosophies may be characterized as either more empirically or more rationalistically inclined. Plato, for example, we would call more rationalistically inclined, and Aristotle more empirically, even though his science was far from empirical in the modern sense of experimental science. The more empirical philosophers have maintained that reason must justify itself as it goes along by actually making order out of whatever experience comes along, while the more rationalistic philosophies have pointed out that unless the power of reason which is the very source of the idea of "ordering" or "unifying" experience is given pre-eminence in philosophy, there couldn't be any philosophy. In ordering experience reason merely exercises itself; it merely shows in particular and in detail what it always was in principle and in general. Thus the unifying idea supplied by philosophy must be something very like a vindication of reason itself, if the enterprise of philosophy is to be valid.

We need not rehearse here the extremes to which this division could be forced. Such extremes have certainly left their mark on the various schools and their accusations against one another. To take the mildest possible view, it is probably an inevitable division, as well as a fruitful one, reflecting as it does the two sides of the reasoning process, the inductive and the deductive. William James thought it reflected the "tough-minded" and the "tender-minded" temperaments, but that characterization in itself was probably the reflection of a turn-of-the-century temperament, when rationalists and idealists were defensively cringing, while empiricists were tough and tall in the saddle. To try to do away with this division at all costs would seem to be a misguided effort at the wrong kind of unity, and hazardous to philosophy itself. In fact it was James's own well-intentioned effort to close the gap between the two camps with his pragmatism, and the later instrumentalism of Dewey, which at least in part led to the various voluntarisms that regard reason in all its aspects as merely the tool of an irrational will-to-power, or, more Freudlike, as the instrument of subrational desires for "satisfactions." That there is a great deal of truth in what the voluntarisms say about the *way* man uses his reason can be admitted with regrets by philosophers, but the basic ability of reason to arrive at some kind of truth must be affirmed, by philosophers, if philosophy is to continue.

So the division between the more empirical and the more rationalistic philosophies is not to be deplored. The thing to do is to see what kind of pictures or accounts of the totality they give us, and to see how they can be combined. The believer will quickly notice what is hardly surprising, that the more empirical philosophies do greater justice to nature while the more rationalistic ones do greater justice to man. Accordingly, philosophies can also be characterized as chiefly naturalistic or humanistic, but since totality is their aim, each of them ought to be judged by how its ideas do justice to the main concerns of the other. That would be the ideal. But actually what happens is that each of them tries to "read off" the main concerns of the other in its own terms and categories, sometimes even to the point of denying the reality of the other's concerns. And then there is that third reality in addition to nature and man, the religious reality, or God, with which the believer is presumably the most concerned.

The fact is, of course, that neither naturalism nor humanism must *necessarily* concern itself with God. They each have enough to do accounting for each other, or fighting each other. But then there is the claim of the interest in totality. To be a philosopher is to be haunted by the idea of totality, by all there is, by the idea of being that means all that is. And the totality, all there is, both includes empirically man's perennial concern with God, and rationally is the very subject matter of that concern. So both naturalism and humanism have to give good reasons as to why they should not concern themselves with God (such as showing that the concern is over an illusion), or they have to concern themselves with God, or they have to admit their incapacity to do so, they have to be agnostic in principle. All of these possibilities are abundantly represented in the many varieties of naturalisms and humanisms extant today, as well as in those that have been prominent in history.

Concerning the religious reality all philosophies are more tolerant than they used to be. Naturalism, for example, in its present-day or "neo" form, has become marvelously catholic in the range of its outlook and the breadth of its sympathies. Repenting itself of its former narrowness and "crudeness," it reaches out to embrace everything. Nothing which is human or divine is alien to it. The human and the divine are now by definition "natural." Man eating, man reasoning, and man praying are now all equally to be thought of as man "doing what comes naturally." "Nature is what nature does" is the new definition of nature, and man is obviously one of nature's most versatile doers. This new catholic naturalism, empiricism's answer to Hegel, illustrates very nicely how a philosophical notion can get out of hand by stretching itself out to a huge abstraction subsuming everything, or by becoming a vague, mystical attitude to "all there is." What satisfaction there can be in calling everything "natural," I don't know; but from the standpoint of requiring that concepts do justice to reality it simply means that somebody will have to invent a new qualifying term for that "nature" which does not eat, another for that "nature" which eats but does not reason or pray, another for that "nature" which eats and reasons but still does not pray, and finally a new term for the religious man, who eats, reasons, and also prays. And, of course, the same thing becomes true when the word "reason" is used as the catch-all, as Hegel unwittingly taught us.

Turning now to the question of how the more empirical and the more rationalistic philosophies try to do justice to the religious reality, when they do try, we discover two types of philosophy of religion corresponding to the two points of departure, the realistic type and the idealistic type. Realistic philosophy of religion begins with the reality of all experience, including religious experience, and is based on the epistemological belief that minds can grasp reality through experience, and can correct wrong or illusionary experience by more experience. On this ground religious experience must be examined and studied like any other experience, to see what it tells us about the religious reality to which it refers. Idealistic philosophy of religion, on the other hand, begins with the nature of man in his ideal aspect, with his spiritual aspirations and his highest values, including reason, as the real clue to the nature of the divine and to the mode of its action in us. In theory, if reason operates here as elsewhere, they should both be on the right track. What they both discover or define should converge toward a single theory about the nature of the religious reality, or God, in the same way that hypothesis and experience correct and support each other in other fields. I need hardly dwell on the fact that the philosophical results in both cases fall far short of this ideal. But we should remind ourselves here of the warnings of the "cautious" philosophers before judging too harshly such a difficult enterprise, lest we too become concealed perfectionists. Considering the inadequacy of language and the incompleteness of empirical evidence in any field, philosophy of religion must consider itself lucky to be able to say anything at all about the religious reality with which it is concerned.

The believer's difficulty here is not with making allowances, which can surely be done, but with the fact that the picture of God that emerges from both philosophies of religion seems hardly to square with, and even hardly to have much to do with, the picture of God that emerges from and dominates biblical thinking. This fact was the subject of the recent controversy between the "liberal" and the "neo-orthodox" theologians, and on nothing were the two parties so much in agreement as on the fact that the philosophical God is not the same as the biblical God. They disagreed over which picture was nearer to the truth and should be given primacy. Unfortunately, because of the catastrophic historical situation in which the controversy took place, the two parties immediately locked horns over the question of man's sinfulness, so that it seemed that sinfulness itself must account for the difference between the philosophical and the biblical picture of God. They never got around to discussing the creatureliness of man's knowledge, because the difference had already been attributed to his sinfulness. Now, while no Christian would wish to deny that the Bible witnesses to man's sinfulness, it also witnesses to his creatureliness, and makes quite an effort to keep the distinction clear. So it is also a different thing to affirm that man can and does use his knowledge sinfully (the subject of Section 4 of this chapter) and to inquire into what that knowledge is capable of, whether used well or misused.

The difference between the philosophical God and the biblical God is much more evident in the idealistic philosophies than in the realistic, because their picture of him is more definite. To paint the picture of the Absolute (as he is called) by the idealistic technique, one must first of all have in mind an idealized picture of man, man at his present or future best, and then one must enlarge, or rather extrapolate to the infinite, all of man's definable virtues and excellencies, his reason, and his other "spiritual" qualities. Whatever ideal man is, the Absolute is more of the same. What one gains in this way is a philosophical defense of spiritual reality and spiritual values that can be used polemically against any materialisms or naturalisms which would like to reduce this reality and these values to "accidental" or "natural" manifestations of the physical interactions that constitute the stuff of the universe. Undoubtedly the need for polemics against the crudeness of early materialisms gave cogency to the project of delineating the idealistic God, but we have seen how more recently all distinctions have become happily blurred; and no doubt "catholic" naturalism could manage to take the idealistic God to its bosom, if he can be regarded as nothing but the deification of man's highest values.

But this fact hardly helps to solve the philosophical problems of biblical Christianity. In contrast to the biblical God, who everywhere stands over his creature, the work of his hands, whom he commands, judges, condemns, loves, forgives, and saves, the Absolute of idealism is more like a picture of the creature blown up to the size of the Creator. In idealistic philosophies of religion man is everywhere the master, and God is man's masterpiece: the prize-winning picture in a "one-man show" displaying the man's capabilities. However, the picture does not really contain him, the artist, and he cannot forever fool himself in that respect. It is the peculiar characteristic of every immanental philosophy that man in the act of comprehending it observes that he stands outside of it, and that he can accept it as true only by limiting or ignoring his own transcendence of it. In idealistic philosophies of religion man actually transcends God, and is then embarrassed by his own residual transcendence.

The picture of God that emerges from realistic philosophies of religion is much less definite than the above, or perhaps it would be better to say that several, many, pictures emerge. These could possibly be the pictures of many gods, but, if their presupposition is monotheistic, they must be regarded as different pictures of the same God. If religious experience is taken as the given, the realistic philosopher of religion who wants to do justice to the religious reality must be willing to take seriously all the many "varieties of religious experience." This means the comparative study of religions first, and then also some kind of classification or typology of the various beliefs and the types of religious experience associated with them, or the special experiences emphasized in the different religions. Here there is likely to be a considerable convergence between philosophy and psychology of religion, both trying to find out and to describe "what happens" in a religious experience. But philosophy of religion cannot stop short with phenomenology. It must be prepared to interpret the religious reality, to elaborate some theological doctrines in terms of what it has learned on the empirical level. And this is where the rub comes. For this philosophy must try to validate the two presuppositions on which the empirical approach to religious experience rests: first, that it is possible to devise criteria by which genuine religious experience can be distinguished from nong nuine experiences; and second, that from the regularities or similarities or "laws" of the religious experiences selected as genuine, it is possible to infer something of the nature of the religious reality to which they refer, namely God.

The first presupposition is hard enough to validate, without prejudging the whole case in favor of the philosopher's own notions of genuine religious experience. What is usually done here is to try to eliminate superstition and magic, or, probably the same thing from a more psychological standpoint, to try to distinguish "immature" from "mature" religious experiences. This in itself can be a risky and even a touchy undertaking, especially if applied tactlessly to the "great religions of mankind." But then there is the second presupposition to be validated: how to arrive at legitimate inferences about God from those religious experiences that have been adjudged genuine or mature, seeing that even they comprise considerable variety, both historically and contemporarily. Is this variety important or isn't it? If the variety is regarded as basically unimportant, some attempt is made to reconcile the differences or to explain them away, and we then get a "syncretistic" philosophy of religion, the patchwork God that corresponds to the conclusion that "all the religions teach the same thing."

As for further attempts to characterize what it is that all the religions teach, the more they try to do away with the differences, the more they tend to reduce to statements that are philosophically and theologically trivial—such as, that all religions teach that it is good, useful, or necessary to be religious; or that they all teach the golden rule; or that they all try to solve the problem of suffering. On the other hand, if the variety of religious experiences and teachings about God is taken as important, and is allowed to "let stand," then here the realistic philosopher must perceive the same limitation of his method that operates in any other empirical undertaking: he must conclude that the "evidence" (of religious experience on the nature of God) is inconclusive, as of the present.

Now into this last and most hospitable of religious philosophies, which we might call religious empiricism *cum* differences, the Christian religion in its biblical perspective will, of course, fit as well as any other, and will be made as welcome as any other. But only if it is willing to regard its own specific bit of "evidence" on the nature of God to be just as inconclusive as that of all the others. Here one is reminded of the saying that to be impartial in religion is to be irreligious. One can, of course, try, and perhaps should try, to be as impartial as one can, but if some of these collected religious teachings do not strike one as more true than others, and therefore worthy of holding on to or "embracing" (as we say, he "embraced" Islam), the whole business will resolve into "reverent agnosticism," for the attainment of which philosophical investigation would hardly seem necessary. For example, it is hard to see how a Christian believer can bear witness to the sufficiency and finality of God's revelation of himself in the Christ, and then at the same time say that this bit of religious evidence on the nature of God is inconclusive.

It would seem from a Christian standpoint that both the idealistic and the realistic philosophies of religion supply the believer with a decidedly inadequate, not to say wrong, interpretation of the religious reality, to which he and they are trying to do justice in philosophical terms. And it should be clear by now that the disagreement between Christianity and other religions and various philosophies is really not about the *existence* of God, but about his *nature.* The question about his existence can be disposed of, and usually is unconsciously disposed of, by the many variations of the traditional "ontological argument." This used to be stated as the argument, that if a highest being can be thought of, it must exist. Turned around, this "argument" merely says that if anything at all exists, there must be some aspect of it that can be regarded as highest. What this "argument" urges is not the proof that something exists which previously did not, but that there is some aspect of that which exists to which man ought to be religiously related. Now if either psychology or theology can show that man is such a being that he must be religiously related to something, whether a self-set goal, a bona-fide religion, or a religion surrogate, then, presto, we have disposed of irreligion as illusion, and after that there remains nothing to argue about except the *nature* of the highest being, or that to which man ought to be religiously related.[2]

The problem before us is why philosophy gives the Christian believer such an unsatisfactory picture of the *nature* of the religious reality, compared to that which he gets in the biblical revelation.

Idealism, no matter how much it tries to exalt the Absolute over actual men, always collapses back into some kind of radical immanentism, spiritual pantheism, or man-deification. Realism gives a patchwork—perhaps implying religious pluralism, or polytheism?—or declares the evidence inconclusive. The problem we are here touching on is the one that is traditionally discussed under the unfortunate rubric of "reason versus revelation," or, even worse, "natural versus supernatural revelation." But under whatever rubric it is discussed, it is a real problem. In a strict sense the word "revelation" should be used only for the purpose of designating a supernatural revelation, since the kind of thinking that is covered by the term "natural revelation" is not different from the ordinary processes of philosophical thinking. Natural revelation is nothing but philosophical thinking applied to the religious reality, and we have just seen how this kind of thinking issues in pantheism or pluralism or inconclusiveness or agnosticism.

But what is wrong with these results, especially the first two, which are more positive? What is wrong with either pantheism or pluralism, if reason alone be our guide? What could be more reasonable to expect than that if man has to worship something, it will have to be either the whole or some part or parts of the whole? In fact every religion and every theistic philosophy can be interpreted as somehow worshiping the whole or the part, except Christianity, which worships a God who is neither the whole of this world nor some part or parts of it, but is rather the creator and redeemer of the whole *and* the parts. So it is only if one has a criterion of divinity such as is given in the biblical accounts that one can, and must, weigh the philosophical results and find them wanting.

I suggest that there are at least three categories of biblical thinking which philosophy does not seem to be able to do justice to and remain philosophy, so that when it does try to use them, it changes them to something else. These are the concepts of transcendence, mystery, and freedom. Philosophy has these words in its vocabulary, but when it uses them it means something quite different by them than when biblical theology uses them. By transcendence philosophy means something like beyondness; by mystery, the not-yet-known; by freedom, the indeterminate. Whereas, in regard to the biblical God, transcendence means his otherness, mystery, his hiddenness, and freedom, his lordship and sovereignty over the world. About *such* a God one can only say with Hamlet that there must be more in him than could be dreamed of in any philosophy. About such a God the traditional "unifying" philosophy would simply have nothing to say. The fact that philosophy over and over again tries to approach the Christian God, to "capture" him in its own terms and categories, is merely an indication of the "existential situation" of man, who, in and through all his searching after truth, betrays his need for God. And having mentioned the "existential situation," we must now consider existentialism as a third major possibility among contemporary candidates for the office of unifying idea, or group of ideas.

Existentialism and the philosophical stumbling blocks: transcendence, mystery, and freedom

The point of departure in existentialism, the given, is neither "raw" experience nor the power of reason, but a special kind of experience reserved for human beings, that of being in "the human situation." "What it means to exist" in the way that only a human being must exist is the object of description in existential writings. The method is that of introspective psychology, but the descriptions may be made the metaphysical basis of an ontology, on the grounds that man is the only being that knows he has being, and is in a position to tell us what it feels like, from the inside, to be a being. Man is the only thing-in-itself that is in itself. In fact man could never even have conceived the notion that other things might be things-in-themselves if he did not have this unique, "inside-story" vantage point on being. Consciousness of self is the "inside story" on being, and it is the truth of this story that both empiricism and rationalism presuppose when, for example, they have to assume the "general similarity of all minds" in order to validate "public knowledge." But existentialism is not interested in, or is even hostile toward, this public knowledge, because of the way it tends to ignore or misrepresent the human situation in its authenticity, from the inside.

There are many different ways, both metaphorical and literal, both emotional and unemotional, in which one can set about to describe the "human situation." For example, one can put the thing in terms of a drama, and then point out the peculiar position of man as one who would like to be actor, spectator, and director all at once. Where this philosophy is oriented toward Christianity, it maintains that if the drama is to be successful, man must stick to his script and leave the directing and spectating to God. His script, which is the evangelical faith, gives him some small understanding of his own part in the play, but, though at first he may be tempted to speculate as to how the drama looks from where God is sitting, he is ever more and more constrained, by his very position on the stage, to pay attention to his lines.

The existential viewpoint recognizes the fact that man lives facing the future; that he must constantly make decisions; that the evasion of decision is itself a decision; that the external determinants he would like to use in helping him to make decisions are themselves in process of change, or ambiguous in relation to him; and finally that, being morally responsible for the use of his time, or "on stage" all the time, he really cannot take time out, or step out of character, long enough to acquire such wisdom as would enable him to predict the future by studying the past or intuiting the eternal. He is thus constantly thrown back on faith, back to his script. Under such conditions the "truth" cannot be for him a matter of observation and appraisal. The truth for him can be only his part in the play, that which he acts out. The question of whether the plot of the play might be better understood from a realistic or from an idealistic standpoint is an idle question for him, since merely to think about it he has to step "off stage" and thereby lose his place in the play, and in that case the play no longer concerns him. His difficulty is that being a creature of time he cannot stop and start the play at will. He must eventually choose between being an actor inside the truth or a spectator outside the truth—that is, without the truth.

Or, less dramatically, the "human situation" can be described in terms of a Socratic search for truth, turning away from the "outer" to the "inner" in obedience to the oracle: know thyself. As a quest for self-knowledge it is nothing new in the history of European thought. But modern existentialism must be appreciated as a revolt against any philosophy or any theory of knowledge which presumes to give answers to man's questions without first of all asking what sort of being is this creature who wants to know, and why does he want to know. That the idea of truth, whatever it may be, and the idea of man, whatever he may be, are somehow inseparable is at least the common denominator of all existential viewpoints. It is also the common-sense intuition that the meaning of life must be the meaning of my life or it is not the meaning of anything.

Kierkegaard, who is falsely hailed as the father of modern existentialism, used the existential "dialectic" never as an end in itself but always as an offensive and defensive weapon in a battle on behalf of the Christian faith deliberately planned to meet what he thought were the special apologetic and evangelistic needs of his historical situation, and, therefore, the Kierkegaardian existentialism should be regarded rather as the exception than the rule in existential philosophizing. And Kierkegaard himself should not be called the father of modern existentialism (especially as he would scarcely admit to the paternity of most of his imputed children), but rather the re-awakener of the existential interest in European thought. All during the time that Kierkegaard's works were still cocooned in Danish, the ground was being prepared for the emergence of existentialism as a philosophy in much of late nineteenth-century and early twentieth-century literature, poetry, and drama, which rebelled against the scientific and industrial civilization that was dehumanizing man.

Existentialism should be given credit for restoring man as man to the centrality of thinking, and for attempting to describe the "human situation" as accurately as it can. But the popular idea that it is a philosophy somehow tailor-made to fit the Christian believer, and that it also solves the problem of his relationship to the traditional philosophy that conceives itself as a quest for objective truth, must, on closer examination, be considerably modified. The existential viewpoint seems to fit the believer so well because it is, among other things, a summons to action, and the believer is certainly called to action by his faith. The picture of him on the stage may be a reminder that, whatever the verdict of philosophy may eventually be, there are some things he must *do* before his time is up. Taken more radically, it is a deliberate abandonment of philosophy in favor of a description of man's situation such that faith as against philosophy is accounted the better solution to his apparently desperate predicament. It attempts to reassure the believer that, the human situation being what it is, he has chosen the better part. But it is a question whether anything human can reassure the believer in this respect, even the human situation, and an even greater question whether he can permit himself to regard his faith as the best solution to a desperate predicament.

Existential thinking is equally congenial to any view of life that centers around the need for action, even the most anti-Christian, and the injunction that for man who must act and decide there is no time to indulge in speculative philosophy is scarcely a solution to his relationship to speculative philosophy, for it is precisely *in action* that he encounters it, in so far as it has influenced and continues to influence the concrete actions and driving beliefs (for example, in politics) of individuals, communities, and states. For in spite of all that may be said against speculative philosophy for setting itself too far above the storm, the fact remains that in every age it is the popular versions of the dominant philosophies that become the half-conscious dynamics of society. According to some of the existentialists themselves it is not a question of speculation versus action, but of "authentic" versus "unauthentic" existence (Heidegger). Even for the Christian believer the script that is his faith cannot be thought of as an unambiguous directive for action in the midst of those ambiguities of existence that arouse all other men to spiritual distress and give urgency to the philosophical quest.

Existentialism should be given credit for attempting to deal with the difficulties raised by the concepts of transcendence, mystery, and freedom, not always in relation to God, but rather as these concepts appear to be partially characteristic even of man, thereby showing themselves as the real "gremlins" in the philosophical description of man as well as God. For example, if the self-transcendence of man, its subjective expression as freedom, and its "objectve correlative" in the "mystery of being" are all real and inescapable characteristics of human life, how can philosophy "deal" with them, without in the same instance contradicting their true character as transcendence, freedom, and mystery? Existentialism has faced the fact that if what we loosely call the spirit of man is truly free, it must always remain to some extent unexplainable, unpredictable, or nonrational, since to be explainable is to be determinate according to some nature. It has called attention to the empirical "emptiness" of man's freedom, to the impossibility of describing or grasping it in the same categories as nature, without thereby misrepresenting its real character as freedom, its real transcendence of the determinate, and its real implication in mystery. It has thereby revealed and affirmed the inadequacy, on the one hand, of any kind of naturalism, whether naïve or sophisticated, which simply denies or ignores these qualities in man, or evades the whole issue, and, on the other hand, of any kind of rationalism which tries to "corral" these qualities, to capture them and squeeze them into something rationally manageable, thereby rendering them all once more determinate according to some kind of nature, even though conceived as "spiritual nature."

To some people existentialism has appeared as a movement that spells the doom of philosophy because it has revealed not this or that error in someone's logic or mode of thinking but the very impossibility of the task itself, in view of man's freedom, self-transcendence, and mystery. Those who have the interests of philosophy at heart therefore tend to attack modern existentialism as a philosophy of nothingness, a pure nihilism, a destructive, totally negating irrationalism. But a less absolutistic view of philosophy than is implied in the use of the word "doom" for these difficulties might suggest that the existential analysis is a potential corrective for both realism and idealism in their destiny to meet each other half way in an admittedly limited and partial description of reality.

If a transcendent God is unmanageable for philosophy, a partially transcendent man must be at least partially unmanageable. Where then does this man stand? How is his partial transcendence evident to him? A good deal of existential philosophy preoccupies itself with the phenomenological analysis, or what would be better called the "pure description" of this man who is aware of transcendence, freedom, and mystery. He seems to stand at an elusive vanishing point which can never become an object of thought to him because it is the point from which all thoughts are surveyed, all perspectives are taken, both subjective and objective. Nor is it even a stationary point, but one that is constantly in retreat before itself, because it transcends itself, or "passes beyond" itself, backward or depthwise into the mystery (though forward in time), in every effort to understand itself, and every determination to identify itself with something thinkable. Yet it knows that it is there by this very process of self-transcendence, which also has the effect of making the man a foreigner in the world, one who tries but never succeeds entirely in identifying himself with something in the world. It is customary to call this point outside his own thought and feeling and desire his "spirit," in contrast to his soul, which is merely his mental life, and the body, his determinate nature. Unfortunately the word "spiritual," by virtue of these very efforts of identification that the man tries and then transcends, has become loaded with intellectual and affective associations; whereas, the real meaning of the self-transcendence of the self can be better appreciated by realizing, as the existentialists have done better than others, that it is actually empty of content. It is the unthinkable that thinks, the unfeelable that is aware of feelings, the unwillable that originates the willed act, the invisible spectator of the presented image.

The realization of the empirical emptiness of this transcendent aspect of man has expressed itself in existential thinking in various ways, affirmatively and negatively, religiously and antireligiously. The "freedom" of man and the "mystery of being" which are the subjective and objective ways of expressing the awareness of the transcendence, and whose reality is, as it were, "guaranteed" by the transcendence from being reduced to something else or somehow explained away, have been used separately or in conjunction to describe what the characteristics of "authentic" or "honest" existence are, the results ranging all the way from the proclamation of the most hopeless and final despair to the exploration of the most intimate and precious aspects of human love, and (by analogy) divine love. That man is made for death, and that man is made for love, are the two apparently equally consistent "conclusions" that one can draw from the fact of his transcendence, freedom, and mystery.

The negative and supposedly nonreligious existentialisms (Sartre is "sorry there is no God"; Heidegger is "waiting for a god or for the gods to appear.") have concentrated rather on the freedom of man as the main problem, whereby the mystery of being becomes for them the "nothingness" of meaning provided by the objective world in which man is truly a freak. It is all very well for idealism and realism in their separate quests for some kind of objective truth to discover all kinds of essences and relations in the objective world: this merely gives emphasis by contrast to the freakishness of man who, because of his freedom, has neither essence nor any established relations with the world; for whom, therefore, all this wisdom is an affront, utterly ambiguous, basically "nothing." The only honest way to live is to look this nothingness square in the eye, and then to be willing to live as the freak that one is, "condemned to be free."

The researches of the negative existentialists consist more than anything else of literary and psychological studies of the states of man that reveal to him his existential situation: anxiety, fear, despair, uncertainty, frustration, homelessness, guilt, the ambiguity of choices, the feeling of being trapped. At this point it should be noted that although it is assumed that the honest or authentic life is one that will be planned in rational consistency with these conditions, suicide as a consistent conclusion is only obliquely considered and seldom recommended. It is assumed that the subject will not be *that* consistent, that he will survive the existential crisis somehow, that he will gaze into the vertiginous abyss of nothingness, feel in his entrails the agony of despair, the unbearable loneliness, the nausea of empty freedom, and then ask what to do next. And sure enough, there on the far side of the crisis, existentialism will be waiting for him, holding out the answer. The answer, the thing to do next, is to take this empty freedom, the cause of all the mischief, and turn it into a slogan and a battle cry, a mandate for action, just sheer action for the sake of exercising the freedom and nothing else. One must become *engagé*, involved, committed, precisely to give freedom something to bite on. Thereby one creates oneself, makes one's own essence, which appears in the rear as the backwash of the forward-moving voyage of free involvement.

Of course, there is the danger of losing sight of the nothingness as soon as one becomes involved, for one can become involved only in something definite, such as politics, religion, art, which all have the appearance of being the manifestation of some objective truth about the world. One becomes a communist, a Christian, a social reformer, a poet, each of which has a certain rationale, as well as a certain discipline behind it, that makes it distinguishable, one from the other. Existentialism is willing enough to admit that all philosophy, all religion, all politics, all art, in so far as they try to give answers to the burning existential question, what is the meaning of life, are to that extent "existential," but it is its avowed purpose to make man face the fact that there *is no answer* to the question to be found either in nature or in man, and that man must *invent* the answers himself. That is what the philosophers have been doing all through the ages, inventing the answer, except that they have tried to support their inventions by drawing upon observations of nature, human nature, the possibilities of both indicated by reason and imagination, and the wisdom of past experience. But the negative existentialism considers these supports to be *illusory* and wants the answer of each individual to be adopted in full consciousness of its purely invented character, of its having *no* support in the objective world, the latter being axiomatically meaningless or the existential question would never have arisen. What is "true" in these pseudo answers is that they constitute an externalization, one might almost say a muscularization, of freedom, but this freedom also needs the constant reminder of the nothingness of existence to be aware of itself as freedom.

The affirmative or supposedly religious existentialism has concentrated on the mystery of being rather than the freedom of man, which it regards as only one aspect of that mystery. Mystery, here, must not be thought of as something technically unknowable, or as a not-yet-solved problem, but rather as that wonder-arousing quality which the totality of being has when contemplated disinterestedly, and which clings to every particular so regarded. Mystery is also the awareness through self-transcendence of a depth dimension to being: the dark source from which not-yet-being comes into being. Mystery is also the *surprise* of there being after all something instead of nothing, which is the obverse of the experience of looking nothingness square in the eye.

The affirmative existentialists take an objective attitude toward being, although they denounce the false objectivity which seeks to find the meaning of being in the external articulation of things instead of looking for it in the only being that knows it has being, the self of man. Self-knowledge, not in the sense of arbitrary or private subjectivism, but in the Socratic sense of the discovery of a structure-of-the-self that can be universalized, is the true road to ontology.

The affirmative existentialists admit that much of the description of man's condition undertaken by the negative existentalists is true, but only because man is in a state of disease and being, therefore, is not itself. These nihilists, they complain, are trying to accommodate us permanently to the disease instead of bringing us back to health. Martin Buber, Nicholas Berdyaev, and Gabriel Marcel, to name only three, all speak in one way or another of the broken or shattered or dismembered condition of true being, as exemplified in the manifold horrors of modern civilization. They explore the successes and failures of person-to-person relations, person-to-thing relations, person-to-god relations. They examine the nature of love, the different kinds of love, the nature of creativity, the empty freedom, and the full freedom. They probe the meaning of history as a lesson book which manifests the mystery of being positively or negatively for those whose sensibilities are sharpened through self-awareness. They become religious when in various ways they make the ontological identification of being with God, the mystery of being thereby becoming the cloak under which this happens, and something of this mystery clinging both to God and to man at the depth of self-awareness. Man's self-transcendence somehow passes over, in this mystery, into God's transcendence, and may even be thought of as the image of God in man.

The negative and the affirmative existentialisms are not so different from the traditional philosophy as would appear at first glance. They correspond roughly to a concretized and personalized realism and idealism respectively, and both have been traumatized into the study of self-awareness by the impact of historical events rather than by the logical development of ideas. Negative existentialism is in a sense the *reductio ad absurdum* of a realism that blithely connects everything in the world but forgets the main connection, the one with man, which then takes its revenge by cutting itself off to spite the world, and reveling in its ability to do this—in the defiant subjectivism of freedom for freedom's sake; or, where the temperament is more pessimistic, in the stoic determination to endure the world for freedom's sake. The affirmative existentialism is a kind of chastened idealism, chastened at least of the claim of speculative reason to be able to effect the salvation of man. It is a back-to-Socrates movement, which, while it does not necessarily issue in Platonism, must hope eventually to be able to disclose those spiritual values or activities that self-knowledge reveals to be the condition of true, unbroken, or fulfilled being. The charge of idolatry can be brought against negative existentialism for what amounts to the worship of human freedom per se, and the charge of pantheism can be brought against affirmative existentialism for a too-ready identification of the being of the self with God, although here the existentialists could defend themselves by skillful use of the "mystery" to allow for divine-human differences.

As long as existentialism confines itself to pure description, the delineation of things as they are with respect to the human situation, it seems to be both negatively and positively more accurate and less one-sided than either traditional realism or idealism have been, and to that extent it represents a mutual *rapprochement* between realism and idealism whereby, ignoring theories of knowledge that may separate them, they can pool their descriptive resources. But when it comes to prescription, to telling man what to do next, how to live, or what to believe, the answers given are just as unsatisfactory from a Christian standpoint as previous attempts. If all that is required of a philosophy is to make room for faith, the negative existentialism certainly does that. It makes more room for faith than either realism or idealism has made in the past, but on the condition that all faiths be considered purely human inventions in answer to the burning existential question.

The believer, aside from the fact that he cannot permit the Christian faith to be put on a par with all other "inventions" in this field, cannot admit his faith to be a human "invention" at all. His faith is a response to a Reality, which, while it may be subjectively apprehended in the inner parts of the spirit, is nevertheless there apprehended as objectively real, as logically and ontologically preceding the believer and independent of him. It is the divine source and sustenance of all, not the private and willful invention of the believer. Here he finds himself all at once in sympathy with traditional philosophy in its quest for an objective truth with which to answer the existential question, for the reduction by the existentialists of all objective meaning to private "inventions" suddenly reminds him that the Christian faith has its own objective content: it implies that the world is this kind of a world, not that kind, and not any kind that I choose to make it. And he sees that traditional philosophy, by its very attempt to support its inventions by some kind of evidence or structure in the world of nature or of human nature, also does not regard its answers as pure inventions. A creative element is certainly involved in attempting an answer—that is, in gathering and expressing and universalizing the elements of the answer from what is given in experience in a particular way—but if for this reason the philosopher would have to regard his answer as "pure invention," he should not succeed in convincing either himself or anyone else that an answer had really been found to the question of what is the meaning of life.

On the other hand, if all that is required of philosophy is to increase man's self-knowledge, the affirmative existentialism certainly attempts to do that—but to what purpose? Surely not to give him "disinterested" knowledge of the meaning and center of all interest! (This is the butt of all of Kierkegaard's jokes about philosophical absent-mindedness, the professor's forgetting that the knowledge is about him.) It must be to tell him what "the good" is, and how his life can be "saved" instead of "wasted." But here a Christian anthropology would have to insist that without Christ no true self-knowledge is possible, he being the criterion which defines both what the good is for man, and what man is when separated from the good; the standard which is the revealer of grace and the yardstick of sin. With this dogmatic assertion philosophical anthropology passes over into Christian theology, and from description into prescription. In other words, from a Christian standpoint it is not enough to describe man in ideal terms, in the terms of his structure of spirit, his personhood, his participation in transcendence, mystery, and freedom, even his sickness and health, without facing up to the fact of what man is in actuality, what *he has done in history,* and *to Whom* his doing has been an offense. But to do this is to face the fact, not the theory, of revelation. This fact is or is not, and to assent or dissent to its factuality is to affirm or deny the entire biblical perspective in terms of which the man-God-Christ relationship is defined. Here is no longer philosophy, but the challenge of the evangel.

What makes Kierkegaard's existentialism "exceptional" is that he never for a moment lost sight of the biblical perspective, never allowed his existentialism to slip out from under its judgment and become something on its own, a new humanism apart from the biblical God. Thus while his existentialism was both negative and affirmative, both driving to despair and affirming the true good for man (which can also drive to despair if this good is seen as out of reach, or to be had only on terms that man refuses), he had the Christian criterion by which *despair* could be condemned as *sin*, as the absence of faith in the most radical sense. In his *The Sickness unto Death* he describes as one of the dialectical developments of despair (which is the sickness unto death) precisely that defiant defiance of despair which is the basic attitude of the modern negative existentialism.[3] But Kierkegaard would probably have smiled over the "seriousness" of their despair, since they do not consider the possibility of suicide but rather regale themselves with metaphysical horror-thrills and then go on living as before. They do not really want to be cured of their despair, so that one must wonder whether such despair is not after all a romantic or a theatrical pose.

The Christian critique of philosophy as a rescue from idolatry

The fact that philosophy seems incapable of doing justice to the real differences in the several aspects of reality without ending up by reading off one part in terms of another, or by reading off the whole in terms of one of the parts, has an innocent and a guilty aspect. Previously we called this the creaturely and the sinful aspect. Surely there would be nothing sinful in the mere fact of the creatureliness of human knowledge, if man were willing to admit its limitations and size them up correctly. But he prefers to fall either into a hopeless, irresponsible skepticism, or else into the making of preposterous, universe-encompassing claims. It seems that what he would like to have is either complete knowledge and complete control—or, no knowledge at all and therefore complete irresponsibility. He doesn't like the idea of creaturely knowledge, and his sinfulness shows itself historically not only in his perennial unwillingness to admit and size up its limitations correctly but already in his tendency to misuse what little he does know, and even to misuse the very act of knowing. So deep is the idolatrous tendency in man that it shows itself in the very way he plays the part of being a "knower," in what he thinks the possibility of having knowledge means for the "human condition." Let us take a cue from the existentialists and see if we cannot first describe idolatry as it arises in the very heart of the "existential situation," rather than in its objective results in the history of philosophy, using whatever Christian insights are relevant toward making this situation clear.

Man's relationship to this own knowledge has sometimes been compared with owning something, like money, which can be piled up and even hoarded, but superior to money, because it is something no one can take away from the owner. The comparison would be more correct if the money in the analogy were specified to be paper money or scrip, subject to sudden and unpredictable inflations or deflations in value, according to the ups and downs of some very remote center of world trade. For it is not the case with man that he is born ignorant and then just grows up, picking up knowledge as he goes along, but rather that his whole accumulation of knoweldge is at any given moment subject to a change of meaning, a sudden rise or fall in value, and even to the threat of no meaning at all. The world is a kind of opaqueness and density that presents itself to him piecemeal, but he is not able to grasp it piecemeal, still less to understand it piecemeal. There is in man a lack of sympathy with what is simply present as given, an inability to grasp immediacy, to understand particulars as particulars, that contrasts sharply with the all-pervading love and understanding of God for his creation.

With God, to know and to love is the same thing. He creates and beholds that it is good. With man, knowledge and love are not only separate acts but they are separated by the dark barrier of the self which must first be overcome in an act of commitment. Only the particular exists for God, who counts the hairs of our heads and the falling of sparrows, for only the particular can be created, loved, and sustained as he creates, loves, and sustains the world in every particular. But for man the particular is a stumbling block—in its discreteness it baffles him, in its independence it offends and even threatens him, and he is quite incapable of loving it for its own sake. He can only love it, or hate it, or ignore it, in some web of meaning that includes himself. The very word "particular" betrays the fact that he has to have a world, a wholeness, a totality, into which he can fit the particulars as parts, before he can make peace with them, accept them, let them be themselves.

This situation in itself would not be hopeless. The fateful or tragic makes its appearance because man is unwilling to understand this silence between himself and the particulars as the mark of his finitude, the badge of creatureliness. Nor is he further willing to appreciate the fact that God has not left him helpless in this condition, and utterly at the mercy of this finitude, but rather that, by giving him the ability to transcend himself, God has given man the possibility of a human kind of knowledge with which to make his way through the density of particulars. A mere by-product of his transcendence, the ability of man to be a spectator, to form concepts, to make abstractions and generalizations, is surely a quality that places man above the animals, that makes possible speech, real communication, and purposeful action in a world of particulars. By means of this ability he enlarges his naturally limited perspective, and transcends his naturally limited senses; he makes a "world" out of the particulars in relation to himself, and he lives in this world as one who knows this world. But he cannot, or rather will not, understand that this knowledge of his, when viewed from the side of God's knowledge of the creation, is precisely his weakness, his inability to know and love as God knows and loves. On the contrary, he refuses to see it this way, and proceeds to make out of his knowledge his greatest virtue and strength, and to see in it a means of escape from that very creatureliness of which it is the authentic sign.

Observe how man glories in his ability to manipulate and to dominate the particular by means of the general. He is never so happy, so conscious of power, so sure of having triumphed over ignorance (or over the particulars, which represent ignorance to him), as when he has concocted another generalization. Nature loses its terrors for him, and history acquires meaning for him, only in so far as he is able to subsume their particulars under his generalizations; and to form yet more comprehensive generalizations, still more unifying categories, becomes the goal of all his knowledge. Not that he does not try to do justice to the particulars—he is most careful about that, most interested in the exact nature of every particular, as our huge fact-finding apparatus of education and research bears witness. But he is interested in the particular only in its relation to the general, because he does not wish to jeopardize the power and efficacy of his generalizations.

The process of abstraction, which is made possible by the fact that he can survey his own thought from a point outside it, gives him not only the feeling of power but also of emancipation, of a disentangling of his spirit from servitude to the partial and contingent, the transitory and the perishable. His spirit literally soars at this taste of freedom, and he concludes that in this direction must lie divinity: to know this emancipation and this freedom must be to know what God is like, to be like God. What greater glory than this is possible for man? In what other direction can his spirit reach such heights, both of contemplation and of control? Obviously this must be his divine spark. Here we have the origin of all those idealistic conceptions of the inferiority and imperfection of the particular as against the perfection and indestructibility of the idea, and the progression from one to the other that ends only in the absolute idea. But this is also the direction in which realism moves, except that it moves more cautiously and its emphasis is more on control and action than on contemplation.

It is only if one takes the perspective of the Bible seriously, and places one's self within it, that one can say, must say, quite simply: no, *that* is not the direction in which divinity lies. God does not need any clever abstractions or king-sized generalizations in order to understand his creation, or to be free of it. He understands it and is free from it by virtue of having created it, and at the same time he loves it and does not wish to be free from it. The process of abstraction is a device, a tool of understanding which God has placed at men's disposal precisely because of man's creaturely mind and limited sensibility. And yet the way in which man uses this tool, this gift, serves only to alienate him from the Giver of every good and perfect gift, both from him and from his creation. For love is always defeated in the process of abstraction. The more man uses this tool, the more he loses the ability to have a godlike love of the particular, and the more the particular sinks in his estimation and loses intrinsic value.

But isn't it heard on all sides, especially from the mouths of the spiritually minded people, that man is altogether too much in love with the finite world, with "creaturely things"? And so he is—but he is in love with the world with *his* idea of what love is, not with God's idea of what love is. He is in love with the world in so far as it arouses and satisfies his desires, fulfills his needs, provides him with positive and unexpected delights, and titillates his intellect. He affirms by his actions, if not by his words, that it is a good thing to be alive, and this avid vitality, this lust for life, constitutes his love for the world. Only on occasion does this fog of self-centeredness lift sufficiently for him to have a brief glimpse of the world as it is, not for him, but without him, for itself, or for something else, or for nothing at all, and then it is no spontaneous love for it that rises in his breast but rather wonder and awe, estrangement and dread, and eventually the agony of the agonizing moment. Here knowledge rushes to his rescue; knoweldge, the human housekeeper, once more makes a human place for everything and puts everything in its human place. It domesticates the insufferable particulars and makes a little human noise in the insufferable silence that permeates the spaces between them. So knowledge gradually takes the place of love, of that godlike love of the particular of which man is so little capable, and becomes less capable as he increases in knowledge.

It is true that artists and poets make a real effort to approach the particular in its particularity, to remain "open" to it, to refrain from vacant abstractions. In his own private, subjective life of artistic perception the artist certainly tries to come to grips with the particular, to commune with it, to make that silence which lies between him and it say something, to listen long and patiently, to let the forms of his imagination run wild so as to catch even the smallest whisper—like the citizens of New York who ran about with pots and pans during a water shortage to catch the slightest fall of rain. This very attitude of creative receptivity and listening is the expression of a different kind of love of the world than the ordinary man's love, even though it is confined to the aesthetic sphere. It is more godlike in so far as it lets the particular be the particular, be itself, speak for itself, or even remain silent; in so far as it respects the uniqueness and otherness of each particular—for this respect for what one is able to violate but chooses not to is affirmation, and affirmation is already love.

But when it comes to creating out of this subjective intercourse an objectice work of art for all the world to see or hear and understand, it is a different matter, for there thought and abstraction and form enter in, bringing with them that universalizing tendency that is not only inevitable but necessary if there is to be any real communication. One might almost say that the love of the particular defies communication, as indeed many other things defy communication, but how much poorer would be the world of already poverty-stricken human beings in this matter of loving the particular, if the artist didn't at least try! Nevertheless, the realm of art does not escape the tendency of knowledge to take the place of love, for in most cases, and for the reason that the artist is only human, the particular, even if better understood and respected, is used only as a point of departure, the medium, or the metaphor, of some universal truth or feeling or situation in human experience. Art as much as knowledge is lauded for contributing to man's emancipation from the world of particular things, and in their contemplative aspects art and knowledge are certainly similar if not identical; but no one ever bothers to mention that man needs this emancipation because he is incapable of loving the world for itself in the first place.

So much for the things. And now how is it with purely human relationships, with the life of person and person? Well, to begin with, there is a "thing" aspect to the human person: it is a particular object or body moving around in the world; it has its individuality, indivisibility, and impenetrability, occupies space and time, has colors, temperatures, weight, form, excites aesthetic responses. That it is much more than all of these qualities does not deny the fact that it is these qualities also, and all that has been said before about the love of particular things applies as well to man considered as a particular thing. But man must not be considered as a particular *thing:* it is wrong to do so. Here a new dimension enters the discussion, the dimension of right and wrong, and it is applied not to the particularity or the generality of man but to the "thingness" of him. And who says that it is wrong? Why, man himself, as soon as he experiences in his own person what it is to be treated as a thing. That man must not be treated as a thing is a valuable insight only recently rediscovered after the reign of "crude" naturalism in philosophy and science had reduced him to exactly that, but it is an insight not entirely unconnected with man's incapacity to love the things for themselves—for man would not feel so insulted to be treated as a thing if he weren't to some extent aware of the fact that he invariably treats things insultingly.

That man is somehow eternally and inescapably different from things is the insight of a real humanism, which humanism, ever since the Enlightenment, has been illogically and optimistically allied with scientific naturalism, content to ignore the fact that a thoroughgoing and consistent naturalism could destroy humanism more effectively than the most tyrannical despot, and that in fact it was naturalism that paved the way for the tyrants of the twentieth century, who carried out historically the logical implications of man's identification with nature.

That man is not identical with nature is not a specifically Christian insight, however, for Christianity considers man to be a child of God, bearing the image of God, which is something other than his being merely different from nature, though, of course, it includes this as a presupposition. And in the Christian differentiation man is not honored at the expense of nature—he is honored with the image of God because this is God's good pleasure, and nature does not suffer from this elevation, for God has given nature her own kind of perfection. The insecurity of mere humanism as a foundation for democratic principles is evident in this distinction, for while the humanist can agree not to treat the other human beings as things, because he himself does not wish to be treated as a thing, this agreement is in the nature of an enlightened self-interest, which means that it is scarcely binding for him who is not sufficiently enlightened, nor for him who does not see his self-interest served, who feels he can get away with something less exacting. But for the Christian it is a mandate from on high: he is not to treat the people as things because God has made them for himself, and in the last analysis they belong to God, and not even to themselves. And that means he is not to treat them so even if they permit it, and even if there is no danger of his receiving this treatment in return.

But the problem of the relationship between persons is a little too simplified if we pose it as merely the obligation not to treat persons as things. For just as there are different ways of treating things as things, there is an even greater variety of ways of treating persons as persons. And here the strange incompatibility of knowledge and love—as man understands knowledge and love—shows itself with even more tragic impact than in the case of things. The gist of this tragedy can be stated very simply: everybody wants to be loved, but few, few are either willing or able to do the loving, and so knowledge is again called to the rescue, to occupy the place left empty by the deficiency of love. When man is honest, he sees in himself a disheartening incapacity to love more than a very limited number of people, and even to love these few in anything but a limited way. The very thought of being required to love large numbers of people as individuals is somehow glutting to his imagination. This is noticeable in the reaction of man to the death of others: the death of a friend moves him deeply; a catastrophe fatal to dozens upsets him somewhat; the death of thousands scarcely touches him. A kind of fatigue of the imagination overwhelms him, setting a limit to his understanding of what happens to others, and a kind of protective insensibility surrounds him, setting a limit to his compassion.

But he is at heart ashamed of this. He will not admit that this too is a mark of his creatureliness, but insists rather that it is because no sufficiently worthy object is offered to him for loving. He wants to love something imposing and grandiose, like some ideal of humanity, or mankind in general, and he thinks he can do this by abstracting the qualities he admires in the few persons he really loves. In other words, he submits the collection of abstract human qualities achieved in knowledge about human beings to a value judgment, and then proceeds to love humanity or mankind in the sense that it is the actual or potential bearer of the values he considers the highest. In this process the particular person sinks in his estimation, the love of particular people becomes something inferior to the love of collective groups, or humanity at large, and the individual is loved, not for himself, but because of the best qualities of humanity that he embodies or represents.

But this is not what God intended. Nowhere in the Bible does it say that you are to love mankind, or humanity at large, or any abstract quality, or any collectivity, but "thy neighbor." God knows all about man's limited capacity for love, but he did not intend that man should build upon this very limitation a kind of structure of knowledge that satisfies and consoles his ego at the same time that it hinders him from exercising even that limited love of persons of which he is capable, to its full extents.

And viewed from this angle, it becomes evident that man does not even love himself properly. His very egoism is no true love of himself as this particular one that he happens to be, but is rather the endless and restless collecting of knowledge, of proofs, of evidences, to the effect that he is really such a fine one as he is capable of loving. No one has expressed this so vividly as Martin Buber in his study of the I-Thou relation, where he describes the "erotic man" as one who in all his pretended dialogue with others is forever monologizing, forever holding up a mirror to himself, to see how he is making out. He says:

> Many years I have wandered through the land of men, and have not yet reached an end of studying the varieties of the "erotic man." . . . There a lover stamps around and is in love only with his passion. There one is wearing his differentiated feelings like medal-ribbons. There one is enjoying the adventures of his own fascinating effect. There one is gazing enraptured at the spectacle of his own supposed surrender. There one is collecting excitement. There one is displaying his "power." There one is preening himself with borrowed vitality. There one is delighting to exist simultaneously as himself, and as an idol very unlike himself. There one is warming himself at the blaze of what has fallen to his lot. There one is experimenting. And so on and on—all the manifold monologists with their mirrors, in the apartment of the most intimate dialogue! [4]

Does such a man really love *himself?* No, for he is busily constructing an idol out of his empirical knowledge about himself to take the place of the self that he does not care to face. And since he does not love himself, he does not love his neighbor, his partner in the dialogue, but only the correlative idol he has built up out of his empirical knowledge about the neighbor. And this sentence can be turned around, for since he does not love his neighbor as that particular one, that irreplaceably other one that he is, neither can he affirm himself in his own otherness and particularity, his right to be the one that he really is. Out of such delicate reciprocal relationships is the fabric of human relations constructed, which is why the harm that is done by man's willingness to substitute knowledge for love has such a terrifyingly cumulative and all-pervasive effect. For we are all born into a world in which love has already been defeated—the fallen world, fallen away from God's love, and therefore also from true human love. To live humanly in such a world requires the grace of the redeeming God, who, in spite of apparent defeat, is determined to restore the broken relationships. Since the relationship of I and Thou is in all directions such an intimately reciprocal relationship, the unlovingness of man both for the I and the Thou is ever and again the new cause and the new effect of more and more unlovingness—and who is able to break this vicious circle? Who can love the enemy where every man is born and reared into enmity with himself and others through the enmity of himself and others? Here there is nothing to do but to wait for the grace of God.

But the believer can do something, for he has already received grace. He can at least recognize this situation for what it is, plumb its depths, avoid attempting any easy solutions, and hold himself in readiness. Unfortunately many Christians think that the solution lies in putting on a terrific act of Christian brotherliness, which by its very enthusiasm and indiscriminateness convinces everyone that it is nothing but an act, and which offends every particular Thou that it encounters. Such an externalizing Christian either unconsciously or well-meaningly commits the same sort of idolatry that already infests the whole domain of community among men, for he substitutes his "idea of how a Christian should behave" for the actual behaving, for the placing of himself before another in that openness and expectancy in which the miracle of grace might happen. Clergymen, of course, are particularly plagued with this temptation, especially as they themselves have continually to do battle with the fact that they encounter from their fellow men little real understanding as particular persons, but only endless variations on the "idea of how a clergyman should behave."

Nevertheless, the believer can try to remain aware of the dangers that beset love on all sides, not from knowledge itself, but from the tendency of man to substitute knowledge for love. And this only the believer can really do, for only the believer has God's love as his standard of love. In the light of this standard the believer can at least understand that the particular thing ought to be loved, not only because it serves this or that purpose of man, but because it is a part of God's creation, and that the particular person ought to be loved, not just because he is the bearer of certain excellent qualities, but because he is a child of God, lost or found, even where he is not the bearer of the best qualities. The awareness of this "ought" will not in itself make him able to love in this way, but it will make him humble for himself, and will make him healthily suspicious of any grandiose rhetoric coming from the direction of philosophy about the love one should have for mankind, and about devotion to high ideals.

This little survey of the different ways in which man tries to use knowledge as a substitute for love might be entitled the "varieties of of idolatrous experience." We all indulge in idolatry, not only in relation to God, but in relation to ourselves and other people and even in relation to things. In the act of idolatry the object idolized is never really loved for itself, but is rather venerated for what it can "do" for the one who offers his veneration. And since it is concerning an object we know, or think we know, that we can best discern what it can "do" for us, it is knowledge, and especially abstract knowledge, that becomes the fateful vehicle of idolatry.

From a more objective standpoint the idolatrous tendency in man has contributed its share in making the history of philosophy almost the history of the stretching and distortion of one partial truth after another in the effort to make such a partial truth do for an ultimate truth. Every new philosophy that comes along is usually founded on a truth that has been sorely neglected by its predecessors, but it immediately proceeds to build on this one truth such an imposing structure of conceptual relationships and logical implications as practically to crowd out every other truth if it does not fit into that conceptual scheme, and thereby it not only distorts that one truth but also paves the way for the next philosophy to do the same with the most obviously neglected truth.[5]

But, after all, isn't such truth-stretching what we almost demand of philosophy when we ask that philosophy should supply us with a set of unifying ideas with which to make sense out of the meaning of the whole? The *whole* is a very large order. The Bible doesn't pretend to make sense out of the *whole*, but only out of the *one thing needful* for man to know, and that is the God-man relationship. And the Bible doesn't pretend for a moment that the form of its knowledge is anything but creaturely. Stories, chronicles, songs, legends, dialogues with God, exhortations, promises, threats, pleadings, witnessings, letters, sermons, memoirs, visions, testimonials—these human, all too human, forms of communication nevertheless manage to convey what philosophy over and over fails to convey: the uniqueness, the wonder, and the urgency of that relationship. And this creaturely knowledge of God's relationship to man also makes more sense out of certain historical situations, and certain personal predicaments, than the abstractions of philosophy are able to make—which is the real reason, I submit, why some of the neo-orthodox theologians turned their backs on philosophy.

While philosophy was repeating logical formulas, or drawing caricatures of man, the Bible was making sense out of an agonizing and catastrophic historical development, the two world wars, not only showing men to themselves in their true colors, but calling them once again to repentance, and to faith in the only source of their being and hope: to the God who was not mocked. And this kind of sense the Bible made directly, without first being translated into philosophy, as the nineteenth century had demanded that it must be translated, before it could be acceptable to intellectuals. Even apologetics seemed outmoded, for if all sorts and conditions of men could understand what the Bible was saying about their historical situation, what need to drag in philosophy? Or perhaps it was history itself, economic, political, and theological history, that became the new domain of apologetics.

It is because the Bible does make sense, out of both historical and personal life, that the believer enters the field of philosophy holding on to "cherished beliefs," which he is not willing to give up even where philosophy gives him no encouragement or justification for retaining them. For he knows he has the one thing needful, and will not be quick to trade it for the very dubious and unconvincing account of the meaning of the whole that the entire history of philosophy presents. But having the one thing needful is also a great responsibility, and because the biblical faith is also a kind of knowledge, knowledge about the nature of God and the nature of man, the responsibility is in part an intellectual one, that falls naturally upon the more intellectually inclined believer. He cannot just sit by and watch philosophy do what it seems perennially determined to do—ruin itself as well as man, by its persistent tendency to make the part do for the whole, and to substitute knowledge for love.

It would seem, then, that the believer might find himself more in sympathy with the cautious philosophers, the logic men and the language analysts, than with the unifiers, for the former at least do not make any claims to have, or even to be able to obtain, interpretations of the whole. Having the one thing needful, the believer might think he could afford to "wait out" the sciences—to wait, that is, for the more exact kind of knowledge they give, at least in certain areas, before recommending action. But that is sheer unrealism in regard to the "human condition," as the existentialists have pointed out to us. Not only is man always forced to act before the requisite knowledge is available to make the action quite rational, but all the major decisions that have to be made are in areas of experience where the knowledge will never be as exact as in science, and perhaps not even cumulative—except for an imaginary Hegeloid type of being, who could survey the whole of history from the standpoint of eternity in order to learn its lessons.

In the next chapter we shall see what may be expected of science in that direction—and what may not. But it is sheer utopianism to expect men to live in a spiritual vacuum, pending better knowledge. The spirit of man needs a unifying idea as the body needs to breathe, and denied it in one place, will seek it in another. The task of Christian evangelism is to lead men to the place where they will recognize the unifying idea in the one thing needful: God's revelation of himself in the biblical accounts of the God-Christ-man relationship. The task of the philosophically inclined believer (either in addition to evangelism or alongside it) is to use the same revelation as a criterion by which to judge the wholeness and ultimacy of philosophical "unifying ideas," in a perennial and piece-meal effort to rescue philosophy from idolatry.

Chapter IV

FAITH AND SOCIAL SCIENCE

The scientific standing of social science

WHEN CHRISTIANITY FIRST ENTERED THE WORLD, IT HAD NOT ONLY TO distinguish itself from Judaism; it also had to define and defend itself over against Hellenistic philosophies, the public mythologies authorized by the Roman Empire, and the semiprivate, semioriental, mystical salvation religions. All of these were going concerns at the time, engaged in interpreting in some way the nature and destiny of man, and therefore properly competitive in relation to the new religion out of Nazareth. Now there exists in the world a going concern which had no parallel in the ancient or even in the medieval and the renaissance world, which claims to be neither a philosophy nor a religion, but which is yet concerned with interpreting something of human nature and social destiny to modern men. I refer to social science, an enterprise which because of its anomalous position and peculiar claims requires separate treatment from either natural science or philosophy in its import for the Christian believer.

The existence of the social sciences as a going concern engaging the attention and energies of intelligent people creates for the Christian believer the practical problem of establishing some relationship to the particular kind of knowledge that they claim to be able to deliver. He needs to find out if this knowledge can be of any use in the furtherance of Christian objectives, especially where he feels called to be a laborer in the vineyard of Christian social relations. Being a laborer is not a matter of good intentions but of creative struggle with the raw material, which in this case is human nature as manifested in social life, so that if there is any possibility that the social sciences might be able to give the believer some special understanding of social relations and social organization, he cannot afford to ignore them, any more than, say, a Christian doctor could ignore new medical knowledge that could be used in the service of healing.

The Christian believer, then, approaches the social sciences with a bias in the direction of the practical. In this approach he should be in the teachable and unargumentative mood of one who merely seeks the best means of achieving some desired end. He should not be on the defensive because he is a believer, nor should he be condescending; he should not preach to the social scientists, and least of all should he try to pick a quarrel on the famous subject of the alleged conflict between science and religion. All this should be so because he is interested only in using the practical findings of the social sciences for the achievement of certain Christian objectives. But anyone who has ever tried to do this knows that this admirable situation does not obtain. From the very beginning, from the words "practical findings," the believer finds himself plunged into a philosophical and terminological jungle. He feels himself surrounded by obscurely hostile attitudes and modes of thinking, and drawn inevitably toward the center of a confused battle of interpretations.[1] Except he pretend to himself that he is a giant of faith, he certainly finds himself on the defensive, needing sometimes to take another look at his faith in the light of this new and curious atmosphere, and he finds many occasions where he would like to pity some of the social scientists and preach to others.

The difficulty encountered here gradually resolves itself into two apparently opposite concerns. As soon as he asks for the "practical findings," he discovers that these are by no means as certain or unambiguous as could be desired by one who wishes to use them to guide action. His first concern, then, is over the scientific standing of the social sciences and how this affects the reliability of their findings. His second concern, which emerges more clearly after he has had some acquaintance with the battle of interpretations, is the question as to whether it is appropriate to deal with certain human problems by the method of the sciences at all.

First, then, the question of the scientific standing of the social sciences. The term "social sicences" will be used here to cover sociology, social and educational psychology, anthropology, economics, and political science. A question arises concerning physiology, pathology, and medicine: don't they also concern themselves with man? The answer is that they concern themselves with man in those respects in which he is identical with animals, as witnessed by the fact that they are able to use animals for experimental purposes in the place of man. The social sciences, as the term will be used here, comprise those studies which are scientifically concerned with the peculiarly human characteristics of man, so that animals cannot be used as human substitutes, except in borderline cases. Next, we must consider what it means to be scientific. Here, due to the fact that popular opinion and cultural pressure have been allowed to influence even professional thinkers, wishful fantasies of various degrees of intellectual respectability abound. We live in an age in which merely to attach the word "scientific" to any thing, process, advertised commodity, or philosophical notion is to give it standing in the community. Considering all this zeal, it is surprising to find how little real understanding of the structure and method of science exists in the popular mind and even in many professional minds. The only reason for the devotion to science stemming from science itself has been the actual success of the physical and biological sciences in providing man with a type of knowledge notable for its dependability, and its power to produce controlled changes at his behest.

Now it remains a historical fact that science began its career in the world with the study of physical, chemical, astronomical, and biological phenomena, and therefore the concept of science, the idea of what scientific knowledge is as distinguished from other kinds of knowledge, is bound together with this origin. The early scientists did not begin, however, with a preconceived notion of "what science is"; they did not begin with a methodological formula conceived out of pure thought and then applied in practice. This is more nearly how social science began.[2] The natural sciences began with some simple and cautious reasoning applied to some actual measurements and observations, allowing themselves to be guided by the nature of the subject matter, and by the inner logic of every experimental situation. It remained for the philosophers of science to point out that there was a certain regularity in the procedure followed by the scientists, to indicate its essential features, and to define scientific knowledge as whatever conclusions are yielded when this method is carefully followed. I will now indicate this method and criterion of science schematically, and in such a way that I hope every natural scientist will recognize all four of these points as being directly or indirectly involved in his work:

(1) Observation and classification of data. (Chronological, morphological, typological, statistical, according to the subject matter. Sometimes mere description in terms of everyday experience is sufficient.)

(2) Reduction and isolation of variables, and their practical identification with some measurable quantity.

(3*a*) The establishment of correlations between variables. (The method of concomitant variation.)

(3*b*) The formation of hypotheses in terms of the variables. (The method of structural or functional relations.)

(4) The verification of a hypothesis, or a correlation, by means of confirming the predicted variation of the variables under specified conditions. (This means repeatability of conditions, and control over at least two of the variables.)

I have allowed two steps under (3) in order to take care of the extreme variation of complexity in the natural sciences. The mere establishment of a correlation between two variables does not have the explanatory value that a structural or functional hypothesis has, but it is often all that can be said in the case of complex phenomena. The ideal situation is, of course, that (3*a*) should be only a preliminary step toward (3*b*). In the growth of any given science this procedure is not observed in exactly this order, new hypotheses leading to the search for new data, and, in general, the relative emphasis on one or another of these points depending on the existing state of theory and experiment. And, according to this scheme, there are degrees of knowledge within science itself, ranging all the way from merely recorded facts to many-times-tested theories, and also there is a cumulative effect, a logical pressure of the latter upon the former for conformity; for while no theory is ever established beyond the shadow of a doubt, no new hypothesis can expect to ignore, or easily overthrow, a theory already established on the grounds of many other facts. Since this procedure is a logico-experimental procedure, involving both the investigation of empirical facts and the drawing of logical conclusions, the scientific standing of the various conclusions of science may be characterized by these two aspects of the process. Thus there are some theories that are very satisfying from the logical standpoint, which for various reasons, such as the inaccessibility of some of the variables, are difficult to verify experimentally, while contrariwise, there are experimentally verified correlations which are far from being understood as the logical components of a general theory. Of the best "scientific standing," of course, are those conclusions and hypotheses which are both logically satisfying and experimentally verified, which means that they have passed through all four points of this procedure.

Now if these four points may be taken as the method and criterion of scientific knowledge, how do the social sciences measure up according to this standard? At least it must be said that, as of the present moment, the claims of certain social scientists and their philosophical backers that the social sciences, if avidly pursued, will yield scientific knowledge of the "laws" of individual and social behavior such as will enable men to predict the course of human events and direct it according to their pleasure—this claim, when placed alongside the criterion of scientific knowledge, appears somewhat extravagant, not to say fantastic. Of course, when pressed in this way, the promoters of the sciences of man always retire quickly behind the future tense. The social sciences *will* accomplish this *some* day, they say. They are only too eager to admit that the social sciences are in mere infancy now. But this kind of putting off of the proof of the pudding to the indefinite future will not satisfy anyone who, by a careful study of both the scientific method and the subject matter of the social sciences, is led to observe that there are certain limitations and obstacles in the path of this goal that no passage of time or accumulation of facts and theories will remove. The really serious question, then, is not how scientific the social sciences are at the present time but how scientific they can ever be.

No layman can answer this question for himself without some study of the literature of the social sciences, but even a casual survey of the classical works, or of special studies, by anyone interested in the "practical findings" will reveal their most important limitations, if the above four steps are constantly kept in mind. The collection of social data (now an apparently inexhaustible source of Ph.D. theses in the larger universities) shows how an element of arbitrariness and conventionality enters into the constitution of the future "social knowledge" from the outset, for without some criterion of selection and categories of classification invented "on the spot" the potential infinity of data in the multiverse of brute facts that confronts the would-be social scientists would render the whole enterprise unmanageable.

The reduction and isolation of variables, which means methodologically ignoring all but one or two aspects of the subject under study, and their identification with some measurable quantity—such as intelligence with the results of an intelligence test, or wants and desires with the number of dollars spent on their gratification—further increases the necessity for introducing prejudicial elements for the sake of definiteness. This fact, it should be noted, has nothing to do with the desires of the social scientist in the matter. He may desire to be ever so objective and ever so impartial, but if it is a correlation of variables he is after, there must be a definition and quantization of the variable, and this is what gives it the "artificial" character at the same time that it is the only way in which actual collection of data can take place. The devising of questionnaires and interviews, the use of statistical methods, the conducting of controlled surveys and polls, the use of vital statistics and other quantitative data already on record in public archives, and, finally, the "weighting" of factors in the calculation of the correlations—all these are adjustments of the social scientist to the special logic and the special intransigence of his subject matter, requiring decisions and choices on his part that constantly call attention to the fact that the "results" could easily have been different. It is almost as if each social scientist had his own terminology, his own techniques and devices that he tries to justify, and, inevitably, his own list of conclusions, not confirmed independently by others, and sometimes not even intelligible to other workers in the field.

The next step, the formulation of hypotheses in terms of the variables studied and the correlations found, is the greatest temptation that besets the social scientists, filling their literature with a clutter of premature conclusions and unjustifiable generalizations. Apparently the tension of suspended judgment, which is scientifically required by the complexity and inconclusiveness of most of the data, is too much for them to bear; or perhaps the academic pressure for publication may have something to do with it. Certainly the "mere" data on social variables and their apparently haphazard correlations are not satisfying to intellectual curiosity, so that speculation about some broad theory that would account for the variations found seems humanly unavoidable.

But it is just at this point that those who are interested in the "practical findings" must learn to distinguish between justifiable and unjustifiable speculations. Are the proposed hypotheses formulated "in terms of the variables studied"? Are they logically adequate in the sense of explaining differences and similarities and not merely attaching a new label to the unknown? Do they exclude arbitrary evaluations, and do they refrain from implying the existence of entities which it is impossible for science either to prove or disprove? And finally (the fourth methodological point), can they be tested by means of experimental confirmation of predictions based on them? Unfortunately for most of the interesting theories in social science most of these questions have to be answered in the negative. Many of these theories are merely the labeling of the unknown in terms of a special jargon—such as the "instincts" or "drives" of the social psychologists that are supposed to account for people's actions but have about as much explanatory value as the "spirits" and "devils" that were used for the same purpose in earlier times—or the theories are a projection of the philosophical or ideological bias of the social scientist in the form of a huge generality (such as economic determinism, adaptation of the organism to the environment, survival of the fittest, conditioned response) which covers so much ground that it would be impossible either to prove or disprove it.

Now it must be maintained that as private citizens the social scientists have every right, or as much right as all other citizens, to indulge in whatever philosophical preferences they wish—and it is even natural to expect that their world outlooks will be influenced by what they have studied and vice versa. But to allow oneself to slip half-consciously into the assumption that the world outlook of a social scientist is the equivalent of a scientific theory, even if based on his work in a special field, is to bring the whole enterprise to confusion. A scientific hypothesis, as distinguished from all other kinds of knowledge or wisdom or reasonable speculation, must be so constructed in relation to the variables that verifiable predictions can be made on the basis of it.

According to the logico-experimental character of the scientific method the predictions that can be made are of two kinds—the logical implications of a structural or functional theory, and the predictions of future events based merely on the record of their regular recurrence in the past. The former are, of course, more satisfying logically and more fruitful experimentally than the latter. For example, eclipses of the sun and moon can be predicted roughly just on the basis of their regular occurrence in the past, but such accurate predictions of eclipses down to the last second for every part of the earth where they can be observed, as are nowadays made by the astrononomers, can be made only on the basis of the planetary and orbital picture of the solar system with its associated mathematical relations. In the social sciences the same logical pressure exists for a "picture" or "model" of social relations and functions on the basis of which predictions of variations could be made. But here a new difficulty is encountered, and one which can hardly be blamed on the social scientist. For supposing he has constructed a pretty clear social hypothesis complete with predictions, where is the laboratory in which this verification can be carried out? With the exception of a few experiments in educational psychology carried on in special schools, and other experiments on individuals, the laboratory of the social sciences is always history: either recent history (called the present), or past history, or future history. From history the social sciences must receive the data on the basis of which their generalizations are made, and to history they must return to prove the truth of the generalizations, even if future history must be called in as evidence.

And how does history qualify as a laboratory? To put it mildly, history is too big, as a laboratory. The laboratory of the natural scientist was built precisely because he found nature too big for his purposes. Neither history nor nature permit the isolation of phenomena for the purpose of study and experiment. But history has the further disadvantage that it is not spread out before the investigator's eye for the purpose of firsthand observation.[3] In the natural sciences the disagreement on the actual phenomena can easily enough be checked by observation, or by the actual repetition of doubtful experiments, and then only the theoretical connections remain as a question. But the most obvious limitation of history as a laboratory for social experiments is that history is both unrepeatable and unfinished. The so-called social experiments themselves are never finished; they never come to a decision; their consequences are forever accumulating. The sudden changes in history, such as this or that revolution, or change in technology, or in political organization, must be "explained" by the social scientists by some theory that also has implications for the future, but since no time limit is placed on the prediction, it is impossible to tell when it has been proved or disproved, and, therefore, whether even the first "explanation" was really adequate. This is especially evident in all theories that include a cyclical interpretation of events. It may not be too difficult to prove from history that certain phenomena occur in cycles, but it is logically impossible to prove that a phenomenon is not cyclical, since it may always reappear in the future. But even if a time limit is included in the theory, and the predicted phenomenon does not appear on schedule, it is always possible to make excuses for the theory on the grounds that the complexity of history intervened, more time must be granted, and so forth, and again a decision on the theory is avoided. Thus there accumulates a host of pretenders to the scientific interpretation of social development as recorded in history, many of them contradictory, among whom it is impossible to make a decision, because their credentials, the verification of their predictions, are never completed. Nature is certainly more kind to the scientists.

It was stated in Chapter II that there is nothing to prevent anyone from applying the scientific method to anything under the sun (or even beyond the sun) but that the adequacy of the method to the subject matter would show up in the type of results the following of the method would produce. The questionable adequacy shows up in the case of the social sciences when we ask simply: how is the "scientific" exegesis and prediction of human history to be distinguished from the merely good or bad guesses of merely wise men, or of interested scholars, journalists, philosophers, who make no pretension of being scientific and are not trying to prove any social hypothesis? Clearly they cannot be so distinguished, and the whole rigmarole of social science becomes a little questionable if it does not lead to anything more dependable than sometimes good, sometimes bad guesses, which people in all common sense are bound to make anyway.[4]

The interpretation of history is one of the basic activities of the human spirit in all ages, expressing itself not only in the efforts of historians, philosophers, and theologians but also in literature, in epic legends, in myth and poetry and drama. These guesses may be called "analytic-imaginative" rationalizations of history, which everyone is surely entitled to make, but they should not be called "scientific." Yet it appears that when the social sciences enter upon the scientific explanation of history, their hypotheses shade off imperceptibly into just this kind of thinking. Well, then, perhaps these analytic-imaginative rationalizations of history *should* be called scientific! This is what some social scientists recommend when they become desperate over the meagerness of prediction and explanation that is permitted by strict adherence to the scientific method. But this also means to invite the greatest confusion, and we might as well throw out the word "scientific" altogether, and give up talking about "scientific" knowledge as against any other kind of knowledge. Analytic-imaginative thinking takes place in every realm of life, from philosophical and theological speculation to political machination and military strategy, from the planning of our children's education to the buying of the day's groceries. If we broaden the concept of "scientific" to include all of these, we are left with a practically meaningless designation.

The more zealous promoters of the social sciences will object to the above analysis of their scientific standing on the grounds that it is not "fair" to judge them by the methodology of natural science. Obviously, the subject matter is different, more complex, always in a state of flux, difficult to isolate, as became evident in the analysis. Several questions must be asked of these objectors. What, then, *is* the proper method of the social sciences, if it is not the method of the natural sciences? Does not the whole enterprise of the social sciences rest historically on the assumption that a certain kind of valid knowledge of human affairs can be obtained only by applying to the study of man the same method that the natural sciences applied to nature? And is not the dependability of the conclusions of natural science related to a strict adherence to their methodology, so that the hope of the social sciences to achieve equally dependable knowledge depends entirely on their ability to follow this method? And finally, are not the optimistic claims made on behalf of the social sciences—that they will enable man to predict and control his own destiny—made precisely on the hope of obtaining a type of knowledge that only the method of the natural sciences can give?

Actually this objection conceals a desperate and rather dangerous attempt to change the rules in the middle of the game. If, now that it has become evident that some of the more fantastic claims that have been made on behalf of social science will never be fulfilled, we change the rules of the game, and agree to call scientific any opinion, guess, or generalization simply because it is uttered by a "scientist"—then we really throw up the sponge; we give up hope of *any* scientific knowledge of social relations and social variables, and jeopardize the results of much hard work which is conducted strictly according to scientific method and makes no unjustified claims.

Social science is not all guesswork. Especially in such fields as economics, and in some parts of sociology where we deal with relatively measurable quantities, many valuable correlations have been and can be established, and even some cautious predictions can be made. There are regularities in social life, whether taken contemporaneously or historically, and it would not hurt men to know more about them. The fact that these regularities are obscured, compounded, and transformed by irregularities, novelties, new and creative or destructive impulses in history, will be a stumbling block only to those social scientists who are dominated by a passion to *reduce* everything to regularities rather than to be content to deal with whatever regularities are actually observable. To maintain their scientific standing on the highest level possible, nothing is required of the social sciences except that they get rid of their messiah complex: the scientific method will take care of the rest. It would be scientific suicide to try to satisfy the messiah complex at the expense of the scientific method, as the proponents of this objection are trying to do.

The engineers and the pragmatists

It is obvious that many people besides Christian believers are interested in the "practical findings" of the social sciences, and this brings us to the famous question of the relationship of these sciences to the ends or values they can be made to serve. The answers given to this question fall into two general categories, and for the sake of convenience we shall call their supporters the engineers and the pragmatists. The engineers are those who believe that any social science bears the same relationship to values or ends as chemistry bears to industrial commodities whose production involves chemical processes. The science thus "used" then becomes a technology with respect to certain ends or products, but the science itself remains indifferent or passive with respect to any values, ends, or products. It does not decide what ends will be sought. The engineers regard science, both natural and social, purely as a possible means toward an end, and disregard that aspect of science which may be considered an end in itself, a part of the quest for general knowledge in the wider sense. They hold that the question of the validity of ends, or values, either cannot be decided at all or it must be decided by some criterion outside science. They merely say, "Tell us your ends, and we will show you how best to achieve them."

The pragmatists, on the other hand, believe that social science is not merely a means toward achieving an end, but that it is also a means for proving or disproving the validity of ends. The pragmatic dictum concerning truth, that "truth is that which works," means that the truth or validity of values or ends is to be judged on the basis of the results that the following of them actually produced. "Results" is the watchword of the pragmatists. The social sciences need not give up any of their objectivity in order to function in the role of proving or disproving values. Their proper method in this is merely to treat values as facts, and to observe and report what are the actual results in terms of overt acts of the values that people hold. Their claim is that the scientific method, by treating values as facts, is just as capable of distinguishing true values from false values as it is capable of distinguishing true facts from false facts. Social science is thus not just a means to an end but an end in itself. The knowledge it gives is the only knowledge of the "working truth" we can have, and it is the concrete objective and the "proving ground" of the entire pragmatic philosophy.

Now, purely from the logical standpoint, it must be evident that the engineers are on a much firmer footing than the pragmatists. It is hard to believe that the pragmatists should think that they have solved the problem of the truth or validity of values by saying that values must be treated as facts, and judged according to the results they produce, for this only shifts the value problem one step over, namely to the "results." Who shall decide on the value of the "results"? Pragmatically we must then treat the valuations of the "results" as a fact, and see what results *they* will produce, and so on, ad infinitum.

But aside from this rather naïve confusion of "is" with "ought," which the engineers at least do not make, the pragmatists raise the much more complex and universal problem of the scientific determination of motivation in history and in society. The usefulness of social science for the discovery of pragmatic truth rests on the ability of science to show that this particular "value" was the "real" motivation of such and such people in a particular situation, and that it produced such and such actions or results. But motivation is a complicated phenomenon, made even more unmanageable by modern theories of "subconscious" and even "unconscious" motivation, and it introduces subjective factors which are simply beyond the reach of science.

The early social scientists had to face this question. They had to decide whether motivation is a possible subject of scientific investigation or whether it must be left alone, even though without considering at least probable motivation the activities of men do not make much sense. The psychologists were inclined to support the use of motivation as an explanatory category, especially the "depth" psychologists, such as the Freudians, because they felt sure that by their techniques they could unearth the "real" motivations behind the apparent motivations. Such techniques, however, can only discover certain "mechanisms" by means of which the "real" motivations of men, under certain conditions of conflict or frustration, conceal themselves behind "apparent" motivation, or they can reveal the disturbances caused in the personalities of men by a simultaneous commitment to conflicting values. They cannot prove that the holding of a certain value always leads to a certain historical result, which is what the pragmatists want to know in order to be able to judge that value by the results it inevitably produces. Furthermore, as far as the conscious motivations, the deliberate intentions, of men are concerned, it is still the privilege of all men to deceive their fellows to the best of their ability, as every psychoanalyst knows to his regret. Only God knows what truly transpires in the hearts of men, and psychoanalysis may sometimes succeed in bringing men to confess and face what God already knows, but this is hardly a technique for discovering the objective "results" in history or society of the values that men profess to believe in. It merely renders suspect even the most sincere "stated motivation," which, along with guesses as to the probable motivation, is all that the social scientist, and even the historian, can ever hope to learn.

To get around this subjectivity, the early sociologists, like Durkheim and his followers, insisted that social and moral institutions and activities must not be considered as due to the deliberate intentions, the free choices, and reasoned calculations of men, but to "obscure social forces" which have a reality outside the individuals who at any time conform to them, and which it is the purpose of science to discover and describe.[5] The effort to eliminate subjectivity by looking for "obscure forces" as the causes of men's action is, however, an unrewarding process, since their very obscurity does not help with an explanation, while a simple statement of motivation is the most obvious way to explain an act. The choice seems to be between motivations which are admittedly suspect and causes or forces which are admittedly obscure. What then becomes of the hope of social science's being able to show the "truth" of a given value, according to the "results" it produces through those whom it motivates? The hope grows dim. Not only is there the inaccessibility of the data of motivation in the case of real men, but this hope is also based on a philosophically idealized picture of man, one in whom the step from motivation to overt action is as direct and inevitable as that from the premises to the conclusion of a syllogism. For this kind of man, this walking syllogism, no social science is necessary to tell us what he will do. The whole matter can be figured out in the privacy of the philosopher's den, as has been done in those studies called theory of value, which again are something different from the "scientific" proof of the truth or falsity of values.

Let us now return to the engineers. Their attitude toward values is not only more logical but also far more realistic than that of the pragmatists. This realism includes the recognition of the fact that science may be used for evil purposes just as efficiently as for good ones. Such recognition was a long time coming, because science, and especially social science, was born on a wave of optimism concerning human nature, which stressed not only man's ability to predict and control his own destiny but also his moral fitness to do so. The various declarations of the "natural" rights of man produced by the Enlightenment everywhere reflected the belief that those who claimed these "natural" rights for themselves were naturally so unselfish, loving, and reasonable, as to claim the same rights for all others, without exception. The assumed good will was needed to make the rights universal, and this universality in turn was needed to give the rights the appearance of being "natural," so that each natural man could claim them for himself. On the basis of this circular argument all the selfish and irrational behavior of man was declared to be "unnatural," caused by the external coercion of selfish and irrational institutions and customs inherited from the past. How these ever arose in virtue of the goodness and rationality of the "natural" man was never explained. Thus science developed historically in the hands of men who, according to the popular philosophy, could do no wrong, as long as they were not subjected to "unnatural" restraints.

Such a theory of human nature can be, and has been, refuted by history itself for those who have a criterion which enables them to condemn the results which it produced. Certainly those who held to the biblical doctrine of the sinfulness of man in all its severity were the least surprised when historical events began to show the increasing use of scientific knowledge for destructive and cruel purposes. The others, the believers in the goodness of man and of science, "viewed with alarm" this tendency toward the "misuse" of science, and they became worried, curiously enough, not so much over the moral qualities of man, but over the moral standing of science. They decided that science must be saved. Somehow it must be shown that science is not indifferent to values, that it is fundamentally on the side of the angels, that it can show us not only what is but what ought to be. Here we have the origin of the pragmatic use of science noted above. The pragmatists wanted to save science from the harsh realism of the engineers, who with inexorable logic and lurid imagination were painting a terrifying picture of a world where all the assorted motivations of man, good and bad, noble and despicable, were simply implemented and magnified by the techniques of science, and where evil, because of its lack of scruple, was easily counted the favorite in this technological scramble to make use of the practical findings of science.

On this question of science and values the Christian believer is for once in a most advantageous position. For the believer Christ is his supreme value and the criterion of all other values, and he knows that he receives this criterion not by making observations and speculations on human nature, society, or history, but by a special kind of confrontation by Christ in which he, the believer, surrenders precisely that human perspective from which such observations and speculations are made.

He knows, then, that he receives the criterion from some source not of this world, and, therefore, as he approaches the social sciences, he is not expecting to find there any ultimate value, supreme purpose, or philosophical absolute deducible from the study of the facts. But he notices from the special vantage point of his Christian detachment that this is precisely what the unbelievers are looking for in their study of social science, no matter how objective they may try to be in their actual scientific work. Having no transcendent criterion, they are looking for an immanent criterion, and even if they admit that this search belongs properly to philosophy, they do not see why such a philosophical quest should not be aided and supported by a scientific study of human nature in society and history. In this they are quite correct, but this is what makes it so difficult for them to keep their philosophical ideas separated from their scientific conclusions and, conversely, from "projecting" their social hypotheses as philosophical ultimates, first causes, and so on.

The Christian's position is in a limited way that of the engineer, one who wants to use science for certain Christian objectives, but without having any illusions as to its being designed for this purpose. At the same time, and precisely in so far as he intends to *depend* on the scientific findings for attaining certain results, he must patiently expurgate them of the ideological connotations that the unbelievers, in their quest for a "scientific philosophy," are constantly reading into, and confusing with, the bare conclusions justified by the scientific method. A critical analysis based on the scientific method is his best weapon, both against bad science and against pseudo science: against scientific carelessness, on the one hand, and philosophy masquerading as science, on the other.

Inadequacies and dangers of social science

The second concern of the Christian believer is the question of whether even "good" science is the right way to deal with certain human problems as manifested in social phenomena. It would appear from our analysis that the scientific method is most adequate and most accurate when applied to the large-scale statistical phenomena of social life, such as trends and cycles, vital statistics in relation to other phenomena, rates of change and normal distributions, and to the structural aspect of society, including the study of organizations, customs, and institutions.[6] The qualities of social life that are felt as particular and personal pass through the scientific method like water through a sieve. The kind of understanding of the particular and the personal which is sought in literature and art and in personal dealings with people is precisely forbidden and eliminated by the scientific method. Even in "casework" the description of the individual "case" must be in terms that are capable of generalization, and the theory or solution must be in terms applicable to all similar cases. The charming smile and big feet of the individual must not enter into the scientific description, unless the phenomenon under study is regularly related to charming smiles and big feet. The question as to whether the most important problems of human life lie on the large-scale statistical and structural level, or whether they lie on the individual and personal level, is of course the big question, which one had better resist trying to answer in general terms.

It is no coincidence that the science worshipers in general, and social planners in particular, stress the importance of the external arrangements and structure of society for the solution of all human problems, implying that the personal or internal difficulties of men are mere symptoms and by-products of the external disorganization or malfunctioning of society. They do this because the scientific techniques are best suited to deal with this aspect of life, and, in order to feel that they have the only solution, they make this the only aspect worth considering.

On the other hand, many Christians, especially those of a fanatically evangelistic, and those of a rationally idealistic, bent, have erred in the opposite direction. The first have stressed that if only men will save their souls by coming into the Church, the organization of society will not matter; and the second have stressed that if only men will be "good" according to the rational ideal set up for them, the organization of society will take care of itself. Both of these attitudes toward the organization of society are perversions of the Christian doctrines of creation and of man. Against the first attitude the doctrine of creation maintains that this world is a good creation, the good work of a good God. Matter is not evil, as Oriental religions and Manichaean heresies repeatedly maintain, but the way men use it is evil, and even then their materialistic sins are relatively innocent compared with the spiritual sins of pride and lust for power, in which the material things are used as means, rather than as immediate satisfactions. The Church is not of the world, but it is in the world, to work and to do the redeeming will of God. It should never forget that all men are the children of God, not just the faithful, and that precisely for this reason they are able to corrupt his creation, to their own distress. The disorganization of society must be considered by Christians as the judgment of God upon a people who both misunderstood and misuse his gifts, not as a phenomenon which does not matter.

Against the second attitude the Christian doctrine of man maintains that man is not, as idealism would have it, a nearly disembodied spirit, free to make an absolute choice and to take absolute responsibility for it, all the rest of him being considered "unessential" and "lowly," or "contingent." Man is a spirit bound to the earth. He is partly free and partly determined, partly responsible and partly exonerable. The earth, no less than the spirit, is his teacher, and even the highest reaches of his spirit, including all of his ideas about God, are bound to the earth for their means of expression. This fact is good, and not evil, because the creation itself is good. Christianity does not begin with the romantic idea that man is a spiritual giant, that he needs only to be told what is good and he will straightway strive for it, and that in this striving he will achieve the triumph of his spirit over the base material which is arrayed against him, and thus not only hasten the arrival of the perfect society of spiritual men but also participate in the divine strivings of the Absolute. How different from this is the doctrine of the incarnation, in which God does not disdain to reveal himself to men by taking on their creatureliness, thus not only showing them his mercy and goodness, but also giving them a divine object-lesson on the use of the creation!

The organization of society is an intimate mixture of material, human, and spiritual components, and it is the business of Christian thought to set up criteria of social organization which will intepret the function of society as permitting the fulfillment of man's real needs in all three of these levels. The Christian doctrine of human nature and human destiny provides for all three of these relations—man's relation to the earth, man's relation to his fellow men, and man's relation to God—and places them in a meaningful order. The Christian criterion of social organization must be no less comprehensive. Social *disorganization* must be judged in terms of the failure of a society to meet these needs rather than a failure of this or that economic or political "system" to function according to its claims. The latter standard always leads to the introduction of another "system" with another set of claims, without any regard as to whether the newest system can be made to serve the real needs of men, or whether it is a mere antidote for the breakdown of the previous system.

The Christian critique of society, therefore, shall not confine itself to the pointing out of the selfish motives in the functioning of a system, for to do this would be to ignore the fact that both the selfish and the unselfish motives of men, if carried out without regard to man's true nature, can lead to such deep entanglement in the inner workings of some "system" that even the best motives lead to evil results. This is true, for example, of present-day economic systems, which are run according to the rules of finance, banking, and foreign trade, or military necessity, or the dictates of a political group, rather than according to the actual economic needs of men. Such systems, once expedient but now running according to their inner logic or the precepts of an ideology, have lost touch with reality, and not even an angel of the Lord could make them work for the good—that is, for the fulfillment of real economic needs. The existence of such autonomously running systems unrelated to the real needs of men manifests itself in the many paradoxes of social organization of this age: scarcity in the midst of plenty; intense desire for human employment in the midst of mechanical marvels; increased social regimentation in the midst of a vapid worship of freedom; the obligation of Americans to be wasteful consumers under their "system," while the rest of the world daily grows more envious and resentful.

Thus a theological interpretation of social organization which attempts to define what Christian doctrine has to say about the "general, statistical, and structural" aspects of society, the aspects with which the social sciences can most adequately deal, is indispensable for any Christian "engineering." This is sometimes called Christian sociology, but that is a misnomer, for the setting up of a concrete criterion by means of which societies may be condemned and changed is no part of sociology. Christian social theology, in contrast to moral and systematic theology, would be a better name for it. It is an activity that must precede every attempt on the part of the Christian believer to use the results of social science, for without this his efforts are no more Christian than the patchwork and local antidotes of the well-meaning liberals, and the one-sided social schemes of the ideologists.

The obvious danger of social science is the engineering danger—that anyone can use this knowledge for any ends—a danger that by now people ought to be aware is connected with all knowledge that is convertible into a technology. But there is also a less obvious danger, one which obtains even when the knowledge is in the hands of the men of good will. I refer to the inability of this knowledge to provide a "solution" even where the nature of the problem has been more or less correctly analyzed, and the desire to make a change for the better is there. The notion that all you need is knowledge and a goal, borrowed from the natural sciences where it is quite true, can become, in the field of human relations and social change, a quite vicious luring and goading on of mankind to try the impossible, simply because it is conceivable—a perennial form of the humanistic delusion. It did not take man long to discover that in relation to nature knowledge is power. But it seems to be taking him quite a long historical while to learn or admit that in relation to his own nature knowledge and power are not quite the same thing.

The way in which this "humanistic delusion" can be dangerous to men is exemplified in the various psychoanalytic attempts to account for social disorganization or malfunctioning. For example, a society may be regarded as "neurotic" if it contains a high proportion of neurotic individuals, so that it is able and willing to encourage mass neurotic attitudes and responses in its public ideologies. Or the breakdown of a particular social and cultural pattern may be explained in terms used for the explanation of the individual "nervous breakdown": the accumulated frustrations, the inner conflicts, and the defensive reactions of men under unusual stress or sudden change in historical conditions. All this sounds fine and even plausible until we ask: what's to be done about it? Is it possible for a whole society to undergo the psychoanalytic cure? And what does the cure consist of, even in the case of individuals?

Here we encounter a curious phenomenon, the surprisingly ambivalent position of psychoanalysis on the power of human reason. The psychoanalysts are always engaged in the peculiar procedure of declaring, first of all, that the activities of men are mostly irrational—that is, they are due to reasons other than the reasons given by the persons themselves, which are called rationalizations—and, secondly, of attempting to explain the acts in terms of the real reasons buried in the subconscious, a process which might be called a rationalization of the rationalizations of men. According to the logic of this procedure (unless we regard the psychoanalyst as a different species of man) there should be a third rationalization—namely, a rationalization of the rationalizations of the psychoanalysts, an unearthing of the real reasons why the psychoanalysts give the kind of real reasons for men's acts that they do, and so on. This regress is due to the fact that the first rationalization is considered to be a defect of reason: it is considered to be detrimental to the possibility of man's recognizing and reporting any real reasons, any truth by means of which a rationalization could be condemned as false.

Rationalization, however, is merely the process of "making reasonable," of making behavior understandable by displaying in a given case the connection between feelings, attitudes, and acts. It is not always, or necessarily, as psychoanalysis has popularized the word, a defensive or hypocritical concealing of bad motives by good ones. That this is not so, and that the psychoanalyst himself expects his patient to be fundamentally rational, even while declaring him irrational, is shown by the fact that the "cure" of the psychoanalytic method rests on the ability and willingness of the patient to recognize the real reasons for his acts, and therefore to be willing to re-educate or change his attitudes. The analyst guides or helps the re-education by various techniques, such as recollection, transference, reality-testing, to get the patient to change his attitudes to his past, to himself, and to others, but basically he has to hope for a rational understanding of his own difficulty by the individual, especially if the cure is to stick.

On the social level much the same method is used, except that here the public has to be its own analyst. The disorganization of society is shown to be in a dialectical way both the cause and the effect of the individual's thrashing about helplessly between such conflicting attitudes as the desire for freedom and the desire for security, between loneliness and aggression, between frustration and overambition, love and hate, the desire to belong to something and the desire to be the master—and many other such horns of psychological and spiritual dilemmas. Such analysis is in many ways illuminating, but it apparently assumes that the mere recognition of this state of affairs will somehow induce a cure, as if the persons involved could simply think themselves out of the various dilemmas.

Such solutions are verbal solutions: they restate the problem in terms of what ought to be, without saying how this may be reached, and by what power. They assume that man is to be talked into being what he ought to be, or talk himself into it, even though he knows very well that he does not have the power to do this, else he would hardly be plagued with such problems. To know is still not to be. Christian doctrine knows this very well, and knows also that the question of power can be handled only by the doctrine of grace. Even the recommendations of some psychoanalysts to the effect that people need religion in order to become integrated is a far cry from their actually becoming religious, and becoming integrated. However, psychoanalysis can hardly be expected to treat the question of power, will, or strength in terms of the grace of God, so that the knowledge it gives of the problem and the "solution" it recommends tend to verge on a mockery of the patient, or to fall back on the futile repetition of appeals to reason. A hollow sound can be heard in this kind of social criticism—for instance, in the advice that man ought to make himself at home in the universe, in spite of his consciousness, through the psychological problems, that he is not at home in it, or in the journalistic contempt and ridicule heaped by the intellectuals on the contradictions and anomalies of social life, as if the mere challenge to reason were sufficient to induce a remedy.

Thanks to the prevalence of the "humanistic delusion," the believer must be wary of too much uncritical co-operation between psychological and religious counseling. He knows where the power comes from, and why knowledge alone is insufficient to effect a cure. Hence, for the patient's sake, he must expose the mere verbalism of the logical-psychological solution (for example, telling the individual that he ought to feel happy, although he feels sad; that he ought to feel loved, although he feels unloved; secure, although he feels anxious; innocent, although he feels guilty; creative, although he feels destructive; and that he ought to act spontaneously, although he acts compulsively), because there is the danger that knowledge without power may lead to desperation. At the same time he must propose a biblically grounded solution, which cannot be done without bringing the whole force of Christian theology to bear on the particular problem. There is no getting around the fact that it is the *truth* that makes men free, not assorted bits of knowledge, but the ultimate truth about the meaning of human life and destiny, namely God's concern for man, that which Christianity proclaims and Christian theology explains as the one thing needful.

The attitudes of objectivity, curiosity, and control, Christianly examined

There remain to be discussed three attitudes closely associated with science, regarding their appropriateness in the context of a human, as against a nonhuman, subject matter. These are the attitudes of objectivity, curiosity, and control. Regarding objectivity there is much misunderstanding. It is generally assumed, especially in modern religious literature, that it is the "objective attitude" of science to its materials that is objectionable to religion. This is based on a view which considers the religious attitudes to be a matter of emotional, or "subjective" disposition, and the objectivity of science to be an expression of the indifference of the scientists. Both of these views seem to me mistaken. I should rather say that the objectivity of the scientist, when properly understood, and the attitude of the Christian believer have a great deal in common. The objectivity of the scientist is merely a decision on his part to abide by the rules of the scientific method, which means to accept the conclusions that this method leads him to discover, whether or not they support his favorite theory or his preconceived notion of how the matter should have come out. The objectivity of the Christian believer is a decision on his part to abide by the implications of the Christian revelation for the meaning of human life and destiny on this earth, whether or not they happen to coincide in a particular instance with his preference in the matter. Both are submitting their personal preference to a reality which is in some sense outside them, which is not dependent on their current whims, and which, after they have made the decision, exercises over them the same authority that truth exercises over error.

Without this objectivity on the part of the scientist the whole scientific enterprise, method and all, would break down into an inconclusive wrangling over private opinions. The decision itself, which every scientist must make, is, from the philosophical point of view, an act of metaphysical faith. On the other hand, without the religious objectivity of the Christian believer there would be no "thou shalt" in the Christian revelation; it would not be the revelation of God but the musings of a handful of men; and it would never exercise the authority that truth has over error, but only the competitive pressure that always exists between one subjective value and another.

The Christian act of faith determines for the believer the objective nature of the truth that the Christian revelation reveals, and hence it also determines his objectivity toward his fellow men. His attitude toward his fellow men is now determined, not by his personal like or dislikes, though these are not always irrelevant, but by his understanding of the meaning of *their* lives in the light of Christian truth, by his understanding of their being, not just pleasant or unpleasant fellows, good or bad neighbors, boring or interesting personalities, but always and also the estranged or reconciled children of God. His attitude is further determined by the objective command: "Thou shalt love . . ." and not by the subjective feelings of attraction and repulsion, indifference or interest.

This does not mean that Christian love is abstract and general, instead of concrete and particular. It is always the latter, and for that very reason it is realistic and unsentimental. Such a demand as that we should love our enemies is an impossibility, or a piece of hypocrisy, when the love thus commanded is taken to be a subjective attraction for, or a romantic idealization of, those who have injured us. Christian love of one's enemies, not to mention all those who are merely indifferent to us, demands neither a sentimental whitewashing of their faults nor a trumped-up admiration for their virtues. This is an appeal to that ordinary human love which demands a lovable object, and expects reciprocation or turns to hate. Christian love demands an objective estimate of our own responsibility for some of the enemy's transgression, combined with the concern that he should not destroy himself by his own iniquities, or injure others. Thus even in his Christian love for others the believer is objective, determined by a reality that is both independent of, and greater than, himself.

It is necessary, in the case of the scientist, to distinguish carefully between objectivity and indifference. Every doctor knows the difference between the objective frame of mind in which he must diagnose the patient's condition and the concern, or unconcern, that he may feel over the patient's well-being. That he should not let the one affect the other is, however, often interpreted, by men hardened in the profession, in a one-sided way—that he should not let his care for the patient interfere with his objectivity. Whereas, the opposite is just as true: he should not let his scientific objectivity interfere with his care for the patient. There is, apparently, a tendency, a pressure, toward identifying scientific objectivity with indifference toward the subject matter, which is rather ludicrous, or theatrical, since most life situations do not even remotely fulfill the conditions of a scientific experiment. Even in natural science there is no contradiction between a scientist's being ever so objective, and yet passionately in love with his work.

The attitude of curiosity is that mood or disposition which finds everything "interesting." Of course, it eventually also finds things uninteresting, or boring, because it is not simply an intellectual activity but an emotion, even an appetite, which has a satiation point. It is fundamentally an aesthetic attitude, even where it is not concerned with aesthetic appreciation as such. The subject feels detached from the object of curiosity, and yet he expects from it a certain kind of satisfaction for his intellect and intuition, a certain kind of delight found in the observation of structural relationships and patterns of functioning. Curiosity is strong in childhood, because childhood is an unreflecting search for the satisfaction of appetites. Reflection begins only when a degree of satiation is reached, when certain lines of investigation are finished, and the insidious "so what?" which pure aesthetes learn to dread, arises. The believer can hardly object to the proper functioning of curiosity in science, especially as science, in particular natural science, arose historically as the sophisticated child of human curiosity rather than as an instrument of control. But when we come to the social sciences, it is a question of how far curiosity can be allowed to go, for now human beings are its object. But why shouldn't human beings be an object of curiosity? As to certain unessential or external trappings or accidental peculiarities, they can be considered as objects of curiosity: their race or color or upbringing, their language or dress, their station in life or their worldly accomplishment—these may be, up to a point proper objects of curiosity. But when these are identified with, or their being treated with curiosity encroaches upon, that inner reality which is the naked human being as such, that source and recipient of all physical, human, and divine interactions which religion calls the "soul" and which psychology cannot find anywhere because it is not a thing or idea but transcends every content—well, when this core of the human creature is treated as an object of curiosity, the believer must enter a protest. Not only the commandment to love our neighbor, but the entire Christian theology which treats of man as a child of God makes it wrong to treat a human being as something from which one can be detached, while regarding it with interest or amusement or boredom. It is the detachment which is forbidden because men are related to one another in an ultimate way and such detachment, even in an apparently harmless attitude like curiosity, denies this ultimate bond between men. In this way respect for privacy, as embodied in codes of manners that condemn curiosity as ill-mannered, can be the very opposite of detachment.

The most obvious protest of the Christian believer must be against the attitude of curiosity as applied to human suffering. The suffering of one's fellow men is not "interesting," no matter how much the social sciences can claim to learn by treating it as if it were. At this point the idea of a "pure" social science, one which studies human distresses without any intention of alleviating them but purely out of scientific curiosity, becomes an impossibility for the Christian consciousness. The only possible attitude is that of control, with the object of alleviating the distress. We shall have more to say about the controlling attitude in a moment. But if the attitude of curiosity, when applied to human suffering, is obviously unchristian, the attitude of curiosity when applied to the more neutral activities of men, and even to the obviously pleasant and happy experiences of human beings, is none the less so for being less obvious. If we do not feel somehow "involved" in the happiness of others, entering into their real joys and even to some extent being transformed by them, rather than looking upon them from the outside as upon "interesting phenomena," we are still in that deadly detachment from our fellow men that is forbidden by even the most objective form of Christian love. It is in the midst of their joys that men are always skirting the edge of the pathetic, just as in the midst of their suffering they are always skirting the edge of the heroic—but as Christians we must identify ourselves with our fellow men in both conditions, and not seek to escape the creaturely implications of either by taking up some supposedly superior position outside of them.

The attitude of control is much less subtle in its Christian implications than the attitude of curiosity. Again a distinction must be made between natural science and social science. In order to get an idea of the vicious possibilities of the control of nature by man, it is enough to realize that the methods of control are just as efficient in the hands of bad men as in the hands of good men, whatever our standard of the good may be. But in order to get an idea of the vicious possibilities of the attitude of control as applied to men, it is necessary to realize that concretely this means the control of *some* men by *other* men—so that here the methods of control even in the hands of the *best* men must be questioned, because the whole concept of "control" of men by "methods" is questionable from the standpoint of the Christian doctrine of human freedom. And yet we have just finished saying that as far as human suffering is concerned, the controlling attitude is the only one that can be allowed: the only object of the study can be the alleviation of the suffering. The question then revolves around the "methods"—and the implication is that even the alleviation of human suffering must not be carried on by "methods" which transgress upon, or deny, human freedom.

To understand this a little better, let us take a concrete example. It is often claimed by psychologists that a knowledge of the reactions of individuals to a variety of stimuli will enable educationalists of the future to induce certain socially desirable responses in the growing generation simply by conditioning them to respond to certain stimuli in a certain way. This is a "method" of social control which can also be practiced on a larger scale and with an adult population, though perhaps not so efficiently, by such means as persistent propaganda, social or material rewards and punishments, playing on human weaknesses, manipulation of the will of peoples by the use of crowd psychology, and other variations on the conditioning technique. By this means, the social psychologists maintain, practically any desired social end may be achieved. What is not always so clearly pointed out is the fact that this means the division of society into two kinds of people: those who *do* the conditioning, and those who *submit* to the conditioning. Whenever this fact is acknowledged, it is always assumed, especially by the sentimental and righteous American social scientists, or rather social philosophers, that of course it is the *best* men that will do the conditioning, and the *best* social ends that will be served.

Right now we are not concerned with the question of what ends are to be served—but with the fact that a *conviction of the truth* is no part of this method. It is all a matter of "adjustment," "adaptation," "cultural pressure," "the line of least resistance," and other such mechanical concepts of social dynamics. Persuasion of the desirability of this or that end even on ground of reason alone is not included in this "method"; it is also not concerned with enlightened self-interest, but only with controlled reactions. Truth and error, right and wrong, do not exist for it, only adjustment and maladjustment. How can Christian social engineering use such a method, even for the alleviation of suffering? What is the meaning of the results achieved by this method? What is the meaning of "peace," for example, which is achieved by means of the deliberate propagation of lies, by cultural pressure in the form of social disapproval, by rewards and punishments intended to induce agreement, by acquiescence in injustice produced by adjusting one's ideas of right and wrong? Such a peace would not be even the absence of war which conceals the real conflicts of men between actual wars, but which has meaning at least in terms of the convictions and practices of human beings. Such a peace would be the peace of the piggery—the well-run "animal farm." It is not necessary to mention grosser forms of the method of social control, such as the extermination of undesirable people, because even in its mild form, even as a control by means of educational psychology, it has the effect of reducing human life to something subhuman by removing from human beings both the ability and the responsibility for making decisions of true and false, right and wrong.

We are brought to the conclusion that the Christian believer must protest both the attitude of inhuman curiosity and the attitude of inhuman control sometimes associated with social science, and that he must do this on the basis of the Christian concept of human nature, which social science in its own terms can never comprehend. As far as any social engineering is concerned, it must be done according to criteria derived from a Christian social theology, and not according to immanent criteria of social disorganization, which are based on the logical functioning of systems and institutions, rather than on the real needs of human beings, Christianly understood. And as far as the "practical findings" of the social sciences are concerned, they must be purged of ideological distortions due to their being treated by the unbelievers as a philosophy, and whatever is left after such purgation must be understood in accordance with the natural limitations of social science revealed by the scientific method, and whatever is useful in the light of such understanding must be applied in accordance with a Christian concept of human freedom and responsibility.

Chapter V

FAITH AND ETHICS

The ethical temper of the world of unbelief

THE ETHICAL TEMPER OF THE WORLD OF UNBELIEF BETRAYS ITSELF most tellingly in its erratic oscillation between two opposite extremes. On the one hand, it discovers the multiplicity of ethical precepts and rules of conduct that have actually been used in the long course of human history; and, on the other hand, it preoccupies itself with the need for, and the calculation of, a least common denominator of agreement on ethical conduct that could be considered binding on all men. On Mondays, Wednesdays, and Fridays it is quite overcome by the study of anthropology (primitive societies), and sternly proclaims that there are no universal ethical precepts, that all manner of exotic and revolting practices have at various times and in various societies been proclaimed to be "right," and hence the terms "right" and "wrong" as applied to human conduct are meaningless. For the modern mind emancipated from superstition there can be only folkways and mores, never ethical principles. On Tuesdays, Thursdays, and Saturdays it wakes up in the rosy glow of sweet reasonableness, and confidently proclaims that since there are value judgments there must be a scale of values, and, hence, by definition, a highest value, or a most general value. For the modern mind emancipated from superstition there may still not be any absolute value, but there is no reason why there can't be a modest pursuit of the more rewarding values that have been statistically analyzed and pragmatically tested.

This oscillation in the ethical temper of the world of unbelief is paralleled by an equal oscillation in its metaphysical opinion of man, which one some days of the week declares man to be a cosmic accident, and on other days proclaims him by virtue of his reasoning and imaginative powers to be the very architect of the universe:

all nature and even outer darkness are pictured as waiting upon his powerful brain to inject into this chaos the saving light of a reasonable meaningfulness and a practicable goal. Since there is nowhere in the unbelievers' world to be found a principle by means of which to decide between these two metaphysical opinions of man, the shift from one to other and back again is a matter of mood. Even philosophers are classified no longer as idealists or realists but as optimists or pessimists, as if to acknowledge that their view of the universe depends as much on the secretions of the glands as on the convictions of the mind.

The believer becomes aware of this nervous dualism that makes the best of two opposite worlds by taking them in turns, when he observes how this alternating viewpoint is applied to himself, or, rather, to the interpretation of Christian ethics. When the ethical temper of unbelief is in its anthropological, or pessimistic, mood, it considers Christianity to be the peculiar outgrowth of Hebrew folkways and mores, culminating in the appearance of a supposedly divine teacher whose disciples converted his teachings into another set of folkways and mores called Christian culture, a sociological phenomenon that reached its greatest influence in the Middle Agaes and has been on the decline ever since. Christian ethical ideals in their various manifestations are just another collection of ethical specimens to be added to the multiplicity of ethical precepts, which demonstrates the relativity of them all, as well as the absurdity of their absolute claims. Furthermore, if there is any critical norm to be applied to them, it is not the norm of true or false, right or wrong, but the norm of adequacy to modern needs. On this ground Christian ethical precepts are often enough condemned, not only for being bound to "outworn creeds," but for being based on outmoded agricultural and pastoral conceptions of social organization and human relationships.

On the other hand, when the ethical temper is in its rationalistic mood, it invites us to observe in the "essence" of Christianity the crowning value of all systems of value, or the embodiment of a universal moral law, such as the golden rule, or the highest form of self-realization through self-sacrifice (Hegel), to which all other ethical systems are but the mere prelude. Now all is order and harmony, nothing is accidental, and man is only to be congratulated for having hit upon so noble and unattainable an ideal as Christian ethics for the goal of his ethical evolution, because thereby endless progress is insured.

The believer may observe that there is some truth in both of these interpretations, and yet he does not recognize the Christian perspective in either of them, and certainly not in the oscillation between them. He should not expect any preferential treatment for the Christian religion from anthropology, although it is surprising that a mood of pessimism should be associated with a presumably scientific enterprise. On the other hand, he may observe that a most peculiar view of history attaches to the mood of sweet reasonableness, which tacitly accepts the anthropological account as far as the past is concerned, but which equally tacitly assumes that in the future, as of now, starting today, things will be different. For there is no question that the pessimistic mood, the spirit of ethical relativism, when applied to the future, produces a paralysis of the ethical enthusiasm, and even an ethical despair, which, according to both empiricists and rationalists, can and must be stopped. Thus, while we may study anthropology in order to help us to understand the ethical history that is past, including all of its extremes of irrationality, ignorance, and superstition, we must insist on the fundamental rationality of men in order to be able to face the ethical history that is to come, if any is to come.

The subject matter of ethics may be defined as the proper relationship of man to man, or human conduct under the aspect of "ought." Wherever human conduct is discussed or described without any implication that it should or might be any different from what it is (as in news reporting, history, sociological research), we are not dealing with ethics. In so far as the power of reasoning is brought to play on the question of what human conduct ought to be, ethics would seem to be a branch of philosophy, and has traditionally been so regarded. But, as we observed in Chapter III, present-day philosophy can hardly be said to concern itself with the defining of ethical precepts as such. At any rate its two most active schools, the positivistic, or cautious-language analysts, and the existentialists, can hardly be said to be rushing to the rescue of the bewildered ethical questioner with well-thought-out ethical systems. The analysts rather seem to be saying in some revulsion, "Please, don't expect any ethical precepts from us; however, if you already have some, we can give you a semantic analysis of the language in which they are couched." And the existentialists: "Ethical precepts? Haven't we just finished showing you that for man who is free there can be only defiance and despair in the face of endless choices chosen under the necessity to choose?"

Philosophy having thus more or less excused itself from the systematic task of designing ethical precepts, people nevertheless continue to act as if there were some, and even professional moralists exist. These are likely to be historians, journalists, or political and social "analysts" engaged in the moral interpretation of recent historical events or changes in society, with their philosophical positions left unstated. But, thanks to the classificatory tendency of the human mind, there are only a relatively few well-defined ethical positions which have been held in the history of ethical thinking, and these can also be recognized in the writings of the unphilosophical practical moralists, as well as in the "original" ethical deliberations of the so-called man in the street. It is sometimes instructive to pause and think of that street, as well as such other gathering places of this man, as football stadiums, cinema houses, county fairs, as being filled with a restless ebb and flow of unconscious stoics, epicureans, Benthamite utilitarians, Platonic idealists, Aristotelian moderationists, Kantian duty men, cynics, libertines, puritans, perfectionists.

At the beginning of this book it was pointed out that we are supposed to be living in a period of the revival of religious interest, but that on closer inspection this revival would more accurately have to be described as an ethical reawakening, as evidenced by the pragmatic interest in the "ethical dividends" which Christianity is supposed to pay. The two world wars are supposed to have uncovered the ethical vacuum over which our civilization rests: what more natural than to try to fill this vacuum as quickly as possible before the structure collapses? In such a situation it is also natural for the Christian believer to be overly anxious to help fill the vacuum with the substance of Christian ethics. But it is just in this desire to make the Christian ethic fulfill the civilization-saving task that is demanded of it that it becomes all too easy for Christians to trim and pare and slur distinctions, until what one hears are vague exhortations to goodness or to "values" that are neither Christian nor capable of saving anything.

The object of this chapter will be to make distinctions as clear as possible in this confusing field of ethical thinking about man, in order to help the Christian resist this temptation. This will be done first by a comparison of Christian ethics with the traditional "reasonable" approach to ethical problems, which, as most reasonable enterprises, may be divided into an inductive and a deductive approach. After a critique of these approaches from the Christian standpoint there will be a summary of some modern attempts to get at the "grass roots" of ethical phenomena by means of new descriptive terminologies. This part will stress the importance both of realizing where and in what terms what used to be called ethical issues are being discussed by the contemporary world of unbelief, and of not letting these new words for old realities obscure the ethical issues revealed by the struggles of traditional ethical thought, as well as by the uniqueness, difficulty, and incommensurability of the Christian ethic.

The inductive, deductive, and Christian approaches to ethics

In so far as the power of reasoning is allowed to play a determining role in ethical decision (not just in analyzing how men actually act, but in concluding how they ought to act), the approach to ethics is either inductive or deductive. The inductive approach is an attempt to condense or abstract from the historically actual ethical experience of mankind a few dependable ethical principles, in order to conserve the *lessons* of the past for the edification of the future. It assumes that mankind as a whole learns by trial and error and that any set of ethical precepts that have enabled a given society or civilization to survive and to grow are to be noted and commended on that very ground. Appeals to tradition and to "the fathers" belong to this approach, on the grounds that what was found good and workable by the "fathers" is at least not to be disdained by the children. But this approach also recognizes that changing historical conditions may bring changes in ethical insight, presumably in the direction of improvement, as human experience broadens and earlier standards are outgrown. The empirical rules of conduct thus discovered and conserved are, of course, not to be taken as absolute, because this experience is still growing. They can, however, be thought of as gradually approximating, in the course of long historical testing and amendment, a constancy which would be indicative of something absolute in reality. The form of the inductive approach to ethics is the discovery of a scale of values actually operative in human history. The content of this ethic is somewhat indeterminate, since the discovery never is completed and new data are constantly becoming available. The arbitrary postulation of certain values as the highest or the best is discouraged both by the impartial attitude of this approach as well as by the variety and multiplicity of data it must study.

The deductive approach to ethics, on the other hand, begins at the opposite end, at precisely that "something absolute in reality" at which the empirical approach hopes, by endless successive approximation, to arrive. It begins with some kind of definition of human nature and from this deduces what man *ought* to do, what his highest good *must* be, presumably on the grounds that man cannot long or successfully do that which is "against" his nature. Everything ethical then hinges logically on the definition of the primary or essential human nature. Since there is this appeal to logic or rationality in the very form of the deductive approach, it is scarcely odd that the deductive approach is most consistent when reason itself is made the determining factor in the definition of human nature. Thus, although formally such definitions as that man is a pleasure-seeking animal, or a will-to-power, or a bundle of desires, or a projected purpose, belong in the deductive approach to ethics (since they begin by defining the "primary" nature of man), if they do not also pay some homage to reason, they cut the nerve of the coercive force of their particular definition of what man ought to do—namely, the logical consequences for society, politics, culture, religion, and what not, of that particular definition of human nature.

Most consistently, then, in the deductive approach, man's rational nature is taken to be the absolute in reality, and man is defined as the *animal rationale*. With man defined as the rational animal, the object of rational ethics becomes the realization of man's rational nature at the expense of his animal nature. Rationalistic ethics is concerned with the "striving" of reason after those things which "belong" to reason, and the depreciation and avoidance, or at least the control, of the things that belong to man's "lower nature." This is the form of the rational ethic, but in order that there should be a content, a "what" for which the rational nature of man may strive, it is necessary to postulate the "things" that naturally belong to reason. Here we encounter either a host of separate virtues, such as those listed by Socrates and Aristotle (courage, temperance, justice, wisdom), or some mystical union of the idealistic trinity of Truth, Beauty, and Goodness. After these things men should strive, if they wish to achieve their greatest self-realization as rational animals.

In contrast to both of these approaches to ethics we must now place the starkly simple Christian ethic, which begins neither with theories of human nature nor with studies of human experience, but with the will of God. The form of the Christian ethic is the will of God, and its content is the commandment of love. We are to love God with all our heart and soul and mind and strength, and our neighbor as ourself; and we are to do this because this is the will of God for us. Any other "reasons" placed alongside, or in support of, this one reason, such as that this will make us happy or the world more peaceful, however true in their own right, are something of an impertinence, because they seek to improve on the will of God. This does not mean that the will of God is arbitrary: it merely means that God knows better than man what is good for man.

A quick glance at these three approaches to the problem of ethics discloses that the first two, while beginning at opposite ends and running in opposite directions, are nevertheless traveling on the same track. They use the same language and move about in the same universe of discourse. Despite the difference of approach they understand each other very well, and they both know that some day they will meet in some halfway point on the road. Their difference is primarily a difference of emphasis on what comes first, whether we must begin our study of ethics with a description of ethical specimens or with a definition of essences. But the third approach is so incommensurable and self-contained that it appears to have no relation to the other two. It is traveling on a track of its own, and on a track that parallels the other, because the two apparently do not meet or cross at any point.

The most obvious barrier between them is that of language. Both inductive and deductive ethics use the language of philosophical abstraction, which is the language of concepts, definitions, propositions, postulates, and conclusions. The interpretation of human experience in terms of generalizations which invite the consent of all normal human beings is the foundation of both of them. No special visions, no special symbols, no claims of extraordinary experience requiring extraordinary language are considered either necessary or legitimate in either deductive or inductive ethics. In contrast to this the language of Christian ethics seems positively childish. Not only God is treated of in mythological terms, which might be excusable, but man also is apprehended in myth. Here there is no description of human experience in generalizations, but man is treated rather like a figure in a fairy tale. He is called a child of God, he is created by God, addressed by God; he experiences personal reactions, such as love or resentment, toward God; his will clashes with the will of God. Not only God appears to be supernatural in the language of Christian ethics, and certainly unrecognizable as a mere concept related to the natural world, but man is equally supernatural, a spirit consorting with spirits.

Every philosophically inclined believer since the time of the Church Fathers has had to face the problem of whether this difference in language between philosophy and Christianity is something accidental and unimportant, which can be explained away, for instance, by the difference between the liturgical and the teaching functions of the Church, or whether this difference is truly radical, something that can never be quite explained away. We cannot go into this complex question here, which raises all manner of epistemological and semantic difficulties, except to observe that, as far as ethics is concerned, the difference appears to be radical rather than inconsequential.

As a rule philosophy tends to regard the difference thus: that theological ethics is trying to say the same thing as philosophy, but with "poetic trimmings" to make the divine-human relations appear more vivid, somehow, and more urgent, than the generalizations of philosophy are able to make them appear. And theology tries to hang on to the mythological terms without quite knowing why, but simply because it feels a genuine loss when the translation into philosophic abstractions is made. Both are hampered by the absence of an adequate conception of poetry and mythology, such as would recognize in the mythical version of the divine-human relations not "trimmings" but greater *accuracy* in rendering the qualitative content of the relations in question. A few embarrassing questions from the standpoint of philosophy will illustrate the difficulty. What is sin, for example, philosophically phrased? What is God's love, wrath, patience, forgiveness—in philosophical ethics? How can we find a philosophical equivalent of the term "will of God"? Must not the will of God be understood as a final term incapable of further explanation or rationalization? Must not philosophy, to save itself from arbitrariness, constantly object to the introduction of such finally inscrutable terms as God's "will" into any of its arguments and persuasions? And must not every philosophical ultimate, every conclusion it can reach, since it is man, and not God, who is philosophizing, turn out to be a human ultimate, such as human happiness, usefulness, duty, wisdom?

In view of the incommensurability of the Christian approach to ethics with these other two (of which the difference in language is a warning signal and symptom) the desire of the unbelievers to avail themselves of the "ethical dividends" that Christianity is supposed to pay poses a peculiar problem. They want to have the ethic without the divine-human relationships implied in the Christian-mythical picture, and yet, when this ethic is translated into either the inductive or the deductive scheme, it loses precisely those qualities of authoritativeness, commitment, and Christian realism that recommend it as an answer to the world's present needs.[1] Is there then something radically wrong with either the inductive or the deductive approach to ethics? A critique conducted from the standpoint of the Christian approach reveals that both are based on sound logic and good intentions, and, if life were nothing but logic and good intentions, would certainly be destined to meet some day in a perfect theory of human nature that both accounts for, and prescribes for, human conduct. They each have their virtues, from the Christian standpoint, which must be noted, but also their unconscious presuppositions which cannot accommodate the Christian-mythical truths about God and man.

The virtues of the inductive approach to ethics are its teachableness, its willingness to listen to the voice of experience and to profit by it, its critique of ethical precepts by what they produce in the way of human happiness and social harmony rather than by appeals to metaphysical absolutes, and its realistic insistence that the world of ethical relations must be accepted and learned, there must be knowledge of "things as they are," before there can be any meaningful and practicable speculation on things as they ought to be. It assumes, again realistically (and herein lies both its strength as philosophy and its weakness as theology), that the only perspective that can disclose ethical reality to human beings is the human perspective. From this perspective there are, to be sure, many irrationalities, contradictions, and even paradoxes to be found in human behavior—but even in these there are discoverable historical causes and relationships which can teach us much that is for our own good, instead of throwing us into a dither of metaphysical despair. The inductive approach to ethics basically affirms, or tacitly assumes, that this life is likely to be most rewarding to those who learn to accept what must be accepted, and who try to change to their desires what can be changed.

All these are admirable virtues. The acceptance of the givenness of the world and of our life in it has something in common with that acceptance of our human nature and creatureliness which is required by the Christian doctrine of the creation. Such acceptance dismisses wishful thinking, and condemns that cynicism which follows upon disappointed idealism, as well as all bitter reproaches to the world for not being more to our liking. For example, the fact that God created us with bodies, and as separate individuals which are nevertheless not self-sufficient, is something which causes most of our personal and social problems, and yet, unless we accept this reverently as something good because coming from God, we are always in the position of criticizing our Creator for having made us in this particular way. That is actually what idealistic ethics does every time it issues a tirade against the materialistic involvements of the greater number of human beings, their preoccupation with their animal needs and their unwillingness to strive for the obviously better and more spiritual things. The idealists lack sympathy with the very conditions of existence. There is always an atmosphere of aristocratic bitterness about their programs of reform. Their exhortations consist more of sarcasm and ridicule than of persuasion, and they are finally driven, both by their lack of success and their loyalty to their ideals, to actual hatred of their opponents and all who do not support them. No one can be so merciless as a reformer driven by a logical conclusion. The disappointed idealist then performs an about-face and cynically proclaims that there is no soul, not even any reason in man, and that what passes for his ideals are nothing but the by-products, projections, and instruments of his animal needs and passions.

But having said this much on behalf of the realistic acceptance by inductive ethics of the world as it is, as a condition for improving it, we must now state that, from the standpoint of the biblical doctrine of the fall, this very acceptance is based on a misunderstanding of the present nature of the creation. It assumes that, even though our knowledge of the creation may not be perfect, the creation itself, that which we study, is now fundamentally sound, so that a satisfactory, pragmatic adjustment to it is possible at any point in history. This means that human nature also is fundamentally sound, since it is from human value-judgments, properly corrected and harmonized by reason or common sense, that we build up our ideas of what ought to be. Neither our ideas of what is nor our ideas of what ought to be are questioned at their roots, so long as there is a sufficient consensus of opinion about them, and no obvious aberrations or deliberate irrationality in them. This is true even in those ethical systems where the existence of God is taken into consideration, and the will of this God is deemed to be a legitimate goal of striving, that is to say, a true ethical value.

From the regularities and structures found in nature, and from certain admittedly basic tendencies in human nature, the combination of which results in the "natural orders"—sex life, family life, national and political groups, economic, cultural, and religious institutions—from these we can deduce, both by means of their structure and by means of the valuations placed upon them, what the will of God might be, in a general way, and also in particular cases. For example, the facts of sexual procreation would make it seem almost obvious that the will of God is that there should be some satisfactory institution of marriage and the family which would satisfy the sexual and parental needs of the adults, the biological and spiritual needs of the young, and the economic, social, and cultural needs of the wider community. Thus, without making practically any postulates at all about this God, except perhaps a general benevolence toward all men, it becomes possible by factual study, analysis, and induction to lay down a set of rules for human conduct, both personal and social, which may confidently be assumed to be a fair approximation to the will of God. It is the claim of some anthropologists that the folkways and mores of primitive societies are the resultant of exactly this kind of process in less sophisticated and self-conscious form, and that the rules and customs thus created often represent a very satisfactory solution for the demands of both the men and the gods in question.

To this kind of pragmatic and essentially optimistic analysis of ethical problems it may be proper to answer by asking, very well, then, if finding out and doing the will of God is such a simple matter, why aren't the results more satisfactory? Why haven't perfectly obvious and unequivocal rules for human conduct been discovered and accepted by the majority of mankind long before this? Why do wars, injustice and aggression, licentiousness and greed, still cover the earth? And why do these seem to increase in violence and lethal power, precisely in the degree that men become more enlightened and informed, and possessed of better tools of research and understanding?

The realization that the ethical is not as simple as it looks may come even in a secular age to a generation that has seen catastrophic times, but this "discovery" is not one for which the modern age can claim the originality it claims for its technical marvels. It is all to be found in the Bible, written down by "primitive" Jews, and in relation to a world situation much more innocent, simple, and analyzable than ours. The men who wrote the Bible were not so unobservant as to ignore the fact that there are cause-and-effect relations in life and in historical events, but, out of a deepening respect for the ethical dimension in their lives, they were not so naïve as to affirm that from these cause-and-effect relations the will of God could be read off as from the dials of an instrument board.

Instead of asking for more time to study the dials more carefully, they saw in this very uncertainty a lesson concerning God and his creation; and this was a lesson which constituted in its essence not knowledge about something but an encounter with someone, with God himself. God, they affirmed, is partly revealed in his creation: "the firmament showeth his handiwork" (A.S.V.). And through those laws that he has given to men to disregard at their own peril, he makes even the wrath of man to praise him. But he is also a hidden God! He hides himself from men, not only because of their sinfulness, but also because mystery is his prerogative in the face of all who would assault him with threats and demands, even ethical demands. Certainly the story of Job does not present us with the problem of undeserved suffering in order to point to any obvious or humanly satisfying solution. The modern pragmatic solution would be to dismiss with an indulgent smirk Job's conviction of a just God, and to apply chemicals to his sores. This may seem like an obvious and humanly satisfying solution, but only so long as chemicals are ready to hand for all human afflictions, and every attempt to give a deeper meaning to suffering other than physical recoil or maladjustment is forbidden—in other words, only if the specifically human in man is denied at the outset. But the men in the Bible are nothing if not human: they rebel at suffering; they speculate on their ultimate destiny; they accept their blessings as if they were deserved; and they put off with endless excuses the feeling of ethical responsibility which they know very well might bring them face to face with God.

But there is another sense in which all is not well in the creation, and this does not depend on man's ability or inability to discover its laws. For the very laws that God has allowed men to discover become in their hands a provocation instead of a blessing, a burden instead of a joy, and a source of strife and hatred instead of peace and love. Marriage may be a blessing and a responsibility before God, and yet many a man is so blinded by his family attachments that he does not question the means by which he provides his dependents with a comfortable living. Work, even the most spontaneous and creative work, becomes a commodity to be bargained for, or a dire necessity to be fought for, in a world that has lost all sense of "tending the garden." The diversity of cultures and races, instead of filling men with admiration for God's manifold creativity, fills them with feelings of superiority, fear, and distrust—and has to be "explained away" by our anthropologists for men even to tolerate it. The religions of the world, each of them representing a rightful outreaching of man toward the ultimate reality, are, or become, idolatrous and superstitious even before they become corrupt and priest-ridden—so that man is seen to be groping toward his Maker in a peculiarly dense darkness that covers the earth even in the brightness of day. Everywhere men misuse the bounties of the earth, not so much through ignorance as through an intelligent following of their most natural impulses, and then they and their children, in the day of catastrophic reckoning, hurl imprecations at God for "allowing" such things to happen. Everywhere men misread the signs that are written all over the creation, again not through ignorance, but because they have cunningly misread the "law that is written in their hearts," which leaves them without excuse.

Now it is this kind of world, this creation so aptly described as "fallen," that the inductive approach to ethics would have us accept as the beginning of our ethical studies, as the objectively given raw material from the natural laws of which we are to learn what ought to be. The believer cannot help protesting that this kind of acceptance of the world is based on a delusion, on the delusion that there is nothing wrong with the world that a little intelligent foresight would not cure. In comparison to this the biblical story of the creation and fall may be mythical in form, but it is not delusory in content. Neither is it a story of something that happened at the beginning of time, but rather the utterly realistic picture of what happens to God's creation every day. It is the story of man's rebelling against God, using his freedom to corrupt that which God had given him to care for, and this in response to his own desires, especially the desire to be like God himself. Comparing this now with the complacent belief of inductive ethics that life is likely to be most rewarding to those who learn to accept what they must, and to change to their own desires what they can, we see that, because of the "realistic delusion" we are asked to accept that very rebellion of man's will against God by which the creation becomes fallen as something ethically neutral, like the weather, and to encourage man to change the world according to the very desires that have driven him out of paradise, especially the desire to be like God. This is the anti-Christian significance of any system of ethics based on an impartial, empirical study of values or desires and their operation in the world, because both the desires or values, and the world in which they operate, or prove themselves, are simply accepted without any reference to the will of God in regard to them.

The virtues of the deductive approach are most obvious where this method is most consistent—namely, in rationalistic or idealistic ethics. With human nature defined in terms of reason, and reason defined as capable of discerning the good, there is avoided the tragicomic situation (implicit in the inductive approach with its cumulative knowledge) of asking the ethical questioner to wait to the end of the world for the true answer to his ethical problem of today. The standard of the good must apply universally to all men in all ages and be available to every man in his lifetime. Therefore it is quite right to state the good in terms of virtues or values that are final or self-rewarding (intrinsic, not instrumental), for if they are justified in terms of the "results" they produce in history, the typical pragmatic regression is started: by what standard shall we judge the results, and, when will the results be considered complete? Idealistic ethics begins quite dogmatically with the assertion that man is different from the animals, and that what he has in addition to what they have makes him *superior* to them. The early Platonists and Stoics never tire of reminding man that he must distinguish himself from the other animals by using his rational faculties—otherwise why is he a man? Thus Epictetus writes in his *Discourses:*

> Well then God constitutes every animal, one to be eaten, another to serve for agriculture, another to supply cheese, and another for some like use; for which purposes what need is there to understand appearances, and to be able to distinguish them? But God has introduced man to be a spectator of God and of His works, and not only a spectator of them, but an interpreter.

And in the fashion characteristic of all idealism he not only urges man to use this rational faculty which distinguished him from the beasts, or "creatures," but also he eventually identifies it with God:

> What then? are not plants and animals also the works of God? They are; but they are not superior things, nor yet parts of the Gods. But you are a superior thing; you are a portion separated from the deity; you have in yourself a certain portion of him. Why then are you ignorant of your own noble descent?

Succeeding centuries of idealistic philosophy have not significantly changed this concept of the spiritual nature of man, even though they have emphasized now this, and now that faculty of the rational soul as being most rewarding of cultivation. And neither have the centuries changed, as a part of the earnest exhortation with which idealism tries to woo man away from his animal existence, the last question in the above quotation: "Why then are you ignorant of your own noble descent?" Apparently man in all ages has to be told about his spiritual nature, about his kinship with God; he has to be "sold on it," as American idiom would say, in order that he may decide on the cultivation of it, which is the ethical purpose of his life. The dynamic of this ethic is a principle of attraction—attraction to the good, repulsion from evil. In ethics men must be persuaded to believe with Socrates that excellence in rational conduct constitutes not only the highest good but likewise true happiness. "Observe that in the pleasure of all except the wise man, there is something positively unreal and ungenuine, and slight as the rude outline of a picture," he says, in the *Republic*, dismissing the claims of sensual or animal indulgences to make men happy. The spiritual nature of man is thus an addendum in man, which makes it possible for him to be happy in a way that is above any happiness the other animals, or irrational and passionate men, may possess.

The Bible also knows that man has in him something different from what the animals have, but its conception of it is quite different from the rationalistic conception. The Bible does not insist upon it and define it; it does not constantly remind men that they are superior to the animals. In the Bible the spiritual nature of man is taken for granted; it is the absolutely given which originated in the instant in which God created man in his image. By itself it has no eudaemonistic value. Man is decreed to be a spirit, whether he wants to be one or not, and his deepest sorrows are the result of this fact as much as his greatest joys. In his despair and in his separation from God he feels that he is condemned to be a spirit, and, far from looking down upon the animals from a supposedly superior position, he may well envy them their relatively simple and untroubled existence. Neither does he express arrogance toward the inanimate creation—but rather a mood of wonderment toward both of them, and toward his peculiar position in their midst: "When I consider thy heavens, the work of thy fingers, the moon and the stars, which thou hast ordained; what is man, that thou art mindful of him? and the son of man, that thou visitest him?" (K.J.V.) He does not "argue" from the fact of his spiritual nature to his dominion over the other creatures, but simply records his amazement at this before the Creator who decreed it: "For thou hast made him a little lower than the angels, and hast crowned him with glory and honour. Thou madest him to have dominion over the works of thy hands; thou hast put all things under his feet: all sheep and oxen, yea, and the beasts of the field." (K.J.V.)

As it is conceived in the Bible, there is no escape for man from his spiritual nature. Man does not have the choice of being a wise man or an animal. He is an animal who is also a spirit, and his only choice is to be a spirit with God, or a spirit against God. And a spirit who is against God is not an animal but a demon. It is an insult to the animals to describe a man who is fallen from the divine unity (and that is all of us) as an animal, because the animals have a perfection of their own which we do not even understand. Of course, men try to escape their spiritual nature all the time by becoming like animals, but even in this they betray their true nature by showing what miserable animals they make. What rationalistic ethics does not seem able to comprehend is the fact that the spiritual nature of man is aesthetically and ethically neutral—it is not a value, but a structure. As our own structure we cannot deny it, escape it, or think it away by changing our attitude toward it. We simply are, and have to be, this structure.

Now the important question here, for a critique of rationalistic ethics, is, why doesn't it discover that structure for itself? If it is able to maintain that man is different from the animals, why must it interpret this difference in such a one-sided and sanguine manner as to distort both man's understanding of his own problems and his opinion of the animals? The answer is, because if the structure of man's spirit is as the Bible pictures it, there is no *hope* in it, as far as a rational salvation is concerned. If man's spirit is that which may throw him into despair as much as lift him into bliss, what gain is there? The animals may suffer pains and hungers and temporary fears and angers, but they do not have all this with them constantly in memory and anticipation. They do not know that they must die; they do not know ultimate frustration and futility; they are not encompassed about with fears of the unknown, with melancholy, loneliness, anxiety, unfulfilled poetic longings, with remorse over the past and dread of the future, with bitterness and resentment, and with always death, death, death staring them in the face. All this is reserved for man, and precisely because of his spiritual structure. The truth of the matter is that rational ethics *must not* discover this structure of man's spirit, for if it does, it ceases to be a way of salvation. It *must* attribute man's distress to his involvement in material things and animal desires, and must promise salvation by way of rational self-elevation above these, and it consistently does so.

The phenomenologies of ethical experience

The preceding criticism from the Christian standpoint of both the inductive and deductive approach to ethics reveals that, reasonable though they be, they are not merely inadequate, in the sense of incomplete or superficial; they are mistaken as to what man's ethical nature and situation in the world really is. Their mistake is "natural," or inevitable, thanks to their nonchristian presuppositions. But a curious fact of the present ethical situation is that these two reasonable approaches are coming in for considerable criticism also from a nonchristian standpoint, in those deliberations on ethical questions that currently attempt to get back to the ethical origins, to the primitive "what happens" in order to provide a fresh start in ethics.

The primitive ethical act is approachable from many directions, being a complicated affair, ranging from the taboo-reactions of savages to the prolonged soul-searchings of saints and reformers. To try to bring this range under one concept means that universality is sought not in the idea of the good, which changes, but in what men do when they pursue what they believe is good, or avoid what they believe is evil. At the present time existentialism, psychoanalysis, value theory, and semantics, in their several ways, are trying to arrive at a more accurate *description* of what goes on when man behaves ethically. These phenomenologies of ethical experience are the grass-roots movement of the present-day revival of ethical interest. They are in some ways more naïve, more simple-minded, but also more honest, serious, and therefore pathetic (arousing sympathy) than either the pragmatic or the dogmatic efforts to "use" Christianity as a bulwark of civilization for its ethical by-products. Their very seriousness and naïveté remind one that there is here a return in spirit to the situation of the Greeks' musing over man in the academy, the kindergarten of the ethical reflections of Western man.

Existentialism is the most vigorous protest, on a not-necessarily

Christian basis, against the sweet reasonableness of the inductive approach to ethics as described above. The appeal to the "fathers," or to custom, or to common sense, or to some generalized rule of benevolence, such as the greatest good of the greatest number, which is what the inductive method reduces to in practice, produces exactly that dishonesty or unauthenticity of personal existence that arouses the existentialist's anger and disgust. The individual ethical self, instead of facing his choices in full consciousness of the responsibility placed on him, retires in a cowardly fashion behind what "they say" or "people believe" or "custom demands" or "experience shows"—all objective rules that relieve him of the pain, but also deprive him of the dignity, of being a free agent. It is this "safe" way of living that infests the whole realm of ethical relationships with hypocrisy and conventional stuffiness. For responsible men to simply "take over" from the "fathers" what might indeed have been for *them* a hard-won wisdom is cowardly retreat from the arduousness of existence.

As for the rationalistic ethic, according to existentialism, it is simply self-contradictory. Man has no essence, rational or other, but only an absurd urge to make one for himself. If man were the rational animal, he would be static, finished, incapable of growing or becoming, and, having ethically no problems at all, he would have nothing to do. The accent on freedom makes it hard for the existentialists to arrive at any ethical precepts, except perhaps the universal duty to use the freedom and respect it in others. But theirs is a much-needed opposition to the pragmatic tendency to treat the human subjects as so many adjustable and manageable items, to be manipulated for their own good, by rules of thumb or appeals to desires, like a herd of cattle that is to be coaxed and prodded and harried to some goal by the agile and clever cowboys.

Most important of all, the existentialists have succeeded where all other modern ethical discourse has failed, in restoring some specific and vivid meaning to that elusive entity that used to be called the "soul." They usually avoid this word, using in its place such surrogates as "self," the "for-itself," the "being-there," the "subjectivity," the "being-in-a-world," the "existent," the "project," but by actually describing the antics and gymnastics, the situations and relations of this entity, they have forced it back into attention as a something to be reckoned with. No longer can the "soul" be ignored on the grounds that nobody can define it, or that naturalism has explained it away, for it can be described, and in terms that make naturalism itself irrelevant. Most important for ethics is their description of the self-creating activity of the soul, of the fact that in every choice what is decided is not merely what the man will *do* but, at the same time, what or whom *he thereby becomes*, whither his project is going, what essence or being he is making of himself. There is thus left a residue of the ethical decision and act that is quite different from the overt "results" in history or society, but is more like a scar and a growing edge of the person. From the Christian standpoint this description, however strained or philosophically excruciating, must be welcomed as a restoration to contemporary awareness of facts of human nature that could once be taken for granted as part of everyone's cultural heritage, but now need rediscovery.

Psychoanalysis is another attempt to describe what happens when man operates in the ethical dimension—that is, in relation to others. It is an odd mixture of naturalistic presuppositions, scientific pretensions, philosophical scrapings and parings, and mythological insights. Clinical psychoanalysis deals only with the scars, and more exactly, only with the more painful scars of the process of growing and becoming, where the scar tissue presents an impediment to "normal" functioning in the patient's present activities. The soul surrogates it uses, such as the id, the ego, the superego, and more recently the real self and the idealized self, have no more justification in physiological psychology or neurology than the words used by the existentialists, but they have clinical justification: the explanation given to the patient in terms of what ordeals this entity undergoes in the now classical concepts of trauma, complex, fixation, frustration, compulsion, compensation, alienation, gives him a self-understanding such that re-education is possible, and, *mirabile dictu*, the symptoms are relieved.

It should never be forgotten that what made Freud persist in his line of investigation was the even to him amazing fact that an explanation in terms of early sexual trauma or repression actually relieved or cured the hysteria of his hysterical females.[2] From the doctor's standpoint the question of whether the terms of the explanation should be called "mechanism" or "mythology" cannot be as important as the clinical results. In the larger human context, and even for the general theory of psychoanalysis, it is important, since it points beyond itself to just such concerns as that of ethics. Both existentialism and psychoanalysis have shown that in order to have real self-knowledge, such as makes possible self-possession, self-determination, and self-renewal, there must be some kind of "mythology of the self" with which the particular person can imaginatively grasp his own biography, and that it must be, as biography is, in dramatic terms—some kind of enactment or record of a happening, not an object. Psychoanalysis has shown that the "soul" is something much more complicated than either rationalistic or empiricist ethics tend to recognize. This is all to the good and can mean a revitalization of ethical problems, for it points to the danger of trying to conceive the soul in simplistic terms (such as when a puritan ethic conceives of the soul as some kind of monad or substance that either God or the devil gets hold of), and the equal danger of underestimating the toughness and resourcefulness of this complexity by encouraging hypochondriacal self-pity, so that the "patient" of the growing pains is defeated in advance and is casting about for something or someone to blame for his ills.

Another attempt to get at the bedrock of ethical reality is general theory of value. Here the method is much more formal or logical than in either of the above. The idea is that if you can get a general definition of value, you can then more narrowly define ethical values as a species or subclass of the genus value. The problem, then, is to define value as such. Here the science-ridden temperament of the age shows itself in the tendency from the outset to distinguish value as over against fact. To an earlier age the "devices and desires of our hearts" were as much a fact as the structure of plants, but now there are values and there are facts. The facts are handed over to the sciences to ascertain by their method and that leaves us with the values floating in some kind of nonfactual miasma. It might be said that in the middle of the nineteenth century God died at the hand of Nietzsche, and ever since then Value, his heir apparent, has become the *mysterium tremendum et fascinosum*.

General theory of value tries to circumvent this mystery by treating values impartially and objectively, "as if" they were facts, having first distinguished them from facts. Man is the valuing animal, or the value-creating animal, or the animal that cares, or the animal that is governed by interests. All you can do to help such a creature is to show him how he can rationally order these interests in such a way as to achieve the ones he wants the most at the expense of those he wants not quite so much, or those he shouldn't want if he knew better. Theory of value tells you that you cannot have your cake and eat it too, but it does not tell you whether to eat it or to keep it. It assumes that values derive from, and operate it, a structured world that will not permit internal contradiction, but it will not commit itself on the nature of that structure, or cannot, and still retain its impartiality. If man is the value-creating animal, then anything he creates has value. Ethical values are those that permit some kind of life in society, or make society desirable, and their rational or harmonious ordering on the principle of impartiality and the greatest inclusiveness would seem to indicate that a place must be found in the ideal society for whatever vices or evils enough people want badly enough. The more seriously one studies theory of value, the more it appears as a *reductio ad absurdum* of the impartial approach to partiality, which ends in the collecting and cataloguing of scales of value arranged on different principles, as in a museum. As a logical exercise it is valuable for the light it throws on the valuing process.

If existentialism, in its breast-beating, brow-striking fashion had not called attention to the necessity, even the implied inevitability, of commitment or involvement in any action stemming from decision, theory of value in its dry, curatorlike fashion would have succeeded in demonstrating the same thing. Somewhere along the line preeminence must be given to some value, interest, purpose, or concern, if there is to be a harmonizing or integration of the person, and this integration can then be seen as simply an efficient arrangement of assorted interests relative to the major commitment or concern of the person's life. Whether from the logic of rational evaluation, or from the phenomenology of the humanoid type of existence, we get curious confirmation of Kierkegaard's assertion that in ethico-religious matters "truth" lies in subjectivity, in selfhood and its choices. Seen from the outside, "impartially," as theory of value looks at them, these choices of selfhood must necessarily appear arbitrary, no matter what current psychological theories of conation are called in to account for them. Seen from the inside, as by existentialism, the choices are man's fatal prerogative of freedom, and the word "arbitrary" as a term of reproach should not even be used by those who understand the existential situation.

The most sophisticated of these several approaches to the "what happens" of ethical activity is that of language analysis. In this most active branch of philosophy man is defined as the sign-using animal and ethics comes in under the heading of what this animal wishes to accomplish with the signs that it uses in ethical discourse. Sentences like "this is good" are analyzed to mean, "I approve," "I want you to approve," "This will get you what you want," "We ought to do it," or simply, "Hurray!" Such apparently designative sentences as, "Justice is every man getting his due," must be broken down into valuative phrases like the above to show that they are not really statements about anything, but are incitements to certain actions or to reciprocal attitudes in the hearer. The presupposition behind language analysis seems to be that if only people knew "the meaning of meaning" they would be more careful about how they use their language—careful about not mixing up the different types of discourse. In this way misunderstandings and "pseudo problems" would be avoided and real communication established among men. Presumably in this linguistic utopia of the future everyday discourse about facts would be couched in the aseptic language of, say, medicine, while valuative discourse would be efficiently couched in the "evocative" speech of poetry: "I am moving my body toward the building on the corner to exchange money for a pound of that ah! so delicious, so aromatic, even by Omar Khayyam honored and by Christ, crusted—bread."

I do not intend to ridicule language analysis—especially as the further pursuit of this entertaining enterprise seems to be not only raising a few "pseudo problems" of its own but also revealing that at least some of the "pseudo problems," thought at first to be due to inaccurate use of language (such as most of metaphysics), are not so easily disposed of and can even be recognized as reappearing under the guise of a different terminology. For ethics, for example, the making of the distinction between "facts" and "values" might be called a new "pseudo problem" since the real problem of ethics is to make distinctions between some values and others, and to be able to give preference to some over others by means of a criterion that is as much grounded in the "nature of reality" as the so-called "facts." [3] Both inductive and deductive ethics go on that supposition, and language analysis itself is a set of sign evaluations that tries to ground itself in factual reality, the latter taken in terms ranging all the way from the behavioristic stimulus-response cycle as studied in dogs to the idealistic concept of man as the basically symbol-creating creature who by means of symbolic transformation makes a world out of every chaos. At this stage of language philosophies it must at least be questioned whether the analyses actually increase either understanding or communication among men—since, as we shall see in the next chapter, there is something about the communicative situation that makes its success depend upon a spontaneous or intuitive reading off of the sign in its contextual pantomime. Language analysis, by placing a figurative question mark over every word in a sentence, tends to paralyze response and to collapse the communicative situation. The language paradise, as any other, depends on the preservation or restoration of original innocence.

From kindergarten to graduate school in ethics

We must now ask, what is the real object of all these descriptions and attempts at a new or contemporary understanding of man's ethical nature and situation in the world? I do not think that any of the writers in the various fields so briefly reviewed would claim that pure, objective curiosity was their motive. They all want to be helpful in the present critical situation; they want to point a way by which man may save himself and his civilization; and they all assume that better knowledge (more accurate description) is what he needs most of all before he can act effectively. At this point a Christian understanding of man with its serpentine wisdom must be used to point out the usual ambiguities of the situation. Up to a point the quest for knowledge may indeed be innocent and honest—but after a certain point one must ask (mainly of oneself, but indirectly of all): is it really true that man does not *know* what he should do? We are reminded of the situation in which the story of the good Samaritan was told. It is hard to believe that the lawyer who could recite the summary of the law did not *know* who his neighbor was, so that, even if he were not told it, we would surmise that he was "seeking to justify himself."

It is also hard to believe that at this late date in man's bloody and long ethical history he does not really *know* what is right, especially as the very form in which the ethical injunctions are given point to the one place where everyone knows what is right or wrong—in his own person. "As thyself" and "as you would have them do unto you" is the blunt answer to the ethical questioner who keeps asking for more and more knowledge, better and better descriptions of ethical reality—and, if he happens to be a father, he will have to acknowledge that no ten-year-old child needs to be given a lecture on justice to know when an injustice has been done to him. Of course, there is something to be said for putting all this ancient wisdom into contemporary modes of thinking, but it is equally important to recognize the point at which these modes of thinking themselves, or the motives behind them, becloud or evade the ethical issues. It is no use at this stage of history to pretend to an innocent, Edenlike ignorance before the monstrous problems of industrial and political world-community-making that man has brought upon himself, and to put on a Greek-like air of naïveté in order to demand, "Just tell us what is right so that we may straightway do it."

The real ethical issues are not new or contemporary at all, but as old as the history of the Jews and as revealing as the history of Christianity. If paganism may be thought of as the kindergarten and grade school of man's ethical education, the history in the Old Testament corresponds to high school and college, while Christianity in this figure corresponds to graduate school, as far as you can go in the ethical curriculum. The ethical reality revealed in this schooling is that man knows (the law is written in his heart) or can easily find out what is right. But then he either does not wish to do it or he tries to do it and fails. In either case guilt is his portion and from then on scapegoating a driving interest. If, however, he does not even *try* to do what is right and thus find out what the failure consists of, it is very hard to convince him that his demand for more knowledge is one of the many forms of his evasion and self-justifying. The merit of the Jews was that they had tried and failed and in this way became the "preparation" for the gospel. Both historically and doctrinally, Christian ethics rests upon the "undergraduate" ethical experience of the Jews, and, without this experience or something equivalent to it in each man's life, it does not make much sense even to talk about a Saviour. The need for a Saviour becomes an "existential" need and ceases to be a religious theory for those who have repeatedly tried to live by the highest ethical rules they knew, and (in the light of the standard of God's love) repeatedly found themselves in despair or in hypocrisy. Yet it is now proposed to summon Christian ethics to solve the worldly predicaments of a people who are still spiritually and temperamentally in the Greek kindergarten, still uncommitted, still asking what is good, what are ethical "values," and still casting sidelong glances at anthropology.

It is hard to see what can come of this well-meant rescue operation except new misunderstandings of what Christianity is, and new misunderstandings of man himself in his present situation. Of course the gospel must be preached to all nations, but it is the whole gospel that must be preached, not just Christian ethics, for it is the whole gospel that man needs, complete with its so mythical, so childish picture of the God-Christ-man relationships set forth in the biblical accounts. Outside these relationships the Christian ethic does not make sense, neither in what is commanded nor why. For this reason, as the Christian believer will discover for himself when he tries to live out the ethical implications of his faith in the midst of the sinful actualities of historical existence, it is also impossible to reduce the Christian ethic to some expedient rule of thumb or abstract principle such as the unbelievers are looking for in the present revival of ethical interest. The freedom, scope, and difficulty of the Christian ethic are such as to leave the believer no time for speculation on five easy ways to save civilization, for this particular graduate school has the peculiar characteristic that it becomes a lifetime job for everyone who enrolls in it. He is better advised to acquaint himself with the nature and difficulties of the special task to which he is called. A brief "orientation" in some of these difficulties may help him, and will close this chapter.

Some difficulties of the Christian ethic

The Christian ethic is most effectively practicable on the person-to-person level, which is not surprising, since an affirmation of the personality of others and a will to personal communion is of the very essence of Christian love. This fact has led many Christians in every age to concentrate their Christian love on works of personal charity and to leave the necessarily more impersonal relations of groups, institutions, and classes quite outside the scope of Christian ethics.

This in itself would not be bad if the groups and institutions in question were neutral or beneficial with respect to the personal being of those who are involved with them (for example, a society for astronomical research may be said not to threaten or corrupt the personal existence of its members, and there are, of course, many such neutral and even beneficial groups in any civilization). But it is precisely an enlightened and increasingly sensitive Christian love that observes in the operations of its contemporary society the fact that some of the most flagrant and wholesale violations of the personal being of people are committed by groups and institutions, governments and industries, and that it is virtually impossible to live in modern society without having one's existence as a person dependent on, and intimately involved in, the impersonal operations of large-scale groups. This raises the question not *whether* the Christian ethic is relevant to the problem (for it is really only Christian love that can see the true dimensions of this situation and thus pose it as a problem) but *how* it may be applied.

First of all, the believer should observe that there already exist between groups and institutions, partly for the sake of sheer survival, and partly for mutual benefit, various ideas of what constitutes just and equitable relationships and obligations among them. There is nothing intrinsically holy or universal about these ideas of justice which make relatively harmonious relations between potentially hostile groups possible, but the more powerful groups always try to give the impression that this is so. For example, American industry's idea of what is a just and equitable relation between management and labor always presupposes that there is something holy or universally right about the American system of private enterprise and capitalistic production. Similarly, governments based on constitutional law presuppose that the just relations defined by the constitution rest on some kind of "universal rights," although they would be hard put to it to prove their "rightness" on a secular basis, and when hard pressed as nations are scarcely ever willing to extend them to their supposed "universality" inside and outside their borders.

The important thing about these ideas of justice and equity actually in practice between groups and groups, or between groups and individuals, is not whether they can by argument be found to be either universal or reasonable but, from the Christian standpoint, whether they can be used as they are in the service of the neighbor's welfare, or whether they need to be revised, extended, re-enforced, or completely challenged as to their adequacy for this purpose. Justice in this sense is regarded not as an abstract quantity, of which there is "more" or "less" in the world, but as an approximation of love, or rather as the necessarily restricted operation of love in the field of impersonal relations. In this sense a higher justice is always a more equal justice, not because *equality* is to be raised to a universal principle, but because the impersonal nature of the relations and the large number of people involved make it impossible to consider individual needs and special cases. Nevertheless, each of these individuals is a "neighbor," and it is because of the welfare of individuals thought of as neighbors that a more equal justice is to be sought, from a Christian standpoint, and not because of the increase in the world of some abstract quantity called Justice.

As soon as the Christian enters the field of relations between groups in order to change them in the direction of greater justice, however, he is immediately confronted with the problem of *consent*, for changes in the relations of groups can usually be achieved only through the concerted action of large numbers of people of assorted beliefs. In order to achieve consent, he finds he must appeal to all kinds of motives and ideas which are Christianly questionable, such as the selfish interest of the parties involved, or the "universal rightness" of the particular idea of justice implicit in the particular change, or even the threat of coercion by the powers that be if the law permits it. This is bound to have a disheartening effect on his ethical enthusiasm, and it also leads to much confusion in his mind. He cannot help observing that both a legalistic ethic which simply lays down certain practices and principles as "universally right," and an ethic of expediency which simply pursues certain goals by any means whatever, are better off when it comes to deciding between historical alternatives of action than he is with his transcendent criterion of love, which simply reveals to him all too clearly the imperfections of all the alternatives. In fact in the thick of action he finds himself not only tempted but actually trapped into one or another of these positions, either legalism or expediency, by the demands of the situation. He catches himself giving his support to certain historically relative notions of justice or welfare as if they were "eternal truths," and he is drawn, as an alternative to no action at all, to use "methods" of achievement about which he has serious doubts. Small wonder, then, that many a Christian retires from social action entirely, leaving the field clear for those with less insight and fewer scruples.

Actually there is no way out of this predicament, as more and more experience in social action will teach him. The believer must simply face the situation for what it is: the ethical manifestation of the fallen nature of the world, in which a purely good deed is not only often unwanted but also impossible. This, however, is no excuse for complacency in the face of social evil, nor for a paring down of the criterion of love so that it may be identified with what passes for justice or goodness in the sinful actualities of the world. The believer must realize that, in the world as it is, both legalism and expediency are *sometimes* preferable to their actual alternatives, which might be anarchy or oppression. Even the alternative of complete withdrawal may sometimes be indicated for him—but he always has this *sometimes* with him, precisely because the criterion of love never permits him to rest in any solution of social relationships as finally satisfactory, but always indicates a higher possibility. This *sometimes* is the warning signal, pointing to the flexible, unpredictable, and necessarily inventive character of the Christian ethic. It makes each ethical decision a potentially new and primitive act of responsibility before God, not to be justified simply by reference to previous decisions, general precedent, tradition, rules of thumb, principles, or any other of the usual means of arriving at and justifying ethical decisions.

Now it is surely the better part of Christian wisdom for the believer to learn the difficulties of the Christian ethic as soon as he can, out of his own experience and thought, so that he may avoid illusions about his own powers, as well as resist the temptation of easy decision provided by secular ethics. But, on the other hand, lest the difficulties of the Christian ethic appear to be overwhelming and insoluble, as in a purely human sense they truly are, it might be well to remind him that the Christian teaching has a doctrine that enables the believer to carry on even in the face of what is overwhelming and insoluble. This is the doctrine of the Christian calling. This concept is not restricted to the field of ethics, but it certainly has its special significance there. It is essentially a biblical concept—God is calling men to himself, first of all calling them to fellowship with himself, and in this fellowship calling them to do his will in the world. But God does not make his will known by issuing once and for all a set of immutable axioms or eternal truths, the implications of which make it self-evident what must be done in each historical situation—this would be the impersonal, first cause, or "watchmaker" God of the Enlightenment, who gives his creation a push and then retires into celestial privacy. The Christian God is the ever-present, ever-personal creator and sustainer of history, who addresses individuals always as persons, and ever anew by bringing them into new historical situations, and by making himself available to them that truly seek him. He calls them out of themselves and out of their historical situation into communion with himself, and yet in such a way that it is in and through their personal and historical situation that they hear his call.

In the context of ethical decision this means that the men who hear this call do not have to understand all the inner workings of the objective processes of history, all the so-called "causes and effects" that historians try to study, before they can be sure that they have heard the call, or before they can answer it. They do not have to carry the whole world on their shoulders like Atlas, nor pose as architects of the universe, peering over the blueprints of the entire structure before daring to make a move. They have only to make sure that their call is really from God and not the prompting of some innerworldly motive—something each individual can decide only for himself, and never for others—and then to answer the call with the courage of faith, leaving the further consequences and the larger blueprints to God. This does not mean that they can ignore all causes and consequences, for at least the more immediate causes and consequences are part of the personal or historical situation which occasions the call. It merely means that the fact that they cannot understand all the causes nor foresee all the consequences, or that some of the consequences they can foresee appear distressing, need not be the determining factor of their decision, and certainly must not be the excuse for putting off the call with endless rationalizations and sophisticated evasions. They must make their decision on the best knowledge they can get, knowing well that this is always incomplete, but knowing also that there is a strong temptation to put off action for the sake of more knowledge, when it is precisely action that may be the essence of the call.

This concept of the Christian calling also has significance for the important problem of maintaining a basic unity and peace within the Christian fellowship itself. We see how difficult it is to achieve consent with regard to specific social action where large numbers of people of assorted motives and beliefs are concerned: but what about achieving consent on specific issues within the Christian fellowship itself, where presumably the essential motives and beliefs of all the members are more or less similar? Here the same problem of being tempted into legalism or expediency to achieve assent arises in an even more acute and embarrassing form, which only goes to show that the Church is a company of pardoned sinners, an "infirmary of souls," and not a society of sinless saints. Aside from the fact of sinfulness within the Church, however, there remains the fact of honest and sincere differences of opinion among Christians on specific historical and ethical issues, and also differences of emphasis on particular aspects of the Christian revelation. Here it is possible to avoid bitter dissensions and schismatic tendencies within the fellowship of the Church by ever remembering the concept of the Christian calling. The concept of the Christian calling is the subjective, cultural counterpart of the objective, theological doctrine of the Holy Spirit, and it is altogether in keeping with the freedom and lordship of the Holy Spirit over history that he should require different things of different men, in his own time, and according to his own wisdom.

The desire of the believer, as a redeemed sinner, is that his work should increasingly be an expression of the "mind of Christ" in history, and in arriving at this "mind of Christ" he cannot in all humility do otherwise than listen to what others of the Christian fellowship think, or have thought, the mind of Christ to be. But in the last analysis he must consult Christ himself for this enlightenment. And for this reason he cannot impose his own understanding of the mind of Christ on the entire Christian community, so as to exclude those who disagree with him. The unity of the Christian fellowship can never be a legalistic unity, but only the spiritual unity of those who recognize one Lord, whatever may be his separate demands on each of them. This is sometimes very difficult to realize and to admit in the heat of action—and, indeed, the sincere differences of opinion that separate Christians over specific ethical issues must be ultimately put down to the mystery of God's way of working in the world, which can be borne without resentment only by that faith in the integrity of others which is a part of Christian love itself.

Chapter VI

FAITH AND CULTURE

Culture as artistic creativity

FOR THE PURPOSES OF THIS CHAPTER A DISTINCTION MUST BE MADE between culture and civilization in order that the discussion may be narrowed down to manageable proportions. Culture will be taken to mean the artistic creativity of man in the arts and sciences, to distingiush it from civilization, which will then be taken to mean the practical creativity of man in the realm of material and social needs.

It must be admitted that, as far as the realm of artistic creativity is concerned, very little specific help of a positive nature is to be gained by resorting to the New Testament. Both the ethical and the eschatological emphases in the Gospels and Epistles militate against the serious consideration of artistic creativity on its own merits, the whole atmosphere being one in which the question never arises. We are told on all sides that we must drop everything and follow Him. Renunciation and discipleship are the order of the day, not self-realization, or the full life. Even in the letters of Paul the admonitions concerning one's worldly calling have about them an air of watching and waiting, which suggests that while one must do one's work well, and do it for the Lord, one can hardly take it very seriously, for all this shall pass away. How much more must this lack of seriousness apply to artistic work, as against useful and necessary labors, since there is always about art an atmosphere of the ornamental and unnecessary that makes it the logical first candidate for things to be renounced? As for self-realization and the full life, it is precisely by giving them up that we gain eternal life: hence the emphasis on "choosing," "forsaking," "counting the cost." Who that can hate father and mother in order to follow Him, can fail to hate the arts first?

Still less do we find any positive suggestions for the estimation of artistic creativity when we turn to the Old Testament, considered as the background and preparation for the New.[1] Here the prophetic fight on behalf of strict, spiritual monotheism, and against all forms of image worship, puts all human artistic creativity under suspicion. And again, the emphasis on justice and righteousness in the covenant between Yahweh and his chosen people would seem to place artistic creativity in the position of either an escape from the ethical demands of the Jewish religion, or a compromise with the idolatrous cultures of Israel's powerful and prosperous neighbors. This twofold negative attitude of indifference or suspicion which we find in the Bible toward artistic creativity can be better understood if we remember that in ancient times art was never an autonomous activity as it is considered today, an end in itself, but existed largely in the service either of religion or of powerful men. The artist was a craftsman who did not necessarily express himself or his private feelings in his work, but rather fulfilled the desires and requirements of those who demanded his work—priests, kings, and wealthy men.

In the case of religion the charge of idolatry was not leveled at the artist as such, but at those who believed in the religious efficacy of the images he created at the behest of the priesthood. And in the case of art in the service of powerful men, the charge of idolatry again sought to condemn, not the labors of the artist as such, but the power and self-sufficiency of these men over against God, as manifested in worldly display of riches and ornaments. For this reason it was possible to deal with artistic creativity so simply in the Bible, either by ignoring it as unimportant or by condemning it as a vehicle of idolatry. The innocence and naïveté of the biblical writers on this subject is revealed in the fact that apparently it never even occurred to them to see artistic creativity where it is so obvious to the modern mind—in the "poetry" of so much of biblical speech itself.

In our day the situation is not so simple and straightforward, and perhaps also not so innocent. In place of the surprised and ecstatic condition of the early church, which looked forward hopefully to the end of this world, we have a thoroughly institutionalized church accommodated for indefinite survival in the midst of a thoroughly secularized culture and civilization. We have also a somewhat different attitude toward works of art, the enjoyment of which is now regarded as an end in itself, a refined form of entertainment, rather than an exposure to manifestations of religious or magical powers. Thus, while we cannot afford to ignore the warnings in the Old Testament against idolatry, and the warnings in the New Testament about "counting the cost" of eternal life, we must translate these warnings into present-day circumstances. They acquire meaning only as idolatry, and the need for renunciation, can be discerned in the actual life of today, in which neither the worship of graven images nor the life of ascetic retreat appear to be live options for many people. In this matter the Church, if it is to be the perpetually reformed Church, must be willing to be both learner and teacher, for even the most sympathetic reading of the history of the Church discloses how the Church in its relation to culture has repeatedly been betrayed into extremes of asceticism and of worldliness, not only by the direct influence of secular culture, but also by its own misinterpretation of the significance of artistic creativity.

The Church in its history has always been in various proportions simultaneously a creator, user, and denouncer of culture, thereby illustrating that the problem of culture is inescapable, and that it masquerades under the guise of quite different problems. It is not as if cultural activity were something that is left over, a leisurely pastime, after the serious issues of science, ethics, politics, and religion have been settled. All of these have an element of artistic creativity in themselves intrinsically, at the same time that they affect artistic creation externally. What is the pursuit of scientific knowledge, when it is not intended for practical application, but the creation of objects of contemplation, and hence the satisfaction of an essentially aesthetic need? And what does ethics do, as soon as it passes over into action, but reject certain portions of culture and embody itself in others? And what political theory is not in part also an epic and a mythology, which creates dramatic pictures and actions out of historical or logical abstractions? And the Bible itself—is it not like a picture book of God's dealings with men? It is simply that attention is not focused on the artistic creativity implicit in all these activities, but it is there all the same.

When attention is focused on artistic creativity where it is obvious—that is to say, on literature, painting, music, architecture and sculpture, the dance and the drama—it is possible to discern three characteristics of this kind of human creativity which are particularly revealing for theological inquiry. These are its dispensability, its spontaneity, and its expressiveness,[2] the latter including its use as a means of communication. The last of these seems to be a contradiction of the first, for surely if artistic creativity is a means of communication it must be indispensable to any people—but, as we shall see, it is the second factor, its spontaneity, that qualifies its function as a means of communication.

First as to its dispensability. There is always about artistic creativity an atmosphere of the ornamental, the luxurious, the superfluous, the not absolutely essential for existence. In fact, wherever life is being lived on the level of survival, such as among primitive people in great poverty, or among civilized people following catastrophic war or famine, artistic creativity is the first activity that can be dispensed with, at least until some energies are left over from the sheer business of maintaining life. During long adventures of hardship willingly undertaken, such as pioneering, exploration, or colonization, the energies devoted to cultural pursuits are markedly reduced, at least for the time being. When the Church is in dire straits, persecuted, dispersed, or driven underground, it cannot get along without its Scriptures, but it can dispense with music, pageantry and cathedrals. In fact whole movements of voluntary ascetic retreat, or of puritanical severity of life, can maintain themselves with vigor for long periods without benefit of the arts, because the latter apparently do not have any inevitable connection with Christian life and doctrine. During modern total warfare the arts may be used in a limited way, and pragmatically, for purposes of propaganda and recreation, but their exercise in a purely creative way is severely restricted, "put on the shelf for the duration." It would be possible to cite countless illustrations from history to the effect that a certain amount of security, leisure, and prosperity on the part of at least some portion of the population is necessary before the arts can enjoy a time of attention and growth, both as to their creation and their appreciation.

In this evident uselessness the arts themselves have taken some measure of pride. They claim to be the flower, even the finest flower, of civilization, not its roots and stem. They are not astonished when they are ignored in times of distress, and they are more than a little suspicious when someone is determined to make them useful for some ulterior purpose. Furthermore, this uselessness is taken by them to be a proof of the fact that art is an end in itself, not a means to anything else: it is an intrinsic, not an instrumental, value. Obviously it is not necessary for survival, but it may well be one of the positive joys of life that make survival worth while.

The spontaneity of artistic creativity is something which it shares to a degree with all human creativity but which it possesses to a superlative degree precisely because of the afore-mentioned dispensability. Much of human creativity in the realm of civilization is determined, as to the form and direction it will take, by the hazards and exigencies of human existence and historical circumstance, which, so to speak, "call forth" a creative response from man. But what is it that "calls forth" the creative response of artistic activity, seeing that it is not necessary for survival, nor even for a secure and comfortable life? Of course it is not the *artist* who is independent of the exigencies of human existence and historical circumstance, but rather his ability to create. The fact that artists often starve or produce potboilers in order to stave off hunger is merely sociological confirmation of the fact that true artistic creativity is both uncoercible and dispensable. The answer to the above question is that we really do not know what it is that "calls forth" the creative response of artistic activity in the first instance, and we cover up our ignorance by changing the subject and observing that some men have "talent" or "genius" in this respect and others do not. On the receptive side the spontaneity of artistic activity shows itself in the nonrational element in appreciation; in the fact that aesthetic delight cannot be commanded to appear by the dictates of reason, as though it were the answer to a problem in mathematics, but must rather grow, be nourished, trained, and developed, like a live organism. It shows itself in the fact that tastes differ, that tastes change, that tastes have a biography, so that in the end all general rules of aesthetics are general only for those with similarly developed tastes.

The expressiveness of artistic creativity is its most ambiguous characteristic and is responsible for both the use and misuse of art as a means of communication among people. No matter how carefully professional critics and theorists may try to analyze and separate the aesthetic experience from all other kinds of experience, the fact remains that works of art, simply because they exist in time and space and history, and are received by a human consciousness, always mediate information of some sort, alongside the fact that they may or may not produce aesthetic pleasure. They constitute a kind of language, of which the several different arts are different universes of discourse, and this language betrays or reveals, intentionally or unintentionally, all kinds of facts, emotions, states of mind, ideas and feelings and even historical conditions, which the ordinary literal language is incapable of communicating in the same way.

For this reason the culture of any people is considered to be a guide to the "inner life" or the "spirit" of this people, a revelation of its basic beliefs and values, which revelation, for those who can read the language, is far more honest and accurate in its portrayal of them than any abstract philosophy or ideology which they may also possess. And this is so even where its artists deliberately eschew all forms of propagandistic or religious art, even when they concentrate on the production of what they believe to be purely aesthetic goods. The use of art as a mean of communication is, however, limited by its spontaneity, which produces the variety and originality of expression which makes art inexhaustible. For in order that a language may function as a means of communication, it is necessary not only that it should have a great variety of words but that everybody should understand the words that it has. Hence there arises the problem of an elite, which consists of those who "understand the language"—that is to say, those who have developed their taste and susceptibility in new and unforeseen directions—and which excludes from communication those who have not.

The problem of human creativity as such

Now it is precisely the unnecessariness and dispensability of artistic creativity which allows us to examine for its direct theological significance that aspect of human activity which it is so easy to overlook in other creative efforts because of their involvement in matters of practical or moral urgency. This is the sheer fact of human creativity itself. The question may be paraphrased in the words of the psalmist: What is man that God should have given him such a preeminence over the creation that he, by a creativity of his own, is able to change it, to his own and God's joy and sorrow? For that is what is involved in human creativity: man, himself a part of God's creation, using God's creation as the raw materials of his own creations. It is almost as if God, in creating over against himself a creature who is also in his own way a creator, had permitted the initiative in creation to pass out of his hands. Yet this initiative is always there, hidden in the fact that man, even as a secondary creator, is himself created by God.

In the sphere of civilization what is involved in human practical creativity is the free play of imagination, intuition, feeling, will, and reason over the "givenness" of the creation, with the intention of discovering how it will allow itself to be used or changed for the fulfillment of human needs. The same is true of artistic creativity, except that it is a special set of needs that it attempts to meet. In either case, whether attempting culture or civilization, man as creator must first of all be a learner. He must know what is, before he can imagine what could be or what ought to be. This is the sign of man's own creatureliness, that he does not create out of nothing, like God, but only out of something already created given to him. Even the "needs" which he attempts to meet with his creations, and which in a sense determine their nature, are a part of the givenness of the situation.

Now it is a characteristic of artistic creativity, as against practical creativity, that it is a little less conscious of its creatureliness, of its dependence on the givenness of both the materials and the needs, than practical creativity, and this is because of the almost playful, joyful, and certainly impractical nature of the need it serves. If we call this need, for the moment, the need for beauty, it is easy to see how the creation of new and beautiful forms out of shapeless materials might seem a little closer to that *creatio ex nihilo* of God than the making of bread out of wheat to satisfy hunger. And it is precisely in this partial release from the consciousness of creatureliness that men find many of the values they assign to both the creation and appreciation of works of art: the soaring of the spirit above material involvements and petty passions, the inward peace and serenity of contemplation, the feeling of fulfillment of life, of achieving an end that is an end in itself, a momentarily pure happiness.

This self-justifying and self-authenticating nature of artistic creativity (both from the side of the creator and the appreciator, for the appreciator is a kind of re-creator, one who follows after the artist and repeats at least part of the creative experience) must be considered by the unbelievers purely as a "stroke of luck," or, in the words of Santayana, one of the things which "amid a thousand vexations and vanities, make the clear profit of living." The pursuit and enjoyment of beauty has probably saved more of the unbelievers from despair than all their schemes for social salvation put together. At any rate, those devoted to its creation seem to be willing to put up with astonishing amounts of material vexations for its sake. It is well known that, because it is an end in itself, an intrinsic value, art easily becomes the open or hidden religion of any highly civilized and sophisticated people, especially in a time of such relative general security that its enjoyment becomes a reasonable expectation within the lifetime of many. Culture easily becomes not just the finest flower but the god of civilization.

But for the believer the situation is not so simple. To regard the enjoyment of beauty as a "stroke of luck" which makes an otherwise questionable life worth living is surely incongruous with the Christian understanding of life, and further to make this "stroke of luck" the basis of a new religion is only to put the whole enterprise of culture under suspicion of idolatry from the Christian standpoint. But neither is it possible for the believer to dismiss the whole realm of art as a structure of unalloyed idolatry, nor even as a daydream with which the unbelievers beguile themselves, and this is precisely because of its primitive quality as an end in itself, a momentarily pure happiness. For Christian faith there are no "strokes of luck" in the universe. There is only the mysterious providence of God, which may or may not be revealed to man. Hence, beauty known by man as an end in itself, a momentarily pure happiness, must also have its relationship to God, whether in mystery or in revelation, and a relationship to man regarded as God's creature, and a secondary creator on his own. From this standpoint artistic creativity raises two questions for the believer, an ethical question as to its basic egoism, and a religious question as to its relationship to God.

The essential egoism of artistic creativity is rooted not in any superficial conceits or temperamental airs which the artist may give himself but in the fact that he has within himself a source of self-sufficiency that is denied to most men, at least to such a measure, and which therefore cuts him off from the mutuality of human intercourse, the give and take of ordinary living in community with one's fellow men. This does not mean that he is necessarily a solitary person, or that he is self-sufficient in an external way, or that he is irreligious, or ungrateful. He may be none of these. He may be surrounded by family and friends; he may belong to a "school" and gratefully acknowledge all that he has learned from this or that master; he may be religious and even devout; he may be quite conscious of social and political problems. But in spite of all this, if he is a truly creative artist, he has something in himself that he can fall back upon when all these human and humane activities disappoint or frustrate him, and for the sake of which he may at any moment desert all of them.

The horizontal relationship between the artist and his fellow men resolves itself into the question: for whom does the artist create? It would be most gratifying from the standpoint of ethics to be able to say that the artist after all creates for his fellow men, not for himself, and that therefore the peculiar egoism basic to artistic creativity is only an accidental accompaniment of this particular type of work, a kind of occupational disease, like miner's lungs, only in this case an occupational deformity of the spirit. Unfortunately the situation is not so simple. It is true that if the artist depends on his artistic works for his livelihood, they must have some value for others beside himself, so that a degree of consideration for his fellow men is forced upon him by the laws of economics. But this need for considering the market value of his works is likely to be only an irritation and a temptation for the truly creative artist, and its ethical meaning is further vitiated by the fact that almost any person with sufficient ability to create works of art has sufficient intelligence and skill to be able to earn a decent livelihood by some other means. If the ethical meaning of earning a living is understood to lie in the fact that by this means one keeps himself from being a burden to society at the same time that one contributes useful goods and services to the needs of the community, then the artist, by his own choice, removes himself from the category of useful members of society, both because of the hazards of earning a livelihood this way, and because he could probably just as well have done something more useful. The sheer earning of a livelihood, therefore, cannot be the ethical basis for his relations as an artist with his fellow men.

Perhaps the question could be approached from the side of the artist's personal ambition. Unquestionably such motives as the desire for personal renown, public recognition, or even immortal fame, form some part, large or small, in the decision of the man who has a talent to make a career of artistic creativity, and, contrary to popular opinion in an age where false modesty is cultivated as a technique for getting on in the world, such motives are not nearly as egoistic as is generally supposed. If a man sets out to earn the approval and remembrance of his fellow men by means of the works he produces, there is presupposed in this effort, first, a sufficient esteem for one's fellow men that their approval seems worth earning, and, second, a common ground of values intrinsic in the work by means of which the approval is to be earned. When a great artist suffers from lack of recognition, as so many in history have suffered, it is not always his ego that is offended. More often, if he is humanly great as well as artistically, it is his sense of solidarity with mankind that is broken, and it is from this isolation and rejection that he suffers.

In fact, if the question be pushed far enough, it must be admitted both by the artist and the general public that the artist does not create specifically for others, and not even for himself. He creates simply in order to create. He has this urge or talent and it wants to do something, to realize itself. This means that his ethical relationship to his fellow men must be indirect—we can arrive at it only by examining the artist's beliefs about the meaning of existence, including the ultimate significance of his own creativity.

It is necessary to distingiush between two theological attitudes toward human creativity which are apparently close to each other, yet which actually represent almost the opposite extremes among the logical possibilities. There is, on the one hand, the Christian belief that all human creativity comes somehow from God, both the actual energy of creation itself and the partial human transcendence over the world which makes the creativity possible. On the other hand, and separated from the Christian conviction only by a hair's breadth as human thinking goes, there is the belief that this human creativity precisely *is* God, or, to put it another way, that God's creativity is nothing more, and nothing other, than the human creativity, and God's transcendence over the world is nothing more, and nothing other, than man's partial transcendence over the world. This belief is imbedded in many pagan philosophies and religions from the

Greek conception of God as the Demiurge, who wrestles to bring form and content out of the pre-existing, shapeless, meaningless, and resisting Chaos, to modern pragmatic, pluralistic, and realistic conceptions of a God who struggles to be born out of inert matter via the incomprehensible fact of human consciousness and human values.

The entire closeness and difference between these two conceptions of human creativity seem to be bound up with the ontological meaning of the words "is" and "comes from," between which philosophy, with its inadequate means of dealing with the transcendent, can scarcely make a clear distinction. This closeness and this difference can be seen much better by considering real life rather than conceptional formulations, by considering, for example, the theological attitudes toward their own creativity of John Sebastian Bach and Rainer Maria Rilke. Bach wrote his music for the glory of God. He knew also that the power to do this came to him from God, and that this applied to both his sacred and his secular works, that there were really no secular works in the life of one who is consecerated to God. This is the Pauline conception of a calling—that whatever gifts we may have may be employed for the greater glory of God, by our consecration of them to him. In contrast to this, Rilke, who was far from being an irreligious man, who was in fact painfully sensitive to many religious feelings, nevertheless identified his creative ability with the Divine itself, so that, in the end, he had to consecrate himself to himself, rather than his work to God.

From this there follows immediately a difference in the horizontal, or ethical, relationship between the artist and his fellow men. If all creativity *comes from* God, then before God the differences in human endowment of creativity disappear. It is the consecration that matters, and they are all of them, great and small creators, without exception, returning to God what is his own. Furthermore, they are stewards and guardians of something which is not their own to use irresponsibly, but which has been entrusted to them for a limited period under the limiting conditions of God's own love for his entire creation. But if God *is* the creativity, we are in a different world. The great mass of humanity is the manure heap of creativity, which occasionally, out of its secret chemistry, puts out some flower, but which to a large extent must remain ignorant of its own end and purpose. The artist constitutes practically a different species of humanity from the ordinary, relatively uncreative man, and he is a law unto himself. His purpose cannot be to serve his fellow men, even if he should want to, because they cannot understand him, nor to serve God, because he is the spearhead of the Divine himself. He must serve the creativity within himself, which is his essential self, using things and people as means to this end without compunction, as the situation demands.

It is scarcely necessary to comment, on the unchristian nature of this latter view of the world, yet it is an outlook that is found, perhaps not in such extreme or self-conscious form, in all the hidden religious orientation of secularism toward art, and also in the hidden diluted paganism within Christianity. This conception of human creativity is basically a romantic idea, which reveals itself in our supposedly unromantic age in the popular attitude toward the artist as a "queer" or "crazy" person, and in learned psychological disputations on the necessity for self-expression as a means to mental health. The artist who devotes himself single-mindedly to his creativity is regarded with a peculiar mixture of awe, amusement, and envy. The ordinary man may not be able to get away with such eccentricity, but for this frustration he can compensate himself by adopting a hobby. The worshipful attitude toward art of the intellectuals of our day, who regard artistic creativity as the secular analogue of the Quaker "that of God in every man," is the most direct expression of this romantic notion, resulting in the idolization of the lunatic fringe, and fanatical prostration before every new artistic "ism" that comes along.

Perhaps I have said too little here about the real suffering of the creative artist, who must, above all, travel a lonely road and take all the risks and terrors of the unknown in solitude, as though this suffering were an extenuation of the basic egoism of his preoccupation. No doubt instructive volumes could be written about the delicate relationship between egoism and suffering, using the creative artist as the revealing example, and as a warning to the rest of mankind. Our purpose for the moment, however, is not to moralize but to analyze. We are not interested here in dismissing anything because it is unchristian, nor in making excuses, but rather in learning from that which is recognizably unchristian what are the pitfalls and temptations that must be overcome in any attitude toward artistic creativity that claims to be recognizably Christian.

The aesthetic experience and its theological interpretation

In order to put any further content into the two questions raised by the dispensability of artistic creativity—the ethical and religious questions—we must turn now to its second characteristic, its spontaneity. In its original uncultivated and unsophisticated form there is something so primitive and uncalculating about the aesthetic experience that one is tempted to put it in the same class with hunger, thirst, pain, hate, sexual attraction, and anger. It is an immediate reaction or feeling in response to something in the external world, a feeling which takes the beholder by surprise. But this surprise, in so far as it is conscious, is already the work of reflection. At first it is indistinguishable from the aesthetic experience itself, and is submerged in the original innocence of human perception. The child reaches out toward the colored or shiny object with the same sure instinct with which it reaches out to the mother's breast, and takes both equally for granted.

Modern pragmatic and realistic theories of aesthetics have been preoccupied with stressing the subjective side of the aesthetic experience, proclaiming that where there is no appreciator of beauty, there is no beauty, where there is no valuer, there is no value. This is more or less in reaction to the absolutistic arrogance of romantic idealism which deifies individual predilections by writing beauty with a capital B, thereby writing it also into the structure of the universe as conceived by the romantic individual. The realists want to reduce the essential datum of the aesthetic experience to the "I like" or "I enjoy," which is, however, already a conscious reflection about the aesthetic experience, while the idealists want to make this self-conscious reflection into a communion of the absolute Beauty with itself via the individual human consciousness, a kind of cosmic narcissism in the Idea. Both of them forget that long before there is any conscious reflection on what *I* like, or on *what* I like, there is, as a prerequisite for both of these, an experience so immediate, unreflective, unintentional, and unpredictable—in other words, so spontaneous—that the division into subject and object is as yet irrelevant to it.

When men try to describe this experience directly without letting their reflection on it transform it, they have to use such unphilosophical terms as "trance" or "ecstasy," both of which stress the absence of self-consciousness, desire, or intentionality in it. In the primitive and unsophisticated form of the aesthetic experience the individual is so fused with the content of the experience (which content may very well be crude and commonplace from the standpoint of a later discrimination of taste) that he makes no distinction between the particular aspect of the world which assaults him and takes him captive and his own unthinking surrender and willing captivity. There is a kind of union between the person and the object that momentarily defies the intrusion of both self-consciousness and object-consciousness. This is especially evident in children. We say that a child is "entranced" with a toy, and we feel in that moment that he is in a different world, that he is blind to us, blind to himself, and blind to every other object in the environment except the one in which he is, as we say significantly, "completely immersed." Most of us can recall from our childhood that our early experiences of the beauty of nature were also of this sort. Suddenly, in the midst of what was perhaps later described by grownups as a "perfect day," we became aware of the loss of weight and loss of self-consciousness that accompanies the onset of sleep, and in that moment the impact upon our senses and our perception of the sheer qualitative content of the "day" became the sole reality.

With the arrival of maturity there comes both the development of individual taste and the self-conscious cultivation of the aesthetic experience for its own sake. Both of these involve a partial loss of that complete spontaneity which is characteristic of the experience in children. It is a kind of aesthetic analogue of that loss of innocence which is at the same time the fate and the original sin of mankind in arriving at manhood. The imperious "I like" arrives on the scene, along with the imperious "I want." At the same time that the powers of perception become sharpened, intensified, and more discriminating, thereby producing satiation and fatigue with earlier forms of the aesthetic experience, there arises the effort to recapture the spontaneity, an effort which expresses itself in the demand for newness, freshness, originality, and inexhaustibility in works of art. As the development of taste is largely an individual matter, depending on original endowment of perceptual sensitivity, plus the accidental or intentional exposure of the individual to specific kinds of art in greater or lesser variety and quantity, there is an increasing inability to share the experience, or even talk about it, with anyone except those who happen to have similarly developed tastes. The aesthetic judgment increasingly takes on an appearance of arbitrariness and subjectivism, more and more the form of "I like," "it moves me," or "it moves me not," instead of the form, "it is beautiful," "it is dull," or "it is profound."

It is at this point that aesthetic theory makes its appearance, or becomes important, either in the effort to show that taste is not as arbitrary as it seems, or that its arbitrariness is justifiable. The aesthetic experience is dissected and analyzed; psychology, history, anthropology, and philosophy are ransacked for clues and definitions; and, on the basis of these researches, principles are set up. These principles, however, always turn out to be the principles of the *criticism* of art, rather than the principles of art. They may be useful in the analysis, elucidation, and classification of works of art already in existence, especially those which "taste" has already considered worthy of such analysis, and they may help an undeveloped artist to pay attention to those aspects of his work which criticism takes into consideration, so that his work may meet a kind of "minimum requirement" laid down by criticism, his own included. But that these are not the principles of art is shown by the fact that no amount of aesthetic theory will tell a well-developed artist, who knows all about the minimum requirements, where his next creation is coming from, nor how he may have to mix and modify the "minimum requirements" in order to achieve the particular aesthetic effect he desires.

Likewise, no amount of knowledge of aesthetic theory, or principles of criticism, in the possession of an appreciator of well-developed taste will be able to predict, determine, or nullify his reaction to an original work of art which incidentally "obeys" all the critical rules, but which precisely makes them only a vehicle for something new, unique, indefinable, and provocative of the aesthetic experience in the observer. Thus, whether taken from the side of the appreciator or the creator, and whether taken in its primitive or cultivated form, the spontaneity of the aesthetic experience, and therefore also of artistic creativity, eludes the intellectual grasp of it, and refuses to be classified or embodied in general principles. Art, in the end, must be enjoyed rather than understood.

The fact that aesthetic experience, whatever else it may be, and whether taken in its primitive or in its cultivated form, includes the immediate enjoyment of the immediately perceived aspect of things, natural or constructed or imagined, puts the problem in terms of the meaning of enjoyment itself in human life. According to the Christian conception of God as the creator who loves his creation, who, in fact, created because of love in the first place, there can be no question but that the existence of the aesthetic experience in man is a manifestation of God's love for him. That there is beauty in the world, that there arises out of the mysterious interaction between man's perceptive ability and certain sensory aspects of natural and humanly constructed things the pure happiness which is aesthetic pleasure, can by no means, on a Christian account of things, be regarded as anything but the gift of an ever-gracious and loving God, the heavenly Father, who knows how to give gifts to his children. It certainly cannot be regarded as an accident, a stroke of luck, or an optical mirage which snares mankind to strive after an illusion. Neither can it be regarded as a trick of nature or the devil for seducing man away from the paths of virtue, as certain types of moralism seem to regard it. God does not tempt man. God did not make the earth fair in order that men might come to grief over its beauty. Rather it might be said that the beauty in the world is already the first step in God's eternal wooing of man, the first step in that gentle and infinitely patient process by which he educates man to the meaning of the divine love.

But man does not understand it this way. Coming into the world as a stranger, he soon discovers that there is much beauty and enjoyment in it, and he quickly makes himself at home in this domain of pleasure, establishing himself not so much by means of what he is actually able to appropriate for himself as by means of his attitude that all he can get is his natural birthright. It is easy to see that man might display his alienation from God through his reaction to moral obligation, for in that case something is demanded of him, which he can refuse. But in the realm of aesthetic experience nothing is demanded of him, he is given something precious for nothing, and now he really shows to what depths he is estranged from his creator, for just this generosity he cannot tolerate; this treasure cannot be a gift because it is his most private right and possession. Thus the spontaneity of aesthetic experience, which has about it all the earmarks of being the grace of God, becomes soured and turned in upon itself in the act of being appropriated by man. It becomes one with that unfortunate spontaneity with which man claims every pleasure as his own, even as his virtue and reward for being so endowed with sensuous and perceptive talents. In this way God's love is misunderstood in the world before it has scarcely begun, before there has even been raised the question of love among men which is implied by ethical obligation.

In regard to the two questions of the artist's ethical relationship to his fellow men and his religious relationship to God, it would seem that a Christian answer to these questions can be given on the basis of a Christian understanding of ethics and a Christian understanding of the theological meaning of beauty in the world. We have seen in the previous chapter, however, that the Christian ethic is not an ethic of legal relationships but an ethic of love with Christ as its criterion. If we add to this now the view that man's aesthetic experience in the world, in spite of the fact that it is constantly misunderstood and misappropriated by man, must be considered as a manifestation of God's love to man, then there begins to emerge a glimpse of what might be called a Christian attitude toward artistic creativity, both from the standpoint of the artist and the appreciator.

The artist, on this view, is a fellow worker with God in the creation of beauty, and the appreciator of human works of art is one who in this act receives a gift, a token of love, from God as surely as he does when he is moved by the beauty of nature. The creative artist is of necessity both of these at once, one who receives the gift, but in such a manner that he is able also to pass it on to others, and even to multiply it in the act of passing it on. And this view of artistic creativity is entirely in keeping with the ethics of love, for love seeks to express itself in an outward act of which the giving of gifts is the simplest and most straightforward.

We ordinarily think of Christian love to the neighbor as a concern for his bodily needs or his civic rights, but this exclusive concern is, alas, only a reflection of the sad state of the world in which such needs and rights are glaringly denied to so many. Staggered both by the quantity of misery and oppression in the world, and over our own limited capacity for love, we tend to assume that we must dole out our Christian love only to the miserable and oppressed, leaving our relationship to those who at the moment are not obviously in need of help on the secular level of attraction and repulsion. However, to those not in the needy category whom we do love, our family and close friends, we know very well how to express our love, in the gift of companionship, in the gift of mutual enjoyment of shared pleasure, and in actual gifts of works of art and other vehicles of aesthetic enjoyment.

The gift which the creative artist has to give to the world must of necessity be of a more impersonal nature, since he has no way of knowing in advance to whom it will be an actual source of aesthetic pleasure, and yet, from a Christian standpoint, he can hope that it will be that to some, and perhaps to many, that he will never know. This hope may be his "philosophy of art," if he is a Christian, a philosophy of which he may, and very likely must be, entirely unconscious in the moment of creation, when he is determined by the "rules" of his art that he has learned or discovered, and the spontaneity of the inspiration that propels him.

The fact that the artist in the moment of creation does not need any "philosophy of art" to tell him what to do does not mean that he does not need such a philosophy at all, or such a faith and hope, in the case of the Christian artist. For before and after the actual moment of creation he is still a man as other men, one who must necessarily have some doubts and reflections upon the larger meaning of his work, of what he has already finished or is planning to do. He may even in some cases consciously embody this philosophy in his work of art, and this is quite another problem from that of having the philosophy, one which will be discussed under the expressive character of artistic creativity. To summarize this section in the form of the two questions with which we began, it may be said that, from a Christian standpoint, the creative artist is related first of all religiously to God in that he is a fellow creator with God in the creation of aesthetic goods in the world, and, secondly, that by virtue of this relationship he is related ethically to his fellow men as one who receives a gift from God which he transforms and passes on to his fellow men, thus becoming the occasion by which they also receive a gift from God. In this way both the activity of the creator and the appreciator is "to the glory of God" and in fellowship with him, a relationship which, of course, ceases when the presupposition of Christian faith on the part of both parties is removed.

Culture and cultural communication

There remains to be considered the expressive character of artistic creativity. Although in actual experience the enjoyment aspect of aesthetic experience is scarcely separable from its expressive aspect, for purposes of analysis the latter must be isolated in order to throw some light on the concept of culture and the fact of cultural communication. To begin with, language itself must be regarded as an artistic product, for it is evident that the three characteristics of dispensability, spontaneity, and expressiveness apply not only to the manner in which language is used after it has been systematized but to its very origins, and to the successive stages of its development in any literature. There must have been many of our primitive forefathers who knew of the possibility of making certain sounds but preferred to remain dumb, or to limit themselves to only the most unavoidable exclamations and indications, while others took special delight, the delight, in fact, of artistic creativity, in discovering or inventing new and more satisfying sounds for expressing to themselves or conveying to others their growing fund of impressions and meanings. And every language even today has qualities that indicate the nonutilitarian, the creatively free and unpredictable, as well as the communicative aspects of life.

That language is something more than a technical device, comparable with the stone ax or the arrowhead for getting things done, is suggested in the story of Genesis, where God brings to Adam the beasts and birds "to see what he would call them: and whatsoever the man called every living creature, that was the name thereof" (A.S.V.). This *naming of the creatures* establishes men's dominion over them, and is the fountainhead of every later knowledge, but it is also a kind of practice lesson in the use of the gift of speech, which God watches with concerned curiosity, like a teacher. For the whole idea of language, the Word, the addressibility and responsibility of man, is to become the keynote of the meaning of man's life on earth and of his relationship to God.

We must begin the analysis with this basic concession, that whatever human communication is, whatever it may be found to consist of if examined closely, it exists, it happens; just to define it assumes it. But at the same time we cannot help noticing that it does not happen of necessity, and it does not happen without some human effort, and that sometimes it refuses to happen, in spite of much effort. Let us try to picture the situation in which communication between two human beings is most certain, at the same time that it is most primitively simple. It is the situation in which two men are pointing at the same object and looking at each other, perhaps uttering a sound. What becomes certain in this *dramatic act* is that both men, by their gestures, indicate that they each have the object in mind, and each man, by observing the other's gesture, realizes that the other has the same object in his mind. And this does not become certain without the dramatic act, unless they happen to speak the same language, which contains the summary of thousands of such dramatic acts passed on from generation to generation.

This is, in fact, the basic situation in which language is learned, but communication is established even if oral sounds do not accompany the dramatic gesture. The mother holds out the spoon to the child who reaches for it, and now psychology tells us that if he hears the sound "spoon" sufficiently often in connection with this act, he will inevitably associate it with this object. But what the psychologists often fail to mention is that it is the mother who must say the word "spoon" along with the dramatic act of holding it out, for it is between her and the child that the certitude exists as to what object is the center of their mutual attention. In other words, some kind of communication must have already occurred, if the sound "spoon" is to be associated by the child with the held-out object. We can hardly imagine that a phonographic record producing the sound "spoon" in the next room, perfectly audible to the child but not in the circle of attention defined by the dramatic act, would have the same effect of teaching the child the name of the object.

Generalizing this situation, we see that the communicative situation in the form of its greatest simplicity and certitude consists of two human beings plus some objective gesture. Every gesture is objective, as soon as it becomes an object to someone, an event in his field of perception. The words "objective gesture" here must be understood to indicate that the gesture is made objective through the deliberate intention of its author to establish communication. Some "object" in the world, some part of the creation, is deliberately used by the one intending to establish communication, whether this be his own body, or some object in the natural world in relation to his body (as in the pointing gesture), or some object created out of natural objects for the purpose of rendering the meaning clear. Thus anything from a glance of the eye, a facial expression, a shrug of the shoulder, to the obvious use of language and the creation of works of art, may be considered as an objective gesture, intended to convey meaning and establish communication. As such, whether it is simple, like the pointing gesture, or complex, like a poem or a dance, the objective gesture is, however, only the middle term of the communicative situation. It is flanked on both sides by the inwardness of the two human beings, the one who originates the gesture and the one who is intended to receive it, or who, at any rate, does receive it.

From this picture or image of the communicative situation, simplified though it be, we can learn several things. For one thing we can learn something of the existential meaning of culture, the meaning of culture that arises not from an abstract philosophizing over the culture that already exists but from a consideration of the basic situation of existence out of which culture arises. For, whatever else culture may be, it is, in terms of the communicative situation, the accumulation and persistence in time of the "objective gestures" of a people; it is the mark which their efforts at communication have left on the world. The pyramids of Egypt, the temples of the Hindus, the monasteries of the Middle Ages, the football stadiums of America, whatever else they may be, are, or were, in part the "objective gesture" of a people engaged in communication. Such an understanding of culture is elementary, it is only a beginning, but it is a beginning at the right place, because it avoids the creation of the abstract concept of Culture apart from life, as an entity having properties toward which we can take up an attitude or pass a value judgment. The idea of culture as the "finest flower of civilization" is such a concept, and it is some such idea that people have in mind when they demand, for example, that the Christian Church should take up an attitude toward culture, should affirm it or repudiate it. In the Middle Ages the Church did do this—it took up an other-worldly, negative attitude toward the abstract concept of culture as the finest flower of this-worldly concern—and what happened? Only another culture—the culture of the monasteries themselves, as well as that peculiar facet of the culture of all medieval life which reflected the fact that it grew up and spent its days in the shadow of the monasteries.

But if we begin with an understanding of culture that includes the ontological and anthropological "beginning" of culture in the human situation—namely, that culture is, among other things, the middle term, the "objective gesture," in the situation of human communication—we can at least formulate our question in a way that will not guarantee a false answer. We must think of culture as something unavoidable, something that will happen as long as men will try to communicate with their fellow men, and as long as men will be such beings as cannot communicate with their fellow men without involving the creation in the process, without making an objective gesture leaving a mark on the world. Then we can formulate the question somewhat as follows: What kind of culture is the present living reality of the Christian faith actually producing, both inside the Church and in its influence on secular culture, and is this culture adequate and true to the Church's message and purpose, and by what criterion of criticism and reform can it be made more so? Is the Christian culture really communicating the Christian message? In the language of theology, is there a real incarnation of the Spirit taking place? Such questions show that the problem of the Church in relation to culture is not at all a question of a well-defined, finished "something," the Church, being friendly or hostile to another well-defined, finished "something," culture. The very raising of the question in its proper form destroys the possibility of such an abstract relationshp, for it is full of implications of self-criticism, the need for self-questioning, decision, and commitment on the part of the questioner.

Using the term "expressiveness" in its broadest sense to include all possible forms of the "objective gesture" from language on up, we can say that certain epochs of history, or certain peoples, seem to have produced more richly expressive cultures than others—that is to say, cultures which, when we study them, make us feel that we actually understand the most intimate and complex thoughts and feelings of these people, who may be separated from us by hundreds of years, as well as by immense differences in the conditions of life. By this we mean that the contemplation of their culture really communicates something to us, their "objective gesture" really reaches us.

Over all these years and differences, even though it was not intended for us, their culture both reveals and betrays them to us. But in saying this we must realize that we have not advanced logically by so much as an inch, we have not defined or established anything. For we began by saying that the expressiveness of artistic creativity is that quality of its products which enables them to act as means of communication, and now we merely reaffirm this when we say that one culture is more expressive than another when it is more successful in communicating its meaning to us. But we have not succeeded in pinning down or defining that elusive and apparently arbitrary quality attached to both "expressiveness" and "real communication."

This problem cannot be entered upon here because any attempt at an answer would require a specific aesthetic theory with concrete examples from the several arts to make it convincing. But perhaps most people would agree, even without the theory, that when we say a particular work of art is "expressive" we mean that this particular work uses the special characteristics of its raw material or medium in order to manifest, show forth, enact, or delineate, a certain meaning, idea, emotion, shade of thought, or shade of feeling, in a particularly complete, adequate, simple, yet finished manner; and that it does so in a way that is not only accompanied by but mysteriously interpenetrated with, enhanced and mediated through, that happy union of the subject with his perceived object which we have called the aesthetic experience.

From this all too crowded definition it would appear that in discussing actual cultures as against the concept of culture the word "expressive" has to be used in two distinct senses, one normative and one descriptive. In the purely descriptive sense all culture is expressive, even if it expresses only the meagerness, shallowness, ineptitude, or triviality of the ideas and skills of the people who produce it. But when we say that one period of history is culturally more expressive than another, bearing in mind that culture of some sort is inevitable, we mean that certain peoples in certain periods of history have something very definite to say, and try to say it in every possible way, while other peoples and periods are vague, diffuse, disconnected, uncertain, and even poverty-stricken, both in what they have to say and the manner in which they are able to say it. So in the normative sense culture is expressive when it successfully communicates a very important and definite idea which dominates the people who produce it. But the two are not unrelated, for it seems to be the very importance and definiteness of the idea to be expressed which arouses whatever native talents there may be to an aesthetically rich and many-sided expression of it.[3]

The definite and important idea, the saying of which in many different ways constitutes the expressiveness of cultural creativity in a given cultural epoch, is the picture that man in that period has of himself, the idea of his own meaning and being that he lives by. It is the existential self-portrait of man, a portrait which includes ideas of the universe, gods and demons, natural and moral phenomena. This idea being the "what" that cultural creativity seeks to express, it is obvious why the great cultures that are studied in history are each associated with one of the great positive religions of mankind. But it is not correct, according to our analysis of the situation, to deduce from this, in a simple, direct way, either that "religion produces culture" or that "culture produces religion." It is the human effort at communication that in the first instance produces culture, and, of course, the kind of culture it produces depends in part on the "what" of the communication.

The Christian critique of culture as a critique of man

The "what" of the cultural communication being the expression of the idea that represents the existential self-portrait of man in that culture, the Christian critique of extant cultures divides into two tasks, or a single task in two sections: first, the critique of the expressed man-picture by means of the Christian doctrine of man, and, second, a critique of the "how" of the culture, the special skills displayed, forms of the imagination invented, and raw materials exploited, by means of aesthetic criteria. The fact that two distinct criteria must be applied suggests a division of labor and the calling in of experts, but unfortunately there has been too much of that already, causing a dismemberment of the very genius of culture, which is in the *union* of the theological (or simply religious or existential) with the aesthetic factors.[4] Since neither specific cultures nor specific aesthetic standards can be discussed in a book of this scope, only a few of the more general problems can be pointed out. We can indicate how the Christian doctrine of man accounts for the variety and restlessness of cultures, and throw some light on the two related questions of cultural autonomy and cultural elites.

The Christian understanding of man as a partly transcendent, partly immanent creature—a creature in the "image" of God—means that he is ultimately a mystery. The instinct for mythology feels this correctly (as against the tendency of reason to identify him with a logical abstraction) no matter how farfetched or fantastic may be the actual myths invented to interpret the mystery. But he is not a mystery in general, something vague, formless, or foggy, but a mystery in the world, a concrete, particular transcendence over a world of concrete particulars. He is a mystery that is revealed as mystery only in its interactions with the things in the world, a mystery that has relations. There are three of these, reflecting his configuration in the world. They are the relation to nature as to that over against which he stands as somehow different; the relation to his fellow men as to those like himself when he recognizes them as such; and the relation to God or gods or powers as to the source and constituent of his own mystery, which is at the same time the basic relation to himself. This he is in all stages of his development that can be called human: in fact it is these relations that he "develops." It is the mystery, acting and reacting, creating and learning, giving and receiving, in these three directions, that constitutes the life and growth of man. In biblical language, man is a creature of God placed in a world also created by God, and made in God's image, his vis-à-vis, who can meet with him, who can hear his call and answer it from his position in the world, hear and answer in and through the three relations in which he always stands by virtue of being made in God's image.

Man is this kind of being, whether he knows it or not, and even if he thinks he is something else, which for the greater part of his history he does, it is as this kind of being that he ultimately reacts even to that which he wrongly or inadequately thinks he is.[5]

What man is historically, or, rather, what particular men are empirically, the way they "behave," is the silent harmony or the silent warfare between what they think they are and what they really are as members of the category: man. This is the "cause" of that vacillation and instability of the ideals and values of men which show themselves in history as the "swing of the pendulum": between reformism and reactionism, classicism and romanticism, individualism and collectivism, authoritarianism and libertarianism, and so on. Anyone can supply his own list of extremes, in particular fields of value or endeavor, between which he has observed the swing of the pendulum. Man is, in all of these cases, much more than he thinks he is, and in the long run refuses to be strait-jacketed in any one of the ideals that he sets for himself. But—and here is the rub—he seems to be able to escape one of these strait jackets only to tie himself neatly into the straps of another, which in turn shall prove its discomfort. He is, in an expression used by Karl Barth, like a sick man tossing in his bed, who hopes that each new turn will relieve his discomfort, but the sum of his efforts is an endless restlessness. Why can't he find a "comfortable position" in the world and stay in it? Why can't he find an "ideal" of himself which would do justice to his real nature, and live accordingly? Why this rushing around from one partial and distorted view of himself to another? Why does every ideal he adopts, every pose he strikes, every attitude he takes up, however real or sincere it seems at the moment, sooner or later pall on him?

There are two answers to these questions, given by Christian doctrine. The first is the doctrine of original sin, that incomprehensible religious myth to the modern mind, which nevertheless contains such uncomfortable truth, and the second is the doctrine of God's love for man as revealed in the Christ. Man cannot find the "ideal" of himself which would do justice to his real nature, and live accordingly, because he does not *like* his real nature, it does not strike him as ideal. He runs away from it, and this is because in the freedom of his mystery he is alienated from God, not necessarily from some "idea" of God, but from the living God who made him thus. And secondly, he cannot find the "ideal" of himself to live by because his real nature cannot be represented by an "ideal" as he conceives it, a static pattern or an abstract concept, but rather by a set of living, growing relationships in the three directions in which his mystery has relations, the determining relation for the other two, the "saving" relation, being the concrete relationship of love and obedience to the God who loved him first, as revealed in the Christ.

So there is really a double alienation between man and God, the alienation of opposition and that of misunderstanding, and these two are tragically intermingled in the long history of man's various attempts to find a "comfortable position" in the world. Man is the unreconciled species, the one animal in whose face there is resentment, in whose mouth the unspoken reproach: "Why did you make me thus? Why could you not have made me a god? If I cannot be a god, I would rather be this or that or the other." Man does not want to be what he really is, and yet what he really is does not permit him to be what he wants to be, or not for long. In this contradiction man spends his days, making his peculiar demands on nature, elaborating his little religions and philosophies, organizing and conquering his fellow men, or being organized and conquered, building monuments to what he thinks is important or holy, waging war, making merry, singing, acting, posing, and always trying to be something he is not, and trying not to be what he really is. And yet through all this the grace of God is near to him, "nearer than hands and feet," nearer to him than any of his various "ideals" of himself, waiting with the patience of love for his slightest turning, for his "coming to himself" and at the same time to his true home and source of being.

It is possible to recognize the places and periods where man has momentarily (as historical time goes) found a comfortable position in his historical sickbed. It is a time of relative cultural stability. Communication among the people is so easy as to become almost unconscious. People feel at home in the world as they see it, and what they see they take pretty much for granted. It makes little difference if this cultural uniformity is the result of conquest, despotic imposition, gradual development, or the power of a ruling caste—it is the uniformity that matters, the general acceptance of it even by those who want to change some small parts of it. Herein lies the source of the close connection between governments and religions, for governments of all kinds are interested in stable power, and it is religion that supplies the dominating idea around which the desired cultural stability can be built. Hence the ever-recurring spectacle of the powerful ruler who adopts a religion and imposes it on his people, because "the people need a religion"—which is true enough, but the ruler also needs the stability, that state of taking things for granted which is produced by a widely accepted religion and its embodiment in a culture. And this also works in the interest of the institutional aspect of religion, of the priesthood and the cult. So much so that the tendency has always been for some combination of government and priesthood to "freeze" the existing religious-cultural embodiment, permit no further development for fear of upsetting the stability, and to prescribe orthodoxy in matters of faith, morals, ritual, artistic and literary expression.

Such a religious-cultural rigidity becomes in turn a menace to stability instead of its foundation, as soon as the course of events produces intercultural clashes, wars, invasions, new inventions and outlooks, sudden outbursts of creativity, intellectual and geographical pioneering—in short, anything radically and inescapably new. In such periods the truly great government is the "political" government, the government which produces stability, not by means of imposing one religion, but by adjusting the interests of many religions, encouraging mutual tolerance, and posing as the protector of religious rights. Such was more or less the attitude of the Greek city-states to religion, such was the deliberate policy of Rome in its greatness, and such has had to be the pragmatic policy, willing or unwilling, of all states since the religious wars that followed the Reformation. But the stability thus produced is something quite different from that in which there is a uniform religious-cultural outlook and everything is taken for granted. Communication between people becomes an extremely obvious, external affair—there is a great exchange of ideas, much intellectual pioneering, everybody is busy explaining himself to somebody else, nothing is taken for granted. Other conditions permitting, there is also a great deal of artistic creativity of an unorthodox, experimental sort, for some of the new ideas and feelings can be expressed only through this medium. Man is "turning over" again in his sickbed, and for the moment he is enjoying the delicious relief from his previously cramped position, and is busy exploring the special satisfactions of his tentative new position.

But in due course of time reaction sets in, the new position is not as comfortable as he thought, and besides, in turning over, he has aggravated a lot of old sores. He decides it is better to lie still, if he could only decide in which position. Men cast about for a new unifying idea, but discover that this is not so easy to find, because in the general ferment of new questions and explanations, in the much talking and little believing, real communication among men has almost broken down, and it seems as though everyone is talking to himself. At this point some unusually creative and imaginative mind is able to feel with intensity and express with felicity the precise uneasiness of this age, its peculiar ache or cramp, the particular direction in which it feels the need for change; and it is between him and the collectivity of isolated questioners that a real communication is set up. He becomes the genius of his age, the one who represents and expresses the *Zeitgeist*, the nucleus of an original unifying idea, a new philosophy or religion or mixture of the two, or a new interpretation of an old religion. Through him communication among men is gradually reestablished as the new "position" becomes articulated in many different ways. His success is due not to the evident "truth" of the new position, although it is as such that it recommends itself to the intellectuals and through them percolates to the people, but to the intensity of the need for both change and unity, a general change in the same direction, a swing of the pendulum. But in a sense his success *is* due to the "truth" of his position, however fragmentary this truth in itself may be, for it is due to the revolt of man's real nature against the distorted "ideal" of it that has been frozen into the old, traditional uniformity, the recent religious-cultural synthesis: and this in spite of the fact that the "ideal" of man's real nature that is included in the new position is just as distorted, but in a different way, as that in the old.

If this is in part the "story" of culture, this restless exploration by man of various "positions" in the world and their creative expression and communication through language, literature, art, philosophy, religion, and social institutions, it is obvious that from a Christian standpoint actual cultures can never be regarded as simply good or bad or even as accidental by-products of something else. They cannot be regarded as simply good, not even in their creativeness and in the fact that in this they share in God's creativity, because it is obvious that man is determined to use this creativity for his own ends, that he is determined not to be what God intends him to be, but to use his creativity precisely in devising all kinds of "ideals" of what he thinks he would like to be and in expressing these in his cultures. Nor can they for this reason be regarded as simply bad, or sinful, for throughout all these restless researches it is the real man, the child of God as God created him, that is looking for something, wandering over the earth, creating, exploring heaven and probing the mystery of creation, looking within and without, catching the eyes of his fellow men doing the same, getting tired and building himself a cultural world-house to settle down in, only to become restless again and to resume his search.

And neither can cultures be regarded as indifferent or accidental; rather, it is man's fate to express himself culturally, he cannot escape it, for he is such a creature as cannot even try to understand himself without betraying himself. Culture is neither good, bad, nor indifferent, but revealing, and revealing of the specifically human. The believer who is so inclined should study cultures with a mixture of imaginative sympathy, critical skepticism, reverent awe, and serious self-questioning. How can one regard a culture like that of ancient Egypt, its dignified, monumental art, its enthrallment by despotism and the tomb-cult, and its clever solutions to many practical problems, with anything but admiration, horror, and humility? How human they were, precisely in imagining themselves to be inhuman, passionless, statuesque, unchangeable, and, in their rulers, immortal! But something more than this outsider attitude to culture is involved in every study of cultures that is to be more than mere entertainment, and that is precisely the self-questioning that is the requisite of being oneself a creator and participator in a culture, of being inescapably on the inside of some culture, its growing edge. For the believer this means a critical as well as sympathetic study of the kind of culture that has been produced under the influence of the Christian faith, both inside and outside the Church, with an eye both on corruptions and distortions, as well as on positive embodiments of doctrine and practice that might affect the future.

Cultural autonomy and the cultural elites

Two points of current importance for the Christian critique of culture are the question of the autonomy of cultural creativity and the problem of cultural elites. These two points are not unrelated, for they both involve what we have called here the spontaneity of artistic creativity. The autonomy of cultural creativity can best be imagined in terms of extremes: at the one extreme there is the situation where the powers that be, church or state, a victorious political party or a despotic dynasty, simply dictate to the creators of culture both the form and content that their creations shall take, prescribing theme and style for the glorification of the reign of the power in question. Those who think that such cultural dictatorship ended forever with the end of the medieval church hegemony in the Renaissance and Reformation should think of the Republican art of the Reign of Terror in France, and of National Socialist and Soviet art of the present age, to remind themselves that this particular display of power is a temptation which no ruling caste can resist.

At the other extreme there is cultural anarchy, in which every specialized branch of creative activity pursues its own development in disregard of the others, showing much originality and experimentation in certain directions, and a total lack of any sense for the meaning of the whole or even interest in it. This is likely to be a time of general transition, and a time for the flourishing of the elites—that avant-garde of every creative movement which is totally sure of its sole importance, incapable of making itself understood to outsiders, and proud of its consequent exclusiveness.

It is to be supposed that somewhere between these two extremes there lies an "ideal" middle position, an Aristotelian moderation, but this it would be most difficult to define, for one would instantly encounter the question—for what, or for whom, is the cultural situation to be made "ideal"? For the creators of culture the situation is more nearly ideal in the state of anarchy, because then they have that complete freedom which the spontaneity of artistic creation demands. For the people in general, the situation of dictatorship is more nearly ideal, for in that case the largest number of them actually understand what the culture of the day is trying to say. It may be forced on them, and it may be of a mediocre quality, but by the same token it actually performs the function of human communication which is one of the primary reasons for its existence. The middle therefore represents a compromise for both sides rather than an ideal for either.

Now it so happens that the Church, if it is to be true to its message, must also take a somewhat middle position on the question of cultural autonomy. This position is not, however, a mere quantitative "golden" mean between extremes in the sense of the Aristotelian moderation for moderation's sake but rather that concrete and particular moderation that results from a vigilant, conscientious awareness of man's sinfulness, his creatureliness, and his wholeness. This kind of moderation is the core of true Christian humanism, which will not allow man to make himself either subhuman or superhuman, as he is constantly tempted to do in his alienation from God, but insists that he remain simply human, a child of God made in the image of God, as God intended him to be. In this kind of humanism it is not man who is the measure of all things, for, as we have seen, in his "sick" condition he is scarcely capable of taking his own measure, but rather it is God's intention for man that is the measure of all things. To recognize that every field of cultural endeavor must be allowed a relative autonomy to develop according to its inner discipline and genius, at the same time that the understanding and evaluation of it must be governed by reference to the totality of human needs and possibilities, is not to counsel Aristotelian prudence but to insist upon respect for the true nature of men as Christian faith understands it.

In the present age it is both academic and misleading to talk about the Church's "granting" autonomy to cultural activity, for, in so far as this autonomy is a matter of legal right, true cultural creativity will seize it, by violence, if necessary, and, in so far as it is a matter of personal conviction of truth and validity, only a genuine conversion could change it. The Church, then, must follow the slow, unspectacular dual task of conversion and the cultural embodiment of its own faith, on the one hand, and of constant study and criticism of the general cultural activity of the age, on the other.

On the one hand, there must be Christians who are not Christians by accident and poets, artists, scientists, or philosophers by intent, nor Christians by intent and poets, artists, scientists, or philosophers by accident; but who are both in one breath and by one calling. These are the ones who will produce the Christian culture of the future, if there is to be any, and this without regard to the question of whether or not their subject matter is specifically religious.

On the other hand, there must be some Christians who devote themselves to the task of understanding and criticizing all cultural activity, past and present, secular and religious; first understanding by virtue of special talents and sympathies, and then criticizing from the standpoint of a believing interpretation of man's real nature and destiny. These are the ones who will help preserve the Christian culture of the past, such as deserves it, and to point lessons for the future for those who have eyes to see and ears to hear.

But real understanding there must be, and this means a real entering into, and participation in, the live and growing movements of the day. And this constitutes the danger of living in two worlds, the danger, on the one hand, of losing one's faith by complete submergence in the secular world, and the danger of losing one's faith in another way, by complete isolation from the secular world. The salt must not lose its savor, and yet it must be the salt of the *earth*, else it is just as useless as if it had lost its savor.

Perhaps at the present time it is safe to say that, as far as cultural creativity is concerned, it is better for the Church to err on the side of "falling" for some newfangled idea that turns out in the long run to be untenable or unfruitful than to err on the side of cultural isolation for the sake of maintaining "purity of faith." For the Christian Church, in the power of a living relationship to a living God, can always repent and reform, and having done so, it is in a better position to lead others away from the fallacious idea than a petrified orthodoxy, to which every new idea is totally irrelevant, as well as totally unintelligible. There is altogether too much concern within Christianity over making the Christian faith "invulnerable" from the outside, especially as this invulnerability is usually thought to lie in rigid theological definition, legalistic morality, and strategic retreat from the growing edge of every realm of thought and action, instead of such invulnerability's being grounded in the sufficiency of grace, the power of endless renewal and redemption which is the activity of the Holy Spirit in history. On the contrary, a vigorous faith should greet each new idea, or cultural "ism," not with fearful and suspicious dislike, as if God were about to be dislodged from his throne by it, but rather with a calm curiosity, a healthy skepticism, and an adventurous sympathy, in the sure knowledge that not only will God survive the most pompous idiocy invented by men, but also under the suspicion that he might well be able to turn it to purposes known only to himself.

As to the question of cultural elites the Christian faith is in the enviable position of possessing a better answer to this problem than any other religion, or any secular philosophy, has possessed, or could invent. For consider the nature of the problem: it reduces basically to this, that human beings are truly different from one another in some respects, at the same time that they truly have something in common, an inescapable likeness. This simple fact has caused the endless opposition and mutual exasperation, in recent history at any rate, of the theoretical equalitarians versus the theoretical aristocrats. We are still living on the crest of an equalitarian wave which began in the Age of Reason just preceding the French Revolution, as witnessed by the fact that nowadays a totalitarian regime still has to establish itself by making some excuses to the equalitarians, such as a national emergency, war, or the promise of establishing even greater equality in the future.

But signs of the cracking of theoretical equalitarianism are found all over, especially among those people who are concerned with the decadence or survival of Culture with a capital C. These doubting Thomases of equalitarianism, no matter how democratic their political sentiments may be, cannot help observing that a thorough practical application of equalitarianism in society has a devastating effect both on the quantity and quality of the cultural products of that society. There is, first of all, the simple statistical fact, to be recorded without evaluation, that every society has its "best minds," its "average minds," and its "simplest minds," and if equalitarianism is its governing philosophy, its culture must be addressed, or made available to the simplest minds, even if it has been created by the best minds. Now it is a fact that the kind of culture that is handed down through history from age to age is mostly the kind that was created by the best minds of all time, and becomes a kind of international property, whereas, the kind of culture that is originally created by the average or simpler minds—that is to say, "folk culture," which may be of excellent quality—is almost always handed down on a national, racial, or even family and tribal basis; it never becomes international property. In the sense of folk culture what has the Kansas farmer of today in common with the man who tilled the soil in the time of Socrates? Very little—but this should not drive us inevitably to the conclusion that it is with Socrates himself that the Kansas farmer must have the most in common. And yet this is precisely the conclusion which the theoretical equalitarians draw from their politically grounded doctrine that all men are created equal before the law. The culture which was created by the "best" minds must be forced down the throats of the average- and simple-minded, in a popularized form, cutting the nerve of their initiative in creating a genuine cultural expression of their own, filling them full of half-digested, bastardized, and commercialized bits of snob-appeal culture, and at the same time giving them an inferiority complex for not being able to take it straight.

This is the so-called "mass" culture of today, which grinds out its endless pork-sausage imitation of the real thing through the large-scale media of mass college education, movies, radio, television, newspapers, magazines, and best-selling books; and which incidentally turns the delicate stomachs of the theoretical aristocrats, who claim to speak on behalf of the "best" minds. The latter claim that something is genuinely lost in this artificial attempt to make the "highest" creations of culture available to the simplest minds, and, in their angry reaction to this process, they become more consciously esoteric than ever, more than ever devoted to the deliberate creation of a culture that is unintelligible outside a small elite that has to be initiated into its secrets. Thus, what we get out of this practical application of the equalitarian theory is not at all a culture created by the best minds for the sake of all, including the simple-minded—and incidentally this would not be so bad if it were possible, if the best minds actually created for the simple-minded, or as if they themselves were simple-minded, for then we would have a good culture on the "folk" pattern. But this just does not happen. What happens is that two cultures arise, the mass culture and the elite culture, and both are to some extent spurious. They derive their separate character, their distinguishing marks, not from an inner creativeness or individuality, but from being in an artificial and hostile relation to each other.

Now there is nothing in itself wrong or damaging to society in there being two cultures, or even several cultures in a given society, nor even in there being an elite, or several elites. As a matter of fact, it is perfectly natural that there should be these differentiations in culture, since it is the outcome partly of the natural differentiation among peoples, partly of the spontaneous character of cultural creativity. The mischief of hypocrisy and spuriousness arises when the natural differences are "evaluated" according to some theoretical scale of values, some doctrine of the political, social, or theological gradation of people. This is what we run into when we consult the theoretical aristocrats, to see if they have any better solution to the problem of human difference and human likeness than the theoretical equalitarians. For the aristocrats, although they insist on the recognition of differentiation in people, do not do this in an objective, matter-of-fact manner, as a biologist would recognize the infinite yet classifiable differentiation of plants and animals, but rather in such a way that their own "species" or differentiation is without question placed at the top of a scale of superiority, and all others arranged beneath it in descending degrees. These are the aristocrats of "ability," who are supposed to be an improvement over the aristocrats of blood or family.

The aristocrats of ability talk a great deal about the "organic" structure of society, comparing society especially to the human body, with the "best minds" corresponding to the head, the "working classes" corresponding to the hands and feet, and so forth. But let us see how the sinful pretentiousness of man creeps into even this plausible analogy of human society. First of all, it is assumed that the "best minds" will also have the best *intentions* for the general welfare of society—as a last resort one can always appeal to their enlightened self-interest, which, being more enlightened than the average, will be a more powerful social force. The head, it is assumed, will do nothing to damage or impair the limbs of the body, but only concern itself with their happiness as limbs. This is not true even in the case of the human body. The head *uses* the limbs for its own purposes, and often enough damages the whole body, including the head, either through willfulness, stubbornness, or carelessness in pursuing its desires. In fact the proper functioning of the body, whether for good or for ill, assumes the complete will-less-ness and submission of the limbs: a man cannot even walk to the post office if his legs should decide to take a walk in the country because this makes them happy.

Thus the seemingly harmless differentiation according to ability, on this analogy of the body, would develop into an absolute reign of terror, if the "best minds" of any society could agree on what it is they want to do, and into civil anarchy if they couldn't. The whole concept of the "organic society" is only the disguised will-to-power of a group within that society, and it does not much matter whether it is the "head" or the "limbs" that aspire to complete domination of the whole. Those who naïvely and rationalistically assume that an aristocracy of ability would be an ideal pattern for society if it could be made to work should ask themselves by what particular human ability they should most like to have their lives enslaved. For it is no mitigation of this system of society that there is equal opportunity for all to develop their ability, or to pass from one class to another freely, because if this system is to function, there must be complete submission at each freely chosen level to the highest level. It is no use putting the "best minds" at the top if no one listens to them.

Secondly, there is the question of the "best minds" themselves—just what is it that they really want to do? Does this classification include artists, poets, philosophers, and scientists, or merely engineers, technicians, and political experts, and, if so, do the former really want to govern society, or do they want to be left alone to pursue their studies and do their creative work? Suppose that the classification: best minds, average minds, simple minds, is a misleading classification altogether, attempting to represent a real difference in kind as a mere difference of degree? Suppose this kind of classification is like trying to arrange apples, oranges, and pears on a scale of goodness, or even on a scale of usefulness? That such is possibly the true nature of the differences among men is something which neither the equalitarians nor the aristocrats can admit, because by this the first would lose their claims to equality, and the second their claims to superiority. In fact, these two theoretical factions are not so opposed as they appear to be—they both labor under the delusion that mankind can be classified under a theoretical abstraction in degrees, and they support each other in this delusion. The equalitarians play into the hands of the aristocrats by insisting that all men are potentially capable of becoming "superior," as this term is understood by the aristocrats, and hence must be given the opportunity to do so, while the aristocrats simply point to existing differences among men and insist on interpreting them as differences of value, thus playing back into the hands of the equalitarians by giving them a scale of values to the top of which all may equally aspire.

But a Christian understanding of man sees nowhere in the world either "superior" individuals or "inferior" individuals, or "equal" individuals. It sees only different people, different in the mysterious providence of God, and within each differentiation only honesty or dishonesty, openness or dissimulation, self-indulgence or self-discipline, obedience or rebellion, a happy or an unhappy relationship with God. Christian equalitarianism has nothing to do with human talents or potentialities, but only with every man's addressibility by God and responsibility to him, with the equality of men that is constituted by the fact that they are all equally God's property. And Christian conceptions of the "orders" of society have nothing to do with aristocracy, but only with the needs of human life in community, and the different ways in which one can serve his fellow men. Compare, for example, Paul's use of the body as an analogy for the community of the Church with that of the aristocrats for their "organic" society. Here there are no "best minds" at the head, and "simplest minds" to do the work of the feet, but all are members of one body, of equal importance in its work, and Christ is its head. This Pauline analogy will do well for the Church as a supratemporal institution, but for the more mixed and inclusive relations of a society that is in the process of becoming Christian a better model would be that of the family. In any large family whose members are joined by genuine family love, the family tie is deeper than individual differences, and is able to support, permit, and encourage these differences. The mere fact that people are different is no problem, as soon as we are willing to let them be different, as on a Christian view of creation, and in a spirit of Christian love, we must be willing.

In so far as cultural elites represent the getting together of like-minded people for mutual edification and support in the pursuit of a common interest, Christian love will not only permit and support them but will defend their right to do this against all abstract theories that wish to reduce men to identical interchangeable items, or cogs in a machine, or parts of an organism. Such a cultural elite would be simply a group of people who have concentrated their creative energies in a given direction or on a given problem; who in communication with each other about it have developed a set of concepts and a language which they understand because they have developed it, and which perhaps others can understand if they wish to follow its development, but not otherwise; and who themselves feel that such a group is a help, and not a hindrance, to the particular kind of creativity that propels them. Not all creative persons will want to belong to such a group, since not all creativity is stimulated by such an interchange, sometimes rather being dissipated by it. But in so far as such a group represents the withdrawal of a select few from the rest of mankind for the purpose of producing something that is intentionally unsharable, Christian love will feel moved to break down such a group, either from within by understanding it better than it understands itself, and making every effort to communicate this understanding to others, or from without by attacking it with legitimate satire. A true cultural elite, motivated purely by considerations for the inner discipline of creativity, must be *resigned* to the possibility of being misunderstood, but never proud of it, and never quite at ease about it, never quite sure that it is not partly its own fault, its own ineptitude, that makes it misunderstood. And yet, it need not grow desperate over the possibility of being misunderstood, desperate to the point of compromising its creativity to ensure an understanding public, if it has a Christian understanding of the real differences among men, and knowledge of the power that both affirms and overcomes them.

Chapter VII

FAITH AND HISTORY

The problem of historical truth

THE SEVERAL REALMS OR ASPECTS OF LIFE CONSIDERED IN THIS BOOK SO far have already involved us in history, giving us sidelong glimpses of it from different angles. This chapter will take up that aspect of history in which it is regarded in its totality as a single chronological development, or as a panorama stretched out in time and viewed from a high place. The study of history is always partly a search for evidences in support of this or that principle of the interpretation of history, and partly an attempt to get at the bare facts of what actually happened in the past. But, prior to such reflection, history is also simply the recorded memory of the human race, and as such it provides human life with a dimension that is equal in kind, only larger in scope, to the dimension of life represented for each individual by the memory of his own past life. This dimension of life, the memory, is an aspect of man's transcendence over nature, and is found wherever life is being humanly lived, so that not even the most primitive tribe is without some story, folklore, or legend concerning its past.

We teach our children history, not so much because we expect them to learn any lessons from it, or to philosophize over it, but because we feel they should have a background against which, and in continuity with which, the foreground of their lives in the present can be lived. A person who could manage to grow to maturity in total ignorance of history, even the history of his own nation or tribe or locality, would be like a person suffering from amnesia concerning his own life, an embarrassment of the whole personality which fortunately can be more easily remedied in the former case than in the latter. About such a person we could say, quite as correctly as about the victim of amnesia, that he does not know who he is. For no man is born into the world in general, or into general history, but into this particular place and that particular time, and this very particularity is constituted in part by the history of that place up to that time. Who I am, or who you are, is a question that cannot be answered without reference to geographical, national, and social background, language and culture, all of which imply their history. For this reason there is in man a curiosity about history which is not interested in passing judgment on the past, but simply in reconstructing it as fully as possible to satisfy its own hunger for knowledge.

Two facts about history taken as the recorded memory of the race must be noted before we can turn to the problem of historical truth. These are its irrevocability, and its operativeness in the present. Nothing would seem to be so futile an effort as the attempt to undo the past, and yet, because of the operativeness of the past within the present, every effort to change the present is also in some sense an effort to undo the past. Man feels the irrevocability of the past as a kind of fate, or destiny, but its operativeness in the present he feels as a challenge to his freedom, which challenge, the moment he takes it up, results in more irrevocable acts, and hence in the accumulation or growth of more historical destiny or fate for him. Man, in freedom, and challenged by fate, creates more fate, which in turn challenges his freedom. This is the peculiar situation of man as a historical creature.

A real feeling for the irrevocability of the past and its fateful operativeness in the present does not arise in man, however, merely from the study of history that is prompted by curiosity or the disinterested quest for knowledge. History as it is taught in school, a series of dates, battles, invasions, treaties, reigns of kings, memorable events strung out in chronological order—this so-called objective history is incapable of arousing in the student of it any feeling other than the mild or lively interest produced by any other boring or entertaining narrative. It is no wonder that young people are by and large bored by the facts of history, unless they happen to be entertained by a teacher who makes it his business to make history entertaining. For whether they are bored or entertained, in neither case are they really *concerned* about history, for they still live under the illusion that they are living their own lives, and can continue to live them, independently of history. They are, at that stage of their lives, much more aware of their freedom than of their fate. And it is only through the accumulation of events in their individual lives that a consciousness of fate can begin to dawn upon them, as they realize how every free act on their part is resisted, limited, or deflected by the historical medium in which, and against which, it is launched.

Nations living side by side, which have had a turbulent history in common, but which would like to make a new start, establish a new policy, even sign a new treaty, discover that history is not as easy to forget as they thought, and that it keeps cropping up in the most subtle and unexpected ways to frustrate the efforts of the present generation. Individuals who identify themselves with some cause or movement in their nation or in the world, or even in their home town, discover that it is not enough for a cause to be good or reasonable to insure its success, but rather that the very historical circumstances which gave rise to it and with which it must do battle may fatefully change the purposes which were its original intention, and give rise to consequences that could not have been foreseen by the originators. And individuals, living what they believe to be their individual lives, find their "best-laid plans" often gone astray, and that not by accident or failure, but by a concatenation of events in itself quite understandable, and appearing even with the inevitability of a design, but quite unmindful of the individual's own designs for his life. It is in this way, and not by the scholarly study of history, that man becomes aware of its irrevocability, and its operativeness in the present, which means that he becomes aware of it as *his* history, as the extension and medium of his own individual life.

Scarcely any age of the past has been as prolific in the production of a variety of historical attitudes as the present age, nor has any other age reached such an intensity of self-conscious historicism as that which developed after the Enlightenment. Inductive logic and empirical research, the two tools that had been forged by the Age of Reason and had proved so successful in the investigation of nature, were turned upon the subject matter of history in the confidence that, by their aid, real, objective history was about to be able to be written for the first time in history. The whole concept of history itself was changed. It was no longer to be a selective remembering and describing of supposedly significant isolated events, interlarded with and supported by the private political, metaphysical, and religious predilections of the historian, but rather it was to be the impartial, objective, and documented reporting of everything that has happened in the past, without favor or emphasis, and presumably without any perspective other than that of scientific curiosity.

This meant that the subject matter of history was immensely enlarged, for, instead of political and national events constituting its main topic, literally everything was now brought into the historian's scope—economics, geography, climate, population, education, anthropology, cultural and religious institutions—according to the reasoning that a sufficiently objective mind provided with sufficiently comprehensive data could discover the most astonishing causal connections where none had been suspected before. The abundance and reliability of all evidence was to be carefully documented, and probabilities estimated in the same way as in the natural sciences. In fact, history was to become a science, the science of the past, or the scientific reconstruction of the past, a kind of paleontology of man's more recent epochs on this planet. In this way history was to become not only the most comprehensive of the social sciences but also the laboratory and source book of the verification of all of them.

With this naïve dream of the eighteenth and nineteenth centuries we shall concern ourselves here no further, because we have already discussed in Chapter IV the question of the possible scientific character of the social sciences, and all the difficulties noted there would apply even more to history considered as a social science, because of its greater comprehensiveness. There may still be a few people today who think of history as a science, but they are probably worrying about the honesty and impartiality of the historian, as if that alone were enough to transform any study into a science, or else they have lost all realistic conception of what a science involves, and are using the word as a slogan. But the fact that the study of history went through a pseudo-scientific stage at the beginning of this era has left its imprint upon historiography, both in the development of "schools" which reflected the special interests of the several social sciences, such as economics, sociology, geopolitics, and in the development of historical attitudes opposed to the thinking of these schools and interested in establishing the writing of history on a deliberately and consciously nonscientific basis. The former we may call the positivists or the sociological historians, for, whether or not they call their efforts a science, their thinking on history is influenced by a positivistic attitude and the emphasis on sociological factors; and the latter we may call the aestheticians or the metaphysicians, for they are interested in making a "pattern" out of the reasonably certain events in man's historical past.

The aestheticians and metaphysicians in historiography have reacted rather violently against the claims of the positivists or empiricists that history can be made into a science, and they have pointed out not only the huge discrepancy between the subject matter of history and that of natural science, and the impossibility of treating it with anything remotely approaching the scientific method, but they have also pointed out the fact that even if we know all the facts of history with scientific accuracy, the question of making "sense" out of these facts would not be facilitated simply by faithful adherence to the scientific method.

History is first of all a reconstruction. An element of imagination and artistic creativity is therefore inevitable and indispensable for any kind of historical writing at all, so that the so-called ideal scientific historian, who is so impartial and unbiased that he refuses to exercise either his imagination or his judgment, and merely wishes to record facts like a machine, would be paralyzed from the outset, the moment he began to examine the verifiability and reliability of the first historical datum. This ideal historian would simply have nothing to say about history. The most he could do would be to collect and preserve or describe the available accounts of what is purported to have happened: journals, state papers, newspaper articles, military communiques, treaties, birth certificates, memoirs, archeological remains, without making any claims for their relative veracity or their causal connections—but in that case we would not call him a historian, but a keeper of the archives. Every actual historian, no matter how great his desire to be impartial, finds it necessary at every moment to exercise imagination, selection, evaluation, guessing, generalization, logical deduction from incomplete evidence, picturization, verbalization, deliberate omission—all this and more with regard to every datum and every claim that comes into his ken, just in order to set forth "what happened." But then, in addition to this, he has to exercise all of these faculties all over again in order to assign plausible causal connections with regard to "what happened"; otherwise his history will still not make any sense, or it will be a hodgepodge, in which the reader is expected to supply the causal connections himself.

The category "what happened" has in it an ambiguity, as if all events could be equally well understood simply by being equally well described. Let us examine a little more closely the concept: what happened. A traffic accident occurs; the police arrive on the scene; and from the configuration of the vehicles and the bodies, plus the accounts of eyewitnesses, if any, plus their knowledge of the laws of nature, the police try to reconstruct "what happened." From the standpoint of the traffic law a description of this event such that it would yield a reasonable certitude as to which party made the first false move is all that is needed, and all further attempts to understand more fully "what happened" are simply dropped. But there is literally no end to the variety and scope of causal connections that could be traced by an inquiring mind from this so-called accident, beginning with the mental state of both drivers, involving the whole nature of man and the world, and ending nothing short of such questions as providence, destiny, fate, God. Thus the question of "what happened" becomes the question of the comprehensiveness or sketchiness of the description of the surrounding and antecedent conditions of the event, or a question of where to draw the line at which description is considered sufficient to become explanation.

Every historian has to decide where to draw this line, where to stop the description and explanation both of events and their causal connections, and it is into the repeated making of this decision that there enter the many vague and subtle predisposing factors that constitute his conscious or unconscious, stated or assumed, historical attitude. Strictly speaking, the historian cannot even begin to write the history of anything unless he already has some idea of the kind of categories of explanation he is going to use, as well as of the kind he definitely means to reject or ignore. And if he expects his history to have any logical consistency at all, merely to be readable as a narrative, he is pretty well forced to adhere to the same general category of explanation throughout, and to refrain from jumping around between one category and another, referring, say, one event solely to economic conditions, another to the will of God, and a third to the operations of evolution.

Almost all historians, whether this is consistent with their avowed philosophy or not, adopt the journalistic expedient of describing and explaining human events in terms of human wills, desires, and actions, at least at the outset, because that is the most easily understandable explanation to one human being of anything that another human being does. It is only later, in reflecting or speculating over the merely human causes of any event that has been described, that these are generalized or abstracted into the "forces" of this or that, the actions of large, impersonal "causes" or conditions. This is partly due to the limitations of the process of narration itself, the verbalization, simplification, and summarization necessary to describe the activities of large masses of people. There is no escape from this limitation of a verbal attempt to convey a nonverbal reality. Even the most journalistic and objective historian has to describe a battle in terms of the "powers" on each side, the "English" or the "rebels," or some other abstraction, since he cannot give the individual desires and motivations of each soldier. And yet, when it comes to assigning causes and tracing relationships, it is these abstractions that become the terms of the thesis, rather than the myriad individual motivations that must have contributed to the event.

Here the difference between "nature" and "history" as subject matter whose truth we wish to investigate comes into evidence. An event in which even a single human agent is involved must include the human motivation as part of its description and explanation, or it is incomprehensible. For example, in any story dealing with a murder mystery the "mystery" is not solved unless both means and motivation are indicated, for if the means alone are made ever so clear, but no motivation is indicated, the murderer must be adjudged insane, which is only another way of saying that a human act cannot be "explained" without reference to motivation even if insanity has to be appealed to as a type of abnormal motivation. History is the story of human acts, whether sane or insane, and hence history must be the reconstruction not only of means but of motivations, and this is where, as the aestheticians and metaphysicians of history-writing maintain, history passes over into literature, and this literature itself passes over into philosophy, theology, and mythology, according to the individual historian's basic beliefs. For while the reconstruction of the means of any event is challenging enough to all the scientific and logical faculties of the historian, and even in the presence of much objective evidence requires the exercise of considerable imagination and judgment, the reconstruction of motivation is dependent on the total personality, the humanity, the depth and breadth of sympathy, the capacity for vicarious experience, the talent for expression, and other subjective characteristics of the individual historian.

History, then, is inescapably literature. It is creative writing which takes as its point of departure certain objective evidences of varying reliability, and seeks to reconstruct on the basis of these, or at least not in contradiction to them, a plausible "story" of what happened in the past. To raise the question of "historical truth," therefore, means to raise the question of truth on many different levels—on all the levels of knowing, interpreting, imagining, and believing that are involved in any literary enterprise.

One man's history may be unusually faithful in the consideration and analysis of objective evidence, documents and such, but its analysis of human motivation may seem to others to be superficial, oversimplified, or prejudiced. Another man's history may be again faithful to the facts as far as they go, but the motivation may be so twisted or generalized as to lend support only to his special philosophy of history while discrediting all others. Still a third historian may have such deep insight into human nature, and such an imaginative command of the supposed situation, that he can make out a very convincing story where the objective evidence is most uncertain, if not nonexistent. Still another may use history to adumbrate and illustrate an inspiring philosophy of one kind or another, but only by taking great liberties with the objective evidence, or by introducing large abstractions that cover so much ground that by means of them one can prove anything. And so it goes. In raising the question of historical truth, one finds that historical truth must of necessity include and contain every other kind of truth: scientific truth, philosophical truth, psychological truth, religious truth, artistic and literary truth, and so on endlessly. This is because history is both the medium in which the quest for truth by human beings must be carried out in all its many-sidedness, and it is at the same time itself one aspect of the truth: that is, the truth that man is such a creature as has had this kind of history.

In order not to be overwhelmed from the start by the comprehensiveness of the subject matter of history, every historian as well as every student of history must set up some criteria for the criticism of historical writing. Thus, so far in this chapter, just in order to be able to talk about history at all, we have had to use such terms as objective and subjective, empirical and metaphysical, means and motivations, events and their causal connections. Such ideas, since the subject matter can hardly be discussed without them, give a clue to the manner in which one might approach written history critically, without either throwing up one's hands in despair over the possibility of any kind of historical truth at all or swallowing gullibly that particular version of history that strikes one as most pleasant and comfortable to believe. If history is a mixture of the subjective and objective, a critique which wishes to discriminate between the relative veracity of one account and another would do well to consider both the subjective and the objective factors involved, to see what justice has been done to both in each case. Again, if human acts can be explained only by an account of both means and motivations, any history which deals cavalierly with either the one or the other would be more suspect than one which summons all its resources to reconstruct both. A "good" history carries with it a certain sort of conviction, similar to that of a convincing character in literature, a feeling that this or that event or movement "could have happened" in the manner described. This conviction is one of the many subjective factors involved in the study and writing of history, and without it the most comprehensive collection of documentary evidence is useless and unreal.

The influence of Christianity

All philosophies and religions may be divided into two kinds, according to whether or not they take history seriously. The most prominent of the nonhistorical varieties of thinking and believing to have captured the allegiance of the world have been the general system of Greek philosophy, on the one hand, and the Oriental religions, on the other. In the case of the Oriental religions history is devaluated because it is the realm of transiency and flux just as much as nature, with its recurrent cycles of birth, growth, and death, and salvation consists of the submergence of individuality and change into the unity and uniformity of being itself, the thoughtless, desireless, imageless peace of nirvana. In the case of Greek thinking, history is devaluated because, along with nature, it is the mere appearance or imitation of eternal and unchanging heavenly essences, and salvation consists of man's transcendence of both nature and history through reason, ending in contemplation of the eternal. In this case, history is not quite as severely negated as in the Oriental religions, for man uses both nature and history as teachers and guides to help him find the eternal essences; he uses them as steppingstones in his rational ascent. A positive relationship to history, where all of history is conceived as a single, purposeful plan or drama having a beginning, middle, and end, originated with the people known as Israel, and both through Judaism and Christianity has since influenced Western thinking in every department so greatly that it is now most difficult for Western man to imagine himself living in a purely negative relation to history. The tremendous activity, aggressiveness, and dynamism, for better or worse, of Western civilization, in contrast to the static resignation and relative peacefulness of Oriental peoples, is the most obvious manifestation of this difference in attitude toward history, and this period of nonhistorical thinking is now under Western impact coming to an end in the East.

The word "history" has at least two distinct meanings. It is used to indicate "what actually happened" and also the accounts of what happened, which, as we have seen, are always and inescapably already interpretations of what happened. But since there is no way of getting at what actually happened except through the interpreted accounts, the first thing to do in considering history as the raw material for a philosophy is to decide whether or not this represents a vicious circle, or whether this intimacy between history and its interpretation is not one of its basic characteristics that must be recognized from the outset. The intimacy between history and its interpretation is what is meant by the subjective-objective characteristic of history, and it presupposes the freedom of man to change the course of history, since it indicates that history itself is influenced by man's interpretation of history to some extent, and that there is no such thing as a purely objective human history to which man's interpretation is added as an extraneous afterthought. Man's interpretation of history is itself a part of history, not in the accidental sense in which everything can be considered part of history, but in the crucial sense that the future course of history at any point in time is partly determined by men's interpretation of the meaning of the past, so that history itself resounds with the repercussions of true and false interpretations of history.

But, on the other hand, lest the freedom of man be overestimated, and his role in history depicted as that of lord and master, it is important to note that the decision as to which interpretation of history to adopt as a guide to action, and hence as a determinant of future history, is never made by man in a historical vacuum, some realm of pure logical essences without history, but always in the context of the historical situation that calls for the decision, and that is itself the consequences of previous decisions. Thus man seems to be constantly called to reinterpret history because his own previous interpretations of history have so altered the course of history that the original interpretation no longer holds. Presumably, the more true an interpretation of history, the less it should have to be changed as a result of its own influence on history, which, on the contrary, it should be able in part to prophesy. And, conversely, an interpretation of history is discredited in the eyes of men when it influences history in such a manner as to disappoint the expectations that are based on it.

The present interest in history, for example, has appeared partly as a result of certain catastrophic developments in real history that disappointed expectations based on the optimistic philosophy of endless progress and increasing rationality which inaugurated the modern period. At its inception in the Enlightenment the modern period had, on the whole, a rather negative attitude to real history, the past, although its attitude toward future history was most positive and optimistic. It simply rejected the past as a comedy of errors and superstitions, and maintained that real, meaningful history, the history of rational man, was just about to begin. The doctrine of evolution was taken over from nature and applied to history, for by means of it the errors and superstitions of the past could be readily explained as the early stages of the evolution of man from barbarism to rationality, thereby discrediting the past without hurting anyone's feelings or holding anyone responsible for the darker pages of history. Evolution became the time machine for converting history into progress according to the formula that the future must be better than the past because it is further "evolved."

The plausibility of this interpretation of history was based certainly on the prosperousness of the "times" that seemed to go hand in hand with it, rather than on its intellectual standing, so that one cannot help wondering how long it would have flourished unchallenged on scientific and philosophical grounds, if history had not stepped in to discredit it by large-scale events displaying unprecedented barbarism and irrationality even at this late stage in evolution. It could have been discredited on intellectual grounds, for the idea that the kind of changes that have occurred in man's history can be equated or even compared with the kind of changes of biological form occurring by mutation and transmitted by the germ plasm, such as the biological theory of evolution postulates, is so silly when examined critically that only the most prejudiced and shoddy thinking could have been satisfied with it. The term "evolution" applied to history was just a slogan or rallying cry for lending false scientific support to an unusually optimistic outlook on the historical prospects of man, characterizing a period of great advance in man's knowledge and power over nature. But history itself discredited the theory, and in a much more painful way, by showing, in totalitarian states and world devastations, that modern man was not only no more evolved away from barbarism and irrationality than many of his superstitious and erring ancestors but was even less evolved, or had actually "regressed," in moral and spiritual goods, which the new theory had incidentally thrown overboard in the process of reducing man to an evolving animal.

With the arrival of the world wars there then appeared a new interest in history, and this time modern man took his look at history with not quite such a superior eye, and not quite such "disinterested" scientific curiosity. Even those hardy progressive evolutionists who refused to abandon the theory in essence admitted that it might need to be revised, that actual progress was neither as steady nor as steep as the theory predicted, and that a study of history might yield some lessons from the past as to the causes of "regression" and their possible elimination. But most people wanted to study history because they were fed up with the one-sidedness and superficiality of evolutionary progressivism and suddenly felt a queer sympathy for various less progressive periods of man's history which seemed to do greater justice to the total human situation in spite of their evident errors and superstitions. Thus there appeared nostalgic studies of the Middle Ages, nostalgic studies of ancient Greece and Rome, and even some naïve "discoveries" concerning Oriental modes of thinking and living. Men turned to history for help in living, because they felt a great need and lack, if only for certain values that the modern viewpoint had simply overlooked or eliminated. But they soon discovered that the problem was not so simple as to permit either a deliberate return to the past or a simple taking over from the past what was desirable and adding it on to the present way of thinking and living.

History was not just a grocery store, a "super" market, where one could go shopping for forgotten values and thus make one's present life into a meaningful whole. For each of these forgotten values was somehow inextricably connected not only with a certain historical situation that could not be repeated but also with a certain view of life, a philosophy or religion which could not easily be reconciled with the modern outlook, and without which the value in question was merely an empty form. Such values as the sense of community, a feeling for human dignity, moral responsibility, communion with God, spiritual wholeness, vocation, could not be simply "adopted," or commanded to grow on an intellectual and spiritual subsoil that essentially denied their validity. There was nothing for it but to question the theory of evolutionary progress and all its associated doctrines to the roots, a painful process which only intensified the general sense of inadequacy, desperation, and catastrophe in which men were already living.

At this point it would perhaps be best to bring the believer back into the discussion, lest he should get the impression that he with his Christian faith somehow stands outside of, or exempt from, the general crisis through which modern man is passing. To begin with, it is the Christian faith and its historical preparation in Judaism that is largely responsible, through its interaction with Greek and Roman thinking, for the positive historical consciousness of the Western world. A biological theory like evolution could never have been adopted as an *optimistic* interpretation of history in a culture which did not already have a positive relationship to history—that is, which did not live both in the remembrance that something important had already taken place in history, and in the expectation that some kind of consummation was the goal of history, and was even now lending an eternal significance to all the partial, fragmentary, and abortive struggles and consummations that constituted the stuff of history. To the Oriental mind, for example, and even to the Greek mind in its speculation on nature, the idea that the present multifarious forms and species on the earth have evolved from fewer and simpler forms would not in the least have suggested the positive value judgment implied in the word "progress." On the contrary, it would have meant only the increase and proliferation of that very individuality, particularity, and transiency from which the human soul needed to be disentangled either by way of submergence in undifferentiated being, or by way of striving after unchanging essences. The ground was prepared for the progressive evolutionary concept of history by the eschatological consciousness of the Christian Church, which, in spite of its apparent other-worldliness, gave the Western world a positive relationship to history in such concepts as the Creation, Augustine's City-of-God, City-of-Man philosophy, the drama of redemption, the second coming of Christ, and the kingdom of God. The Christian religion is not only the one religion above all others that takes history seriously, but it is also responsible directly or indirectly for all secular and even anti-religious philosophies that try to take history seriously.

The Christian Church is also more directly and immediately responsible for the particular way in which the Enlightenment tore itself away from its Christian moorings in order to seek a salvation in history by political and industrial means, and then for the present catastrophic times by the faithless manner in which Christians all too readily capitulated to politics and industry. If Christians tend to think of the present catastrophic times as the judgment of God upon sinful man for wandering away from the truths of the Christian faith, they had better not forget that this judgment falls first and foremost on the Christians themselves, who should have known better. Just as Luther did not identify the Turks with the Antichrist, but the pope, who should have known better, so the Christians of today should not be so eager to trace catastrophe to secular modes of thinking and living, as to repent for themselves and for the Church, which should have known better. For the Enlightenment came into the world partly on a wave of sincere conviction that the medieval church in its arrogance and power was deliberately stifling certain aspects of God's truth, as well as on a wave of disgust at the intransigency with which that church resisted reform. The Reformation, in the particular tragic, schismatic, and warlike form in which it actually happened, should never have been needed, and, however much we may prize the truths which it defended, we cannot help wondering if the same truths could not have been restored, as well as new truth admitted, without breaking the Church into fragments and scattering God's people, had there been more humility, love, and faith on all sides. At any rate, it should never be forgotten, at least by the believer, that the present critical situation of man must not be ascribed *solely* to his sudden desire to be his own master under the power of reason, but also to the historically crucial lack of humility, love, and faith on the part of Christian believers.

Three modern interpretations of history

The fact is that the Christian believer of today is surrounded by several conflicting interpretations of history, not one of which is independent of Christian influence positively or negatively, and every one of which seeks a salvation for man within history which is erroneous from the standpoint of the Christian interpretation of history. These interpretations may be classified into three kinds and for convenience labeled the heretical, the heroic, and the pseudo-scientific interpretations of history. The heretical interpretation of history in the modern period is the revolutionary-utopian interpretation which believes that it is the goal of history to establish on earth a political-social-economic utopia by means of a certain kind of organization of society through force or consent or both. This is a heretical interpretation of the Christian idea of the kingdom of God, not because the organization of society toward greater economic and political justice is irrelevant to the kingdom of God, but because the insistence upon the sufficiency and finality of this goal rests upon a non-Christian understanding of the true nature of man.

Present-day communism is, of course, the most extreme and self-conscious form of this heretical interpretation of history, but in a milder, less logical form this interpretation of history is the driving force behind most of the political, social, and economic reform movements sponsored by democratic, liberal-bourgeois society, by newly awakened "backward" peoples, and by that segment of liberal Christianity which is concerned to promote the "social gospel" to the exclusion of all other aspects of Christian truth. It is heretical because it ignores both the transcendence of God and the partial transcendence of man, which is to say that it ignores the fact that the full meaning of truly human life cannot be realized or consummated merely by the organization of the most harmonious organic society imaginable, a fact that has been brought out recently by various satirical literary pictures of the ideal society that awaits us, whose harmony can be achieved only by reducing man to a well-adjusted, socially and medically conditioned animal. Man the happy animal, and not man the fellow spirit created in God's image, is the subject of this social-utopian consummation of history, where happiness is identified with the maximization of pleasure and self-realization, plus the minimization of conflict and frustration.

We have already discussed the socially-medically controlled society in the chapter on the social sciences, with all that it implies in the way of the dehumanization of man, and the division of society into those who control, and those who are controlled, and we need add here only the observation that if this is indeed the true goal of history, then it is a crime against humanity not to accomplish it in the most obvious way, which would be for a few courageous souls to perform a small operation on the brain of every child at birth, so as to transform the controlled part of mankind into a species of happy imbeciles.

This interpretation of history is also heretical because it ignores either the reality or the true dimensions of sin. The social-control utopians understand well enough that there is something wrong with man that makes him self-destructive and socially intransigent, but they cannot realize that it is the spirit of man that is sick, not just the psychobiological organism, because they basically deny man's spiritual structure. Thus their healing misses the point, well-meant and even partially fruitful though it may be.

There is, however, another version of this utopian interpretation, the more rationalistic version, which recognizes at least part of the spiritual structure of man in that it believes him to be a rational creature who ought to be able, by means of his own capacity for understanding, for duty, for love, and for sacrifice, to build a harmonious rational society on earth. This is the earlier version, which has had a venerable history since the time of Plato, which had a democratic-universalistic renaissance at the time of the Enlightenment, and which is now again being revived by the "new" humanists, in a kind of horrified reaction to the picture of society envisioned by the social-control utopians. But humanism, new or old, denies the true dimension of sin by relegating it to the nonrational portion of man's being, which it seeks to eradicate. It believes that reason itself is impervious to sinful distortion, so that salvation is only a question of making men more rational. It then beats its head against the manifestly nonrational aspect of man, trying to shame it and blame it out of existence, thereby driving it into direct conflict with reason, and at the same time expecting miracles of omniscience, love, and self-sacrifice from the pitifully precarious rational endowment of man.

In contrast to the heretical interpretation of history, which seeks as the goal of history an imitation of the kingdom of God based on a naturalistic or rationalistic interpretation of man's capacity, the heroic interpretation of history is definitely, and in most cases consciously, anti-Christian. And, curiously enough, this anti-Christian interpretation of history often shows a better understanding of the true nature of man than the heretical interpretation. For it begins not with the rational man, or the socially adjustable animal, but with the heroic man, the Nietzschean man, the demonic man, the man who cannot stand the idea of a God other than himself, and who is the true symbol of unregenerate human nature. It does not want the kingdom of God or any imitation of it. It wants power, invulnerability, self-sufficiency, self-realization, and historical justification for all those who have it in them to demand and appropriate these things. In regard to the Christian God it is not apathetic, condescending, or lukewarm, but politely or rudely defiant. Before Christianity came into the world there were no truly heroic men, for they did not have God as revealed in Christ to pit themselves against. Now the opportunities for heroism have vastly increased, and with them the opportunities for the demonic refinement of the heroic interpretation of history. The heroic interpretation of history has many subtle variations. It can be detected in almost every kind of romanticism; it is the basis of all absolutistic idealisms, even those, like Hegel's, which incorporate Christianity; it is the root of all radical skepticism; it is behind religous and cultural aestheticism; it lurks even in the puritanical, rugged individualism of the American empire-building era, with its worship of the self-made man.

In our day this heroic interpretation of history has broken out catastrophically in two forms, in the very obvious form of vicious nationalism based on the myth of the superior race or the superior segment of society, which, as the bearer of historical destiny, has the right to impose its will on all the lesser peoples; and in the less obvious form of existential nihilism, or heroic-romantic despair. In the latter form it reveals a truer understanding of the real nature of man and his situation in the world and in relation to God than any of the other contemporary interpretations of history, because, by denying man a possible salvation even by means of a superior race or an all-powerful state, it reveals the truly desperate condition of man in separation from God, at the same time that it consciously and demonically maintains the separation as an act of romantic, self-pitying, heroic defiance.

These two interpretations of history, the heretical-utopian and the heroic-demonic, are easy enough to understand as the corruption of, and as the rebellion against, the Christian interpretation of history as the incarnation of God's will for the redemption of mankind from its sinful self-sufficiency to reconciliation and fellowship with himself. Both of them have an implicitly religious undergirding, because both claim to answer the ultimate questions concerning man's destiny and the meaning of his life on earth. The third general type of the modern interpretation of history, the pseudo-scientific, is a little more difficult for the believer to understand in its relationship to the Christian interpretation, for it is too noncommittal to be classified as heretical, and too self-consciously objective to be classified as heroically defiant, in regard to the Christian interpretation.

We have already discussed some of the difficulties encountered in the effort to study history scientifically, or, rather, to reconstruct history scientifically from the objective evidences that are available to us. These difficulties, however, merely limit and circumscribe the possibility of achieving accuracy and certainty with regard to historical knowledge—they certainly do not invalidate the empirical approach to history as a commendable effort to gain whatever knowledge is possible within these recognized limitations. The word "pseudo" in the name I have given to this general type of historical interpretation should not be taken in a derogatory sense, but only as an indication of the scientific limitations of the method, whether these are always recognized by individual historiographers or not. It is certainly no fault of the historian that history is not as amenable to the scientific method as he might wish it to be, although it might be regarded as a fault in him if he refuses to recognize the degree to which this is the case.

What I have called the pseudo-scientific interpretation of history involves, however, something more than this commendable effort on the part of historians to get at the objective facts in the face of the recognized difficulties. It involves what must from the standpoint of pure science be called an ulterior motive, a motive other than the disinterested curiosity with which, let us say, the archeologist reconstructs an ancient city. Now this ulterior motive is nothing to be ashamed of; it is, on the contrary, a most commendable motive, especially from the Christian standpoint, but it must be recognized for what it is, since it determines the subjective goals of this interpretation of history in spite of all the protestations of pure objectivity on the part of its supporters. This ulterior motive is nothing but the desire to learn from the empirical approach to history some law, some regularity, or pattern of recurrence, which might be helpful to mankind in understanding and manipulating its historical existence, in the same way that a law of nature is helpful in the understanding and manipulation of nature. We have already seen, in discussing the social sciences, that there comes a point where the detached curiosity appropriate to natural science must, from the Christian standpoint, be considered a vicious thing, since it implies an inhuman indifference to human destiny. So there is certainly nothing wrong with the *desire* to learn something from history that might be beneficial to mankind. The question is, just what is it that the pseudo-scientific interpretation of history hopes to learn from history, and how does this compare with what the Christian faith claims can be learned from history?

The pseudo-scientific interpretation of history hopes to discover, in the empirical historical knowledge available, some regularities, some recurrring patterns, some upward or downward trends, some cycles or parts of cycles, anything that can be described or compared, abstractly, with a line on a graph plus a description of the various "stages" or points on the line. Even if no such simple geometric picture is attempted, the effort, nevertheless, is to seek similarities within differences, and to correlate trends with trends, the rise of this with the rise or fall of that.

Now it must be apparent from the start that the effort to comprehend history in this way calls for a tremendous activity of the creative imagination, for really stupendous powers of abstraction and analogic representation, not to mention an almost unbelievable insight into the religious, cultural, and political existence of whole peoples of whom we have no more objective evidence than a few potsherds and burial customs. Such an effort is, in fact, constantly embarrassed by both the richness and the poverty of historical data. On the one hand, there is the uniqueness, the specificity and particularity, the many-sidedness and intricate ramifications of even a single historical event, which makes it most difficult to say, in comparing two events, "here there is real similarity, but there, there is real difference." On the other hand, there are the lacunae. To overcome this difficulty the pseudo-scientific interpretation tries more and more to "stand back" in order to see greater and greater portions of history "as a whole," and this means to take larger and larger segments of time, half-dozen centuries or the "lifetime" of whole civilizations, as the basis of comparison or the periodicity of the cycles, and this in turn means that the analogies and recurrences that can be detected become increasingly abstract, almost fantastically so, and the poverty of historical data in certain parts of these vast panoramas becomes in increasing limitation on the verisimilitude of these conjectures and generalizations.

Both the more empirically inclined and the more metaphysically inclined variations of the pseudo-scientific interpretation of history tend toward the consideration of "universal" history as the ultimate logical unit of study, the first for the sake of methodological completeness, the second for the sake of the "eternal." Thus Sorokin, the most empirically inclined of them, claims that only by taking periods somewhere between six and nine hundred years in length can there be demonstrated the alternating cycles of ideational and sensate cultures that he professes to see in the historical data. Spengler studies the rise and decline of Western civilization in comparison with the rise and fall of Greco-Roman civilization, and concludes that all civilizations, regardless of time span, like plants and animals and human beings, follow a law of birth, growth, maturity, decay, and death, a law which presumably determines universal history, both past and future. Toynbee, without this deterministic bias, and with a number of biblical thought forms imbedded in such concepts as challenge and response (vocation), withdrawal and return (prayer), suicide and rebirth (regeneration), claims that no sense can be made out of history unless all civilizations up to date, existing and extinct, are studied as members of a species, as "societies" which may be compared and contrasted for fruitful analogies and significant differences. And, of course, Hegel, the archmetaphysician, simply *defines* universal history as the dialectical self-objectification of the Absolute Idea, and leaves it more or less to his disciples, and all who are fascinated by this concept, to make the facts of universal history fit into this metaphysical strait jacket, a project which at least has the merit that it will assuredly keep all absolute idealists busily occupied from now until the end of universal history.

The chief error to avoid in considering these variations of the pseudo-scientific interpretation of history (and there are, of course, many more than those I have just barely mentioned) is to jump to the conclusion that because there are so many different and even contradictory versions of the story, they must all be wrong. On the contrary, from these differences and even these contradictions we should conclude, history being the complex thing it is, that they are probably all partly true. Every one of them probably contains some element of the truth concerning the cyclic or recurrent aspect of history, granted the categories in terms of which the cycles and recurrences are described. And there is no reason why we should not grant to these historians their various categories, any more than we should not grant a composer the right to write music in whatever form he chooses, or an artist to paint pictures in whatever form he chooses. We already know that even the natural sciences, even the very origin and use of language, contain an element of artistic creativity—how could an interpretation of universal history in terms of recurring elements be anything but an artistic creation, an abstraction-picture, a concept-panorama? Not only that, but we must also grant that an almost endless variety of such history-pictures must be possible since there is hardly any limit that we can set upon the variety of categories and abstractions that the creative imagination can conceive, or reason can devise, now or in the future, in terms of which to describe the cyclic or recurrent aspect of history. For there is no doubt that history has this aspect, or perhaps we should rather say, there is no doubt that the human mind is such as will always see this aspect in any collection of data, but especially in any collection of historical data, which offer possibilities for such seeing as rich and many-sided as human life itself.

The Christian revelation also has its history-picture, but the Christian picture is conceived in theological and mythical terms, and it is a dramatic-personal picture rather than an abstract-impersonal picture. This dramatic-personal picture has been the original inspiration for the historical consciousness of the Western world, even though it has issued in such a variety of historical interpretations as we have indicated. There is, however, nothing in the Christian interpretation that would necessarily deny the cyclic or recurrent aspect of history which the pseudo-scientific interpretation finds so significant in one way or another. On the contrary, man being a mixture of finiteness and freedom, of createdness and creativity, of the natural and the nature-transcendent, it would be very odd if history, like nature, did not display some cyclic or recurrent aspects, even beyond those inherent in its physical and biological foundations, although at the same time this aspect would be united with the other aspect, the unique and unrepeatable aspect of every human being and every human action and every event. (A little meditation on a single rather simple historical event, such as the discovery of America by the Europeans, will show how such an event could be unique and unrepeatable at the same time that it might be part of some general cycle of expansion or migration or empire building.) The question to argue, therefore, is not whether there is this aspect to history, which can be granted, but what significance is to be attached to it.

In other words, we have to ask for the "existential" significance of the cyclic and recurrent aspect of history as the pseudo-scientific interpretation of history assumes or states it, in order to be able to compare or contrast it with the manner in which Christianity sees the existential significance of this aspect of history. And here we again get a variety of answers, some of which would probably be surprising to the historians themselves, if they have never bothered to analyze their interpretations from this point of view.

First of all, we are confronted with a whole plethora of different kinds of determinisms, wherever the simple identification of possibility with necessity is made, according to the argument that whatever has happened several times before is possible, and therefore it must, under similar conditions, happen again. This is a simple transference of naturalistic ideas of causation to the realm of history, disregarding the fact that in the human realm possibility is not always the same as necessity, and hence Christianity denies outright all of these different kinds of determinisms without in the least denying the cyclic or recurrent aspect of history. Whatever has happened in the past may very well happen in vaguely similar form again, or it may not; but even if it does, it will be so intimately constituted of both human freedom and necessity that no one will be able to say categorically that it had to happen as it did. But even where there is no such rigid deterministic bias, if we are still to take the cycles and recurrences seriously, the existential significance of this for man could be only that human life and destiny are different, depending on what part of what cycle one happens to be born into. The meaning of life itself is different, *de facto*, at the bottom of one of Sorokin's sensate cultures from what it is at the top of one of his ideational periods, and it is different at the birth, at the maturity, at the decay, and at the death of one of the completed civilizations. And there is some truth in this, but it is precisely on this *de facto* existence and meaning that Christianity sits in judgment with its ultimate criterion in Christ as to what human destiny ought to be in any period, what it is divinely ordained to be, no matter what part of what cycle or civilization is just then recurring.

And, secondly, there is the whole plethora of judgments upon history in which the cyclic or recurrent aspect of history is seen as the vehicle, medium, or dialectical manifestation of some kind of progress. Since every one of these contains a separate and distinct value judgment as to what constitutes progress for man, and we cannot discuss them all individually, it must suffice here to say that any such conception, or all of them put together, no matter how high-minded or idealistic, must be from the Christian standpoint considered wrong and untrue, if they do not consider the ultimate progress of mankind to consist of man's growth toward reconciliation and fellowship with God in Christ—a demand which obviously dismisses most of them, even while it permits a limited sort of Christian interpretation of the cyclic and recurrent aspect of history on these terms.

History as the realm of sin and grace

It would seem, then, that the answer of Christian faith to the question of what can be learned from history must be that nothing can be learned from history, either from the recurrent or the non-recurrent aspect of it, unless something is first of all learned from God. History is full of interesting and entertaining, or boring and repetitious, facts, but all of them put together, even so as to cover "universal" history, do not spell out any ultimate meaning for any human being, as long as the crucial question of divine-human confrontation in history is left out of the account. According to the Christian interpretation this divine-human encounter can take place without any knowledge of universal history on the part of the human subject, but it cannot take place without a radical transformation of the human subject, such that he becomes through repentance and faith a new being, living a new life, in a new world. The pseudo-scientific interpretation of history—and this is its blind spot—simply assumes that man is in a position to learn something from history just by taking thought, just by sitting up and paying attention to what has happened, while remaining essentially the same unregenerate man, who uses his own unregenerate judgment in deciding what the lesson of history might be. It is the same old story of man's trying to save himself by his own hand, without undergoing that radical and painful spiritual reorientation which is the unconditional prerequisite for salvation. God himself cannot change this prerequisite, and still be God. And God cannot teach any man any lessons from history or anywhere else unless that man be first transformed into a creature capable of learning a lesson from God.

All three of the interpretations of history we have been considering—the heretical, because of its corruption of the Christian concept of human nature and destiny; the heroic, because of its defiance of that nature and destiny; and the pesudo-scientific, because of the falsely superior perspective from which it views the whole situation—make it difficult for a truly teachable Christian attitude toward history to emerge. This teachable attitude must first of all be the dismaying realization that most of history as it has actually happened is something for which man must continually ask to be forgiven. For, whatever else history may be, it is certainly also the graveyard of human attempts at self-salvation down the years, in defiance or disregard of the salvation that God has prepared for all peoples. It is the record of hopes raised, and atrocities propagated in their name, of failure heaped upon dismal failure, of vicious circles entangled in the cumulative effects of past evils.

Scarcely a movement or development of history can be mentioned which, even with good intentions looming large in its motivation, did not turn bad in its realization, or become deflected to other ends. The early church was offered the disintegrating Roman Empire for its parish, an unparalleled opportunity, which it used in part for its own institutional aggrandizement to the point where half of Christendom turned against it in tragic revolt. The relatively co-operative Christian society of medieval feudalism turned into the arrogance of the *ancien régime*, and the protection and spiritual consolation of Mother Church turned into the terror of the Inquisition. But the well-intentioned movements inspired to offset these evils fared no better in their turn. The Reformation, which hoped to restore the proper filial relationship between man and God, turned into acrid, dogmatic sectarianism, on the one hand, and complete denial of religion, on the other. The Counter Reformation, reforming nothing, only tightened the dogmatic basis of disagreements which might have otherwise flowered into a new religious renaissance on the Catholic side.

The Renaissance, hoping to create a new, universalistic humanism, created revolutionary self-determination and vicious nationalism. The French Revolution, with its liberty, equality, and fraternity, became the Reign of Terror, the reign of Napoleon, and then the reign of bourgeois capitalism and nationalism all over Europe. The colonial expansion of Europe, bringing the blessings of Western civilization to backward peoples, brought also untold suffering and exploitation, and created problems for the future unification of the world whose complexity has not yet been plumbed. Industrialism, hoping to liberate man from slavery to nature, created wage-machine slavery, which is distorting man's human structure in a manner that baffles even the new experts on the psychology of human relations. Two world wars were fought for the sake of democratic principles combined with the principle of national sovereignty, ending in an insufferable ideological impasse between two world-uniting powers, which is now thwarting every rational approach to the establishment of a world community of peoples. And so it goes with history. Whether on a large scale or on a small scale the failure of history to live up to its promises and its opportunities is so glaring that even measured against purely human standards it is disheartening. Measured against divine standards, against the Christ-standard, it is one long human offense against God.

It has been the fashion, in recent years, for historians, paleontologists, and astronomers to pool their knowledge in order to construct a time scale for the life of this planet, on which the period of man's recorded historical existence appears as a mere speck in comparison with the hundreds of thousands of years of his prehistorical life, and the even greater aeons of nonhuman hegemony on earth before that. The argument to which this new time scale is supposed to lend support is the complacent long-range view that man has had so little time to "evolve" historically, as a civilized being, that we really should not be so impatient with him. We should give him another million years before judging him too severely. But this optimistic patience ignores the fact that the very appearance of civilized, historical life among men marks the "end" of natural evolution for man, that man's transcendence over nature, however it may have arisen, once it is a fact, spikes the evolutionary process, time scale and all. Man has outwitted the simple, relatively mechanical, long-range process of biological evolution, possibly to his own chagrin, but, having done so, he can scarcely call upon it to save him from his own independence of it, by asking biological processes to do, granted a million years, what the wayward spirit has tried and repeatedly failed to do.

Man is now a spirit, for better or for worse, and must be judged by spiritual standards. Time, for a spiritual being, is something different from what it is for nature. Time is not a span of duration but an opportunity, an elbowroom for choice, another chance to do something, a breathing space for freedom, an emptiness waiting to be filled. Time alone will therefore never save history, no matter how many years we "allow." Only eternity can save human history, by entering into time, by filling the form of time with eternal content—a paradox for the abstract human understanding. And eternity can enter time only through the human spirit, which is a spirit precisely because it transcends nature in the direction of the eternal. The human spirit faces nature in time—but its back is to eternity, which it never sees, but only feels in the background as its depth and source.

History, therefore, brings its own standard with it, one that cannot be applied to prehistorical or biological life any more than the processes of the latter can be applied as criteria to the former. We may think of biological evolution as the incubation period of man's biological organism, and of prehistorical life as the incubation period of man's spirit, but in neither case should we be so impressed by the length of time involved in these processes as to apply it comparatively to man's historical existence, which actually inaugurates a new time for man, the time that is opportunity to be filled with eternity. Only the Eternal can be the criterion of history, if it is truly human history we are talking about, and therefore the study of history, as Toynbee correctly surmises, passes over into theology. But while man keeps looking for the eternal in some aspect of the temporal, and keeps finding an unknown or unknowable God in an untouchable eternity, Christian faith proclaims that the eternal God has revealed himself to man in the fullness of time through his incarnate Son, leaving man without excuse, and leaving history without excuse. History is a failure, not because men did not know what God wanted, but because they did not want what God wanted for them. It is impossible, from a Christian standpoint, to view history with any sort of equanimity or complacency, whether on a long-range or a short-range view, because history is something for which man needs to be forgiven.

And yet history goes on. It still confronts the present generation with opportunities and challenges; it still provides man with a future, which, however clouded by the past, is still a future, another chance, a time in which to meet eternity, an ever-present hope. Man is not such a creature that he, by his own merits, deserves a future. Nevertheless, while he lives he has it, a fact that cannot be Christianly understood except under the category of the grace and mercy of God. The Christian verdict on history is by no means negative. On the contrary, Christian faith sees history as full of the grace and mercy, the healing and restoring, the patience and love, of God, precisely where the unbelievers see nothing. Without pretending to explain everything in history, or presuming to pry into mysteries that are open to God alone, Christian faith perceives that there are healing and preserving tendencies in history, and that these seem to be bound up in a mysterious way with the very structure of the creation itself. This must be attributed to the patience and goodness of God, who refuses to be defeated, and who can use even the selfishness of men to teach them the nature of their true happiness. For instance, men must learn the minimum essentials of living together at all, if they are eventually to learn the secret of living together in love. Therefore, any system of government and any code of justice which permits men to live together at all is already a step in the right direction, and a part of God's preserving patience. And it seems as though the very structure of human nature, with its physical, biological, and social needs, were calculated to drive men together, for the sake of selfish advantage at first, but with an eye to something better. How many more utterly selfish and isolated individuals there would be in the world, for example, if the sexual need did not drive them out of their sinful self-sufficiency into the mutuality of marriage and family life, where they can learn the elementary lessons of a higher kind of love?

But not even the sheer physical qualities of the world felt by human beings can be taken for granted, as having nothing to do with God. The physical processes of biological healing and restoration, for example, are studied and amplified by doctors, but they are not initiated or constructed by them out of nothing. Nature must be accepted and understood if she is to be manipulated by man—and even then such change must be based on co-operation rather than decree. One cannot help feeling sometimes that the very "laws" of nature that men so proudly discover and use were designed in some measure to protect the structure of the creation from the insolent trespasses of human arrogance and impatience. Appalled by atomic power, we can at least perceive some providence in the way nature resists capricious manipulation by the mountainlike stability of her ageless persistence in her ways.

And what of the aesthetic experiences of men in the world—is not the healing and teaching finger of God to be discerned even here, in an area which most people simply take for granted as their birthright of private enjoyment? Who has not felt, after a long convalescence, when the will to live ebbs low, that the sheer beauty of nature is like the coaxing of an unseen, beneficent hand, that blesses life as it beckons? And who has not felt in the presence of great beauty, whether natural or man-made, some stirring of humility and wonder? To be sure, all these experiences can be, and most often are, selfishly perverted, but that is hardly a thing with which to reproach either the creation or the Creator. Even the virtues and excellencies and values which some secular philosophies—and some other religions—invite us to contemplate and pursue are not imaginary; they are indeed most real, but it is the privilege of the Christian believer to regard them, not as objects of competitive striving, but as the bountiful gifts of an ever-gracious and loving God whose patience and generosity make life even in a fallen world a still precious present reality.

The same kind of believing interpretation of history that sees God's wrath in certain of its concrete events and conditions does not fail to observe his goodness and mercy in others. But exactly where or how does one learn this believing interpretation of history, or where does one even hear about it? One does not learn this believing interpretation of history by studying history as a panorama viewed from a high place, and one hears about it for the first time by paying attention to the curious history of the Jews. By studying history as a panorama viewed from a high place, one learns about what Kierkegaard calls the "falsified eternity" and what he warns against when he says about the moment of contemplation:

> It is a foreshortening that is necessary in order that the contemplation may take place. It must foreshorten time a good deal. Indeed it must actually call the senses and thoughts away from time in order that they may complete themselves in a spurious eternal well-roundedness. It is here as when an artist sketches a country. The sketch cannot be as big as the country, it must be infinitely smaller; but on that account it also becomes all the easier for the observer to scan the outlines of that country. And yet it may well happen to the observer, if suddenly he were actually set down in that country where the many, many miles really exist and are valid, that he would be unable to recognize the country, or to make any sense of it, or as a traveler, to find his way about in it.[1]

The "falsified eternity," the foreshortened time, is just what the pseudo-scientific method discovers when it looks for recurrences and regularities down the longest vistas it can find in "universal" history. Here is another instance of how abstract thinking, the larger and larger generalization, leads men astray in case they should regard it as the pointer of the divine instead of merely a tool of creaturely thought. And we in this day of high-altitude flying can learn an even clearer lesson about its deceptivity than Kierkegaard could point. For as the plane first leaves the ground, the flyer certainly sees longer vistas, and is able to perceive patterns in the topology of the country below him that he could never have seen from the ground. But as he increases altitude, there is a blurring of the details, the most marked characteristics finally fade into insignificance, the longest vista becomes a featureless haze, and above the clouds the earth is lost altogether. This ascent of the flyer may be a good image for the mystical ascent of the soul from the alone to the Alone, for it shows just how history fades into insignificance for the mystical view of life. But the pseudo-scientific interpretation of history is concerned to find the significance of history, not its insignificance, by means of the larger and larger generalizations, and is even concerned, at the present time, to learn lessons from the long-range patterns of history. What is the exact nature of this deception? Why is it that the larger and larger abstractions become emptier and emptier of meaning for the traveler down below, who has to make his way through the forest where "the many, many miles actually exist and are valid"? Could it be that God is not to be found by men up there in the stratoliner at all, and that this fact is what makes the eternity viewed from there "falsified"?

Such is the hinted answer we find if we pay attention to the curious history of the Jews. Relatively early in the span of time covered by the study of "universal" history, when as yet scarcely much historical evidence had had a chance to accumulate, there appeared this people who, on the basis of at least inconclusive evidence, namely the exodus from Egypt, conceived the notion that God was *doing something with them in history*, and the positive historical consciousness of the Western world was born. Such a ridiculous tribal prejudice of itself is nothing new in the world, and must cause the modern historian to smile even more out of recognition than out of pity. And yet there was something about the way in which this tribe conceived their God's dealings with them that was destined to become the undoing of tribes and civilizations with far more reasonable claims to the prejudice. Markus Barth calls this peculiar way in which the Old Testament speaks about God's acting with man "The Christ in Israel's History," and in an article of that name distinguishes five aspects of "the relation of God to man that are characteristic of the Old Testament documents": God acts in history; God keeps the covenant; God has appointed a representative; God saves not without bloodshed; God will do greater works. The last aspect keeps the future open, and indeed opens the door through which the spiritual descendents of Abraham can pass from the Old Testament into the New, without a discontinuity in their understanding of "the way of God's acting with man."

The God of Israel reveals himself by his specific acts (not, be it noted, by long-range patterns of cycles or recurrences).

These acts are caused, accompanied, and explained by God's words, and therefore each one of them is a revelation of God. By his acts he proclaims his love and his law, and each time he calls for faith and obedience. There is no institution on earth (not even the dynasty of David, nor the mediating office of the priests, nor the visionary power of the prophets, nor the fertility of motherhood) which is, as such, a bearer of divinity or of revelation. But the ever-renewed evidence, which God gives of himself, the ever-surprising gift of grace, and the daily new rendering of obedience is the link between God and man.[2]

So God speaks to men through historical events, but never in such a way that they could hear and remain unchanged. When men hear God speaking to them through history, they are already different men—they are no longer completely separated from him, even if it is only his wrath and condemnation they see in the events. For no one can feel the grace of God who does not first experience the judgment of God, not only in the form that all have fallen short of the glory of God, but also in the form: "Thou art the man!" This unconditional condition for historical salvation immediately excludes as irrelevent and impertinent all so-called "objective" judgments or criticisms of history by persons who imagine that they stand outside of history, exempt from judgment and responsibility for all of it before the throne of the Most High. Such persons, no matter how great their historical erudition, or even their supposed historical activity, not only do not have any real historical existence, but they also do not have any real humanity. Real historical existence and real humanity are inseparable from the encounter with God in history, which encounter, for sinful man, must always have the character of judgment as well as grace, judgment precisely because of grace, and which from the human side must always be accompanied by a sense of the solidarity of the human family before God, even in sin. There is no separating of oneself from one's fellow men, even those of remote ages, imagining that one is "not like other men," and then trying to be responsible to God for one's own little life, as against those others, who have made history the failure that it is. Historical phariseeism is the basic attitude behind all impartial, objective judgments on history, whether pessimistic or optimistic, predicting doom or utopia, because whoever makes this judgment does not consider himself to be at one with humanity, either in Adam or in Christ.

Only the eternal can save history, but it makes a difference how one conceives the relation between the eternal and history. By seeing history under the category of sin and grace, the Judaeo-Christian awareness of the relation brings the eternal into the very heart of history as its source and standard, since there is no sin except sin against God, and no grace except the grace that is of God. By the same token there is no proper response to the speaking of God in historical events except humility and thankfulness, obedience and love. In the absence of these attitudes, which are the response of faith, whatever men pretend to learn from history is in reality only a reflection of their resentment against the world for not being more to their liking. Men curse life, but try to take it away from them! They expect a great deal from it, and from history too. If they are born into good "times," they personally take credit for whatever prosperity befalls them; and if they are born into bad "times," they curse fate or God, demanding justice, presumably in accordance with their virtue. Having made a failure of history, they want to know why God "allows" such things to happen. History, they demand, must not only make men happy: it must be a theodicy. It is God who must justify himself before men, if he allows history to happen, by giving them whatever they want.

Certainly there can be no Christian lesson-learning from history unless this phenomenal ingratitude of man, and his almost comical presumptuousness, are first of all recognized for what they are, and for the way in which they have stained the various historical ages with spiritual ugliness, neurotic discontent, and that most gratuitous of all forms of human unhappiness, self-pity. As long as there is this everlasting tendency of man to take the good things of this life, and life itself, utterly for granted, and to regard all pain and misfortune as a personal affront, it is impossible for man to size himself up realistically and sanely, as to what he might reasonably expect of historical existence, and what he ought to dismiss as unhealthy wish-dreaming. Yet the curious fact is that awareness of grace always comes as a surprise, surprise both at finding that there is grace, and at discovering what it consists of. And those whose eyes have been opened regarding their true condition before God, who have been surprised by grace, and who have accepted the offered forgiveness, begin to see everything in a new light, to see everything that matters as a gift and a task. Life itself is a gift and a task. Human capacities are a gift and a task. The heritage of the past is a gift and a task. Time, the time that is opportunity and that is to be filled with eternity, is a gift and a task. Even suffering can be a gift and a task, for one who is filled with the grace of God.

Given such an appreciation of history as the realm of sin and grace, what may a believer Christianly think concerning the ups and downs of history, the recurrent cycles, the coming to be and passing away of empires and civilizations, the golden ages and the dark ages from the dawn of history to the present day? He may, and this is indeed a Christian privilege, consider himself liberated from the necessity of taking any of these historical phenomena at their face value, and from taking them too seriously either as triumphs or catastrophes in human destiny. He need not attach a false ultimacy and a false finality either to those happy occasions in some particular time and place in history where a particularly successful counterbalance of opposing forces, combined with fortunate circumstance, has created an era of peace and prosperity, social stability, and cultural creativity, such that the men of that age are tempted to believe that they have reached the peak of historical achievement and are filled with pride and self-glory; or to those other periods when civilizations are crashing, social disorder reigns, creativity is anarchic, cherished institutions crumble, and men are tempted to believe that the end of the world is at hand, since the end of their world is ingloriously obvious amidst hopelessness on all sides. And he will, of course, try to refrain from attaching such false finality to his own time, to the age into which he happens to be born, though this may be considerably more difficult to do than in the case of looking back over past ages.

Whether he be born into an age of prosperity or into an age of catastrophe, the Christian believer need not let himself be beguiled by what the world of unbelief calls success, nor overwhelmed by what that world calls disaster. He can say, in any age, in the midst of any culture, any cycle, any peak or valley of the historical adventure, in the midst of people wallowing in riches or in the midst of people wallowing in despair: "Mine eyes have seen *thy* salvation, which thou hast prepared before the face of all people; to be a light to lighten the Gentiles, and to be the glory of thy people Israel." He can say this, he must say this, without in the least becoming "detached" from history after the manner of historicophilosophical objectivity, and without in the least implying that he stands outside of history, or that the salvation which God has prepared for all people is not concerned with history. And he can say this, he must say it, not because he has such a clever pate that he can make a decent pattern out of any collection of historical data, but only because, and only in so far as, he again and again turns away from the panorama of history in obedience and love to this salvation: to the time that is to be filled with the eternal, the Christ-filled time, the kingdom of surprising grace and truth which is not of this world, but which is even now in our midst.

Notes

CHAPTER I

1. *The Epistle to Diognetus, Ancient Christian Writers* (Westminster, Md.: The Newman Press, 1948), VI, 138-39.

CHAPTER II

1. The relationship between poetry and doctrine is one on which volumes remain to be written in the field of religion. In actual works it appears to be somewhat like the hen-and-egg relation, in so far as they seem to presuppose each other. Thus some of the poetry in *The Divine Comedy* presupposes certain scholastic doctrines, while these doctrines in turn presuppose insights about the God-man-nature relationships which are expressed as poetry in the Bible.

2. Rudolf Carnap, *The Logical Syntax of Language* (New York: Harcourt, Brace & Co., 1937). More specifically, he says in the Foreword, p. xiii, that the conclusion to which the study undertaken in this book leads is: "*Philosophy is to be replaced by the logic of science*—that is to say, by the logical analysis of the concepts and sentences of the sciences, for *the logic of science is nothing other than the logical syntax of the language of science*." (Italics his.)

3. Most regrettable, in this connection, are the attempts by some religionists, and even some religious-minded physicists, to interpret the "new physics" as revelatory of the limitations of science and on *this* account as favorable to religious doctrine. The fact that crude mechanical pictures of the atom must be abandoned in favor of mathematical pictures for which no large-scale equivalents can be found is a limitation of the visual imagination, not of science. There is no reason why the fine structure of matter and energy should resemble anything we know in the large-scale, everyday world, and still less reason to jump to the conclusion that because all is not known or knowable about the elementary particles or waves, something analogous to "free will" or "personality" must be ascribed to them. The believer should, in any case, beware of all reasoning in which science and religion are so related that a defeat of the former is considered to be a triumph of the latter. The real defeat of the scientific method (still no occasion for gloating) will be made clearer, I hope, in the chapter on the social sciences.

CHAPTER III

1. And such statements may be used with different intentions; for example, the scientist deliberately removes all ambiguities from the words in order to identify measurable quantities; the poet, on the other hand, takes advantage of any multiple meanings inherent in the words in order to create new relationships in his structure. The point at issue here is that no radical discontinuity can be claimed to obtain between the different types of knowledge in so far as they can be talked about at all. It is just as logical to complain that the scientific statements are "bad poetry" because they are so self restricted to only the

most abstracted and measurable aspects of things, as to complain that the poetic statements are "bad science" because they contain unmeasurable qualities or particular comparisons that cannot be universalized. Good metaphysical statements, because of their effort to characterize the totality, would probably fall somewhere between the two, and could therefore be logically complained of as being both "bad science" and "bad poetry."

2. The other traditional "arguments" for the existence of God try, but do not succeed, in proving his existence, because they are really statements about his nature. They say, in effect, that God is like a first cause, or like the designer of a design. But they do not add anything logically to the force of the ontological argument, which claims that the existence of anything at all necessarily presupposes the existence of God, or that God is a necessary aspect of existence.

3. In Kierkegaard's own words it appears in what he describes as the third form of despair, the dialectical intensification of despair which arises when the self becomes conscious of the second form of despair: self-hatred, not willing to be the self that one is (the first form was despair over not having a self), and now it decides as an act of despairing defiance to do just the opposite, to will to be itself; to insist defiantly on being itself. "In this form of despair there is now a mounting conciousness of the self, and hence greater consciousness of what despair is and of the fact that one's condition is that of despair. Here despair is conscious of itself as a deed, it does not come from without as a suffering under the pressure of circumstances, it comes directly from the self. . . . In order to will in despair to be oneself there must be consciousness of the infinite self. This infinite self, however, is really only the abstractest form, the abstractest possibility of the self. And it is this self the man despairingly wills to be, detaching the self from every relation to the Power which posited it, or detaching it from the conception that there is such a Power in existence. By the aid of this infinite form the self despairingly wills to dispose of itself or to create itself, to make itself the self it wills to be, distinguishing in the concrete self what it will and what it will not accept." (From *The Sickness unto Death* [Princeton, N. J.: Princeton University Press, 1941], pp. 108-9. Used by permission of the publishers.) In both Sartre and Heidegger there is the consciousness of what Kierkegaard here calls the self in its most abstract and empty form—that is, the mere possibilities of a self, the sheer empty shell of an essence of human nature, which, however, man has only as a possibility because of his freedom, and which he must fill, and does fill, with content and actuality as he goes along in life, choosing himself and making his own essence. The despair Kierkegaard here so prophetically defines is not the despair they *talk* about (despair of meaning in external things felt as the vertigo in the face of nothingness), but the despair *in which they are.*

4. Martin Buber, *Between Man and Man* (New York: The Macmillan Co., 1948), p. 29. Used by permission of the publishers.

5. A recent example and a brilliant one would be the philosophy of symbolic forms. However, the unfortunate effect of Cassirer's and Langer's effort to

make the word "symbol" cover so much ground is that it becomes indistinguishable from "idea" and "concept" at the same time that the word is thus ruined for specialized usage in literature and theology where it is so much needed to take care of images or acts or forms that have a representative as well as a literal meaning. When everything is a symbol then nothing is a symbol, and Mrs. Langer is driven to such devices as speaking of "literal" symbols and "figurative" symbols. See her *Philosophy in a New Key*, pp. 113-15. This is an example of a perennial difficulty encountered in philosophy because of its attempt to achieve unity by reading off the whole in terms of one of the parts. In spite of which it must be admitted that the "reading off" in terms of symbols is a refreshing relief from such stale-grown readings as those in terms of "idea" or "matter" or "law."

CHAPTER IV

1. That the hostility was clearly felt but hard to define by religious writers is shown in the excellent study of the pioneers in sociology by the Rt. Rev. Simon Deploige entitled *The Conflict Between Ethics and Sociology*. He announces his topic by quoting one of the pioneers thus: " 'A large number of philosophers are attracted to sociology and accept its essential position; but they continue teaching theoretical ethics according to traditional methods. They seem unaware that they must make a choice between the two.' Lévy-Bruhl, professor of the history of philosophy at the University of Paris, thus declares the existence of a conflict between ethics and sociology." (Page 1.) Today it would perhaps be more correct to use the word "dissociation" rather than conflict, and to locate the potential hostility more in the sociologist's nonvaluative, "disinfected" talk about moral issues rather than in any new moral precepts issuing from these sciences that could create an either/or with ethics. It is no longer as clear that sociology will some day take the place of ethics as it was in the visions of the pioneers Auguste Comte, Émile Durkheim, and Lucien Lévy-Bruhl.

2. The fact that social science began as a formula conceived out of pure thought (the imitation of Newtonian physics) has in turn influenced its history. After the first wave of enthusiastic programs delineating what social science ought to be came a series of monomaniacal studies, each claiming to explain the whole development of societies from primitive to civilized by means of a hypothetical "primary" or determining factor: climate; geography; population density; division of labor; various psychological instincts in man; various biological processes such as growth, adaptation, survival of the fittest; various economic factors such as farming and herding methods, tools. The number of "primary" factors grew and grew, giving rise to various "sociological schools," each one trying to pile up evidences for its dominant hypothesis, which is in practice how the problem of infinite data was overcome and social science got started. But the logical absurdity of so many factors claiming to be primary aroused its own reaction, this time against hypothesis and in favor of "pure data" in the hopes that the mountainous accumulation of these would prove the sure guide to more dependable theorizing. Now there is

another swing back to theory, on the grounds that data alone, even in heaps, are unintelligible, and only provisional hypotheses can indicate which piles of data are worth correlating with others.

3. "Indeed, there is one problem which no amount of improvement in research methods will ever permit us to overcome, namely the limitation of our knowledge of the past imposed by the unfortunate fact that we cannot interview or test the dead. Historiography and archeology can do remarkable jobs of reconstruction, but they can seldom satisfy the ambitious social scientist in search of quantitative comparisons—a point well made in Paul Lazarsfeld's presidential address to the American Association for Public Opinion Research on 'The Obligation of the 1950 Pollster to the 1984 Historian.' " From an essay by David Riesman (with Nathan Glazer) entitled "Some Observations on Social Science Research" included in *Individualism Reconsidered* (Glencoe, Ill.: The Free Press, 1954), p. 469. Used by permission of the publishers.

4. Riesman, in the essay quoted in the previous note, trying to reconcile the warring camps on the theory-data battlefront, deplores the data-disdainers' slogan: "All this foundation money and all these IBM machines to tell us this, which Tocqueville already knew a hundred years ago!" He calls it an "epistemological mystery," the question of "how we know that an understanding not established directly or by strict reasoning on a sufficient volume of empirical data is a true understanding. I don't propose to unravel this epistemological mystery here: it is enough to observe that the acceptance of the position that only the generalizations founded on irrefutable data are true leaves us to conclude that all understanding of society . . . established up till now is pure illusion; and that all sociology is simply hypothesis awaiting proof, for I believe it can be shown that with rare exceptions even the most up-to-date data support the most up-to-date generalization only as example, not as proof in any (even probability-theory) scientific sense." (Page 472.) It is not, however, an epistemological mystery but the desperate straits of the "existential situation" that make us listen to the shrewd guesses of experienced observers. We listen, for example, to news reportage and news analyses, not because we would not prefer scientifically supported hypotheses as to what is going on, but because that's all the "science" there will be time for before the historical situation changes so that present issues are superseded by new ones. Riesman admits that a true appraisal of the scientific standing of the social sciences may demand such sacrifices of intellect on the part of the workers in the field in the way of present unintelligibility for the sake of future theorizing that the more impatient and zealous are bound to lose interest, or to grow desperate. "In this situation, work which is very far from technical validation, let alone from proving anything important about society, is often desperately seized upon by the promoters and defenders of social science in order to convince themselves and others that they are in a good line of work, and, beyond that, that they could produce far more if they got the funds and the go-ahead orders." (Page 475.) Used by permission.

5. Durkheim feared that if individual psychology or "human nature" were allowed to supply the motives for social behavior, sociology would "lose its subject matter" to psychology. He tried to establish the "social fact," the way of behaving directly attributable to living in society and impossible to explain in terms of the individual. According to him "society is not a mere collection of individuals, but a being which has its life, its conscience, its interests, its history. Without this idea we have no social science." Hence the "obscure forces," through which the individual feels the coercive power of the social mind, conscience, interest, and hence the "collective representations" such as the flag, religious writings and symbols, legal obligations, in which the obscure forces are collectively expressed. He has here touched one of the sorest spots of social science—whether the "social fact" can really be described in scientific terms at all or whether one must call in mystical, mythical, or metaphysical ideas. For the scientific method yields, in such devices as opinion polls, interviews, and questionnaires, nothing more than statistical summations and correlations of individual reactions.

6. According to Sorokin, the way to stop the "waste of time" in discussing what social science ought to be is to look at what it has done, regardless of its theories about itself. I quote his summary here, not because I believe that the theoretical discussions are profitless, but because I think his summary reveals the type of knowledge the scientific method is best suited to give, and that the "waste of time" consists in expecting something that this method applied to this subject matter cannot deliver: "The development of sociology begins to show more and more clearly what its subject matter is. It seems to be a study, first, of the *relationships and correlations between various classes of social phenomena* (*correlations between economic and religious; family and moral; juridical and economic; mobility and political phenomena and so on*); *second, that between the social and the non-social* (*geographic, biological, etc.*) *phenomena; third, the study of the general characteristics common to all classes of social phenomena*." (Italics his.) Pitirim A. Sorokin, *Contemporary Sociological Theories*, p. 760.

CHAPTER V

1. An interesting side light on post-Christian paganism is given by this desire to appropriate the Christian ethic without the divine-human relationships. It apparently never occurs to the unbelievers that the effort to live the Christian ethic, without the constant help of God in a prayer and worship relationship through which both grace and forgiveness restore the ethical subject from day to day like food and drink and elimination—that this effort might turn out to be the most cruel and unusual punishment yet invented to torture the human psyche. How else account for the enormous guilt complex from which all the more prosperous or fortunate segments of our society suffer, and the almost complete lack of happy pagans? By far more logical and kind are the few stalwart unbelievers who resent or deride the Christian ethic along with its theology.

2. See Earnest Jones's excellent biography of the formative years of Freud. One gets the feeling, in following Freud's development and his casting about for explanations, that one is sitting in on the "naming of parts" of a new morphology or anatomy. What if Freud had not had a good classical education, and had never even heard of Oedipus?

3. Signs that language analysis may soon take notice of the "what" that language is about can already be found. Thus Max Black in his essay on Stevenson's *Ethics and Language* (New Haven: Yale University Press, 1944) has this to say finally about Stevenson's theory of "emotive meaning": "A way of speaking about 'emotive meaning' which focuses attention upon the irrational aspects of ethical communication and leaves ethical issues to be resolved by the interplay of generated emotive influence seems not merely inconvenient but almost mischievous. A reversal of emphasis, made possible by a fuller recognition of the informative aspect of utterances, however charged with feeling, may encourage some, perhaps, to search further for a basis of *rational agreement* on ethical questions." *Language and Philosophy* (Ithaca, N.Y.: Cornell University Press, 1949), p. 220.

CHAPTER VI

1. An exception to the rule of silence about artistic creativity in the Old Testament would seem to be found in the place where Yahweh "commissions" the art work and the artists that will be needed for the setting up of the tabernacle and all the religious furnishings previously enumerated: "The Lord said to Moses, 'See, I have called by name Bezalel the son of Uri, son of Hur, of the tribe of Judah: and I have filled him with the Spirit of God, with ability and intelligence, with knowledge and all craftsmanship, to devise artistic designs, to work in gold, silver, and bronze, in cutting stones for setting, and in carving wood, for work in every craft. And behold, I have appointed with him Oholiab, the son of Ahisamach, of the tribe of Dan; and I have given to all able men ability, that they may make all that I have commanded you' " (Exod. 31:1-6 R.S.V.). I am indebted to Charles J. Stoneburner for calling my attention to this passage.

2. These three characteristics should not be mistaken for aesthetic criteria—they characterize the activity that precedes aesthetics, the latter being ex-post-facto judgments on its products. It is especially needful nowadays to be careful about the word "expressive," which tends to be taken automatically as equivalent to "*self*-expressive" or "emotionally evocative." Fuzzy notions as to what the "self" is, as well as the confusing habit of classifying under "emotion" everything that doesn't fit under "fact," have encouraged this sorry usage. But "expressive" means simply what the etymology suggests—to ex-press, to squeeze out like toothpaste out of a tube, to make manifest or visible what previously was not so—and it is just the glory and endless fascination of artistic creativity that it can ex-press so many specific, concrete, multidimensional experiences—not just the physiological affects we lump together under the term "emotion."

3. André Malraux, in his remarkable book *The Voices of Silence*

(Garden City: Doubleday & Company, 1953), touches upon this question of the "what" that a culture communicates. He calls by the name "style" the technical aesthetic means by which a culture becomes expressive—but, of course, "style" is just as hard to define in a general way as is "expressiveness." However, I find myself in agreement with him when he says, "This immanent power of art can be equated to the fact that most works of the past usually affect us *through their styles* (p. 320). . . . After that great moment of art history when for the first time man arose, rejoicing in his strength, in the straight folds of the Auriga, then in the parallel lines of the Panathenaic frieze and the horsemen of the Acropolis, the 'classical' sculptors replaced the hieratic line of Egyptian statuary by their broad shell-like curves and a facile majesty reminiscent of the trophy. Thus we see that what once ranked as absolute beauty now strikes us as the style, followed by the stylization, of the classical age. Both, like those of Byzantium, are the expression of a particular interpretation of the world—an interpretation calling for a special way of seeing before being enriched by it (p. 321). . . . Every great style of the past impresses us as being a special interpretation of the world, but this collective conquest is obviously a sum total of the individual conquests that have gone to its making" (p. 334). Selections used by permission of the publishers.

4. To convince himself of the "union," one need only remind himself of the "bleeding heart" religious pictures as an example of high Christian content combined with low aesthetic standards, or of certain Buddhist or Moslem temples as an example of nonchristian content with high aesthetic standards.

5. There is something tragicomical, certainly theatrical, in the ease with which man assumes that he can be whatever it strikes his fancy to be—like an actor moving glibly from one role to another, except that in real life the acting is for keeps and the results of acting the part are not so easily shed as the role is assumed. Thus he may decide that he is a creature solely of reason, a logical automaton, and straightway proceeds to be that chimera—and it is almost as if the neglected parts of his nature conspired together to permit him to be such a creature, so as to build up secretly a more violent revenge, exploding in an entirely unexpected quarter. Or he may decide that he is a creature of purely material desires and satisfactions and straightway proceeds to be *that*, only to encounter the nemesis of satiation and boredom. Or he may think he is a pure spirit, a god unfortunately trapped in a hostile body—and now there is almost no limit to his arrogance, except the death and putrefaction of his body.

CHAPTER VII

1. Sören Kierkegaard, *Purity of Heart* (New York: Harper & Bros., 1938), pp. 91-92. Used by permission of the publishers.

2. Markus Barth, "The Christ in Israel's History," *Theology Today*, Vol. XI, No. 3, pp. 347-53. Used by permission of the publishers and the author.